FROM MANOR H
GIBSON SQUARE – AND BACK AGAIN

From Manor House Station to Gibson Square – and Back Again

Secrets from the London Taxi Trade

CHRIS ACKRILL

© Chris Ackrill, 2018

Published by Pubcat Publishing

A CIP catalogue record for this book is available from the British Library.

ISBN 978-1-9996881-0-3

Book layout and cover design by Clare Brayshaw

Cover image © Paul Sankey | Dreamstime.com

Production by:

York Publishing Services Ltd
64 Hallfield Road
Layerthorpe
York YO31 7ZQ

Tel: 01904 431213

Website: www.yps-publishing.co.uk

Contents

	Acknowledgements	vi
	Introduction	viii
1	The Knowledge	1
2	Butter Boy	25
3	My Personal Revolution	39
4	Back on the Cab	60
5	How it all Works	69
6	Passengers	108
7	Know Your Enemy	141
8	When Things Go Wrong	161
9	Examiner	192
10	Back on the Cab (Again)	228
11	Examiner 2	240
12	The Years of Change	255
13	Uber	281
14	The Future	297
	Appendix A	308
	Appendix B	319

Acknowledgements

Chris Ackrill has experienced the cab trade from all angles: as trainee on the Knowledge of London in the mid-1980s, as driver, and eventually as a Knowledge Examiner himself.

Chris is the undisputed master of the U-Turn. Following a radical change of direction he started his schooling all over again aged thirty, and settled happily into the world of academia – working himself through the country's colleges and universities, and somehow finding himself on the Bradford University Challenge team.

He resisted the urge to stay at university for ever, and full of misplaced idealism decided to look for a proper job. After eleven years in the wilderness "doing other things" and becoming increasingly disillusioned, Chris became one of the few to complete the Knowledge twice. He returned to the cab trade for good in 2010.

Chris was born in Romford, and as a child moved around the country, living in Hornchurch, Upminster, Northumberland, Staffordshire, and Timperley (the posh bit of Greater Manchester). As an adult he's lived in London, Birmingham, Bradford, Louisiana, and Northampton.

He escaped London many years ago in order to seek the rural idyll of county fairs and scarecrow festivals. His dream is to retire to small town Yorkshire. He currently lives happily with his wife and pets in Bedfordshire, in the Soft South, where the weather's better.

"This book is the best thing to come out of Leighton Buzzard since Kajagoogoo"

(Chris's wife, Maureen)

"The Bob Dylan of the cab trade"

(Chris's mate, Adam)

I'm not going to be drawn into naming the important people in my life, only to upset others by missing them out. I acknowledge anyone who has ever believed in me.

Many thanks to the folk at York Publishing Services for producing this book.

Special thanks to my wife, Mo, for her unwavering patience and support.

I dedicate this book to family, past and present.

Introduction

"The game's dead. Always has been" (traditional)

A man stops me outside the Royal Academy on Piccadilly and asks for London Bridge. We crawl along Pall Mall and around Trafalgar Square. I apologise for the traffic. They close all the roads around Buckingham Palace for two hours every day during the Changing of the Guard ceremony. They say it's about security. I say it's about making the roads hostile to motorists.

I inform the man we're now travelling on the infamous Cycle Superhighway. The traffic stops again. We pull off Victoria Embankment at Blackfriars and try Cannon Street. Cannon Street is crawling because they recently made Bank Junction buses and cycles only, so extra pressure is put on alternative routes. We get onto London Bridge and pass Tooley Street. I say this road's been closed for years, and I don't know when it'll reopen. Perhaps it never will. Thankfully, my man doesn't want Tooley Street. Had he wanted the Hilton, it would entail a long and expensive detour around Bermondsey.

We arrive. He thought he'd do the trip for twenty quid. So did I. A couple of years ago, he would have got change from a twenty. The meter says £32. He gives me a tip, but I don't feel I've deserved it.

He hasn't been to London for forty years and the journey had been an experience. It was an interesting ride for him, but a pain in the arse for me. He probably won't return for another forty years. I feel his pity. He's meeting old friends for a pub lunch at the George Inn. Very nice too. I envy his sizzling steak and foaming tankard of British ale. I'm off to the cab caff for a cheese roll and a Twix.

This is the reality of driving a cab in modern London. If you'd like to know more, please read on…

Polite Notice: *the London taxi trade still operates in a male-dominated environment and I've used male terminology for simplicity. Feel free to convert my gender terminology into politically correct-speak in your head. I've used imperial measurements too. I think this is only fitting in the brave new world of Brexit Britain. I drink beer in pints, and British direction signs are still indicated in miles anyway, so there.*

The London cab trade attracts freaks and misfits from around the world. If you're not insane to start with, you'll certainly need a robust sense of humour to avoid going crackers after a few years on London's roads. It's not for me to say whether I'm on the spectrum of madness or not. Unless you've purchased this book directly, selected from a pile of my belongings on a blanket outside Amsterdam Centraal Station, please assume I haven't burnt out quite yet.

You'll similarly need a sense of humour to get anything out of this book, so if you're in any way irony-deficient, please don't take me *too* seriously. I was brought up on *Monty Python's Flying Circus* and *Viz* comic.

I'm not a great one for facts and figures. Other cab trade writers do it better than I. Current taxi and private hire licensing figures can be checked on TfLs website. Mine were correct as of July 2018.

Right, are we ready to go? Before we set off, please put that burger wrapper in the bin, and keep your feet off the seats. Sit well in your seat for comfort and safety, sir; it could be a bumpy ride.

Many of the following events happened a long time ago. This is how I remember it.

1

The Knowledge

"Why don't you go on the Knowledge?" Andy in the packing room had asked a reasonable question, but the idea sounded crazy. Me, a cab driver? For one thing I couldn't drive. "It's only doing what you're doing now," was the follow up. The idea wasn't something I'd considered before, but the seed was sown.

I was working at the Covent Garden publishing house of Chatto, Virago, Bodley Head and Cape, delivering packages on the company motorbike. My understanding of the mysterious process London taxi drivers have to go through to get licensed was vague. When I came to see Jack Rosenthal's brilliant 1979 film, *The Knowledge* I had a better idea of what it involved. Blood, sweat and tears, mate. Well, maybe no blood in my case; though many years later when I became a Knowledge Examiner, I saw plenty of Knowledge Boys who had been knocked off their bikes in the call of duty and struggled in to the examination room on crutches or with limbs in plaster. That was many years in the future. Back in 1985, I was struggling with the idea of going on the Knowledge.

I'd never given any thought to what I might like to do when I finished school. One day I left, the next day I just waited around for something to happen. I'd had a few dead-end jobs since leaving school at sixteen, and was living with my mum in suburban Upminster, enjoying bacon sandwiches on demand and having few responsibilities. A few pints at the weekend and the new Jam album made for a simple life. I would have probably said that I'd like to be a train driver. In fact, the idea still appeals to me. Many years later when I became a Careers Adviser I actually researched my fantasy option. Yes, I quite fancied pulling my Eurostar train out of St Pancras bound for Paris while making announcements in French. Maybe driving a London cab was the next best thing? I could still pull off the rank at Pancras and practice my French with a phoney Gallic shrug. As surreal as the idea sounded, Andy was right:it was only doing what I was already doing, only carrying people instead of packages, and driving a car instead of a motorbike.

It didn't sound such a big jump up from delivering packages on a motorbike, but it was certainly a lot more serious than anything I'd done before. Taxi driving in London was seen as an elite trade, and was known to be extremely difficult to get into, particularly for someone with a discipline problem such as mine. School breaks at my Essex comprehensive were often spent standing outside the staff room as punishment for various low-level misdemeanours. Applying myself to something so serious wasn't something I was sure I was ready for. Cab driving was a mature person's thing. I was twenty-three and barely an adult. I was little more than a foetus with shoes on.

Rebel without a Cab

I'd always admired the London taxi. As a child, my mum would sometimes hire a cab home to Hornchurch after shopping in Romford, and it was always an exciting experience. The classic shaped FX4 had been around since 1958, and by the 1970s had become old-fashioned and out of step with the times. It was a throwback to another era. It was a strange vehicle: big, black and bulbous; and with the brute functionalism of a First World War tank. It appealed to my rapidly growing rebellious side, and I admired its uncompromising rebuff to modernity. It was slow and noisy, but I loved its solidity and its Tardis-like feeling of space. As the huge mechanical meter clicked over the twenty pence increments that I suspect my family could ill afford, I felt a sense of occasion and privilege. I felt like a rich man riding in a limousine. Pure luxury. I still love riding in cabs today, though in towns outside London taxis are usually boring van conversions.

The Knowledge depicts four trainee cab drivers learning the Knowledge of London, and how their lives, and the lives around them, are affected by the pursuit of something that on the surface appears mundane. When I started the Knowledge myself I realised how authentic this depiction was. It's a riveting piece of work and much admired by cab drivers who regard it as the definitive work on the subject. Not that there are any other films on the Knowledge that I can think of. You don't see television documentaries following trainee cab drivers as you might see doctors, vets, lawyers or teachers. Little is written about the Knowledge experience too, which adds to the mystique. The impenetrable workings of the Public Carriage Office are shrouded in mystery. Even cab drivers are in the dark as far as the PCO is concerned.

Those who start the Knowledge are either scared of it, scarred by it, or are defeated by it. Those who have seen the process through secretly revel in it. Cab drivers of fifty years standing still talk about their experiences on the Knowledge, and reflect on their examiners with a mixture of fear and affection. Would these scary men turn up one day as mystery shoppers and criticise their choice of route? Perhaps they'd even send them back for re-testing?

There were the mysterious drivers, sitting in silence, behind the bullet-proof partition. The idea of myself as an anonymous man of mystery had laid dormant for many years, but I knew I was a bit of an outsider. Hell, yes! Maybe I could drive that big black beetle myself. I could be Johnny Cash and Clint Eastwood rolled into one. The Man in Black, the Stranger in Town. I could be a real outlaw! Subject to strict policies and procedures, of course.

Taking the Plunge

The idea still felt surreal though, when I went up to 15 Penton Street to collect my application forms. The grey, austere exterior of the old Public Carriage Office was matched by the grey austerity within. It felt like an old police station that had seen better days, which is essentially what it was. The PCO was run by the Metropolitan Police and its members of staff were police civilians. It was fitting that the licensing of wartime vehicles took place in such a decrepit environment. This was also where those on the Knowledge came to get tested. I vaguely recall a smell of antiseptic, and a tense atmosphere.

The old PCO represented the last bastion of the British Empire. You could imagine colonial rule administered from here, but run by the folk who never made it to India and were a bit grumpy at only getting as far as Islington.

You were in no doubt that they were the ones in the white linen suits running the show, while we were the Knowledge wallahs serving tiffin on the veranda and keeping them in their cushy jobs. The regime was archaic and undemocratic, but older cab drivers will tell you they were happier when licensing was carried out by the Met. Many years later, the end of the Raj came and the PCO came under the umbrella of Transport for London. By the time the PCO moved to TfL's Palestra building, all the administration was done remotely, and Knowledge candidates were only allowed in and escorted upstairs under tight security. Cab drivers were not allowed into Palestra at all, even to renew licences. 15 Penton Street was a frightening place, but one that I miss dearly.

One minute I was sitting at home wondering if I was doing the right thing, and the next I was nervously handing in a strange official-looking form in a scary office block full of coppers. I had to supply a medical report from my doctor, and to declare that I had no criminal convictions. As the PCO was run by the Metropolitan Police they could check anyway. Knowledge candidates were normally invited to an Acceptance Interview welcoming them to the Knowledge. I missed out through an administration error. Nowadays candidates get an information booklet instead. I didn't even get that.

Without fanfare, my application to become a London cab driver was accepted and I was on the Knowledge. There was no sense of occasion welcoming me to the brotherhood. No inspiring speech by the head of department, no freshers' week to ease me into upwards of three years of study, no fellow students to talk to. I was on my own.

Things happen slowly in the cab trade. The rules and regulations we work under haven't changed much since Oliver Cromwell drew up "The Regulation of Hackney Coachmen in London" ordinance in 1654. We made the transition from horse-drawn carriages to motor-cabs in the first half of the twentieth century, but surprisingly little has changed in over three centuries really. The introduction of the Knowledge of London in 1851 was a major development and was said to have come about after passengers complained that cab drivers couldn't find the Great Exhibition in Hyde Park. Yes, Hyde Park, that huge green thing in the middle of London.

If you're an out-of-towner and wonder what those blokes are doing riding around London on scooters, noting down government buildings on clipboards, I can put your mind at rest that they are not agents of a foreign power. They are Knowledge Boys, and they pose no threat to national security whatsoever. You are called a "Knowledge Boy" regardless of age, just as you are known as a "Butter Boy" when you gain your shiny green badge. Look closely and you will notice that some Knowledge Boys are actually female. They are forever known as "Girls". The object of Knowledge Boys and Girls is to learn several hundred routes in order to pass the Knowledge of London.

To pass the Knowledge you need to know almost everything within six miles of Charing Cross; which, for our purposes, is the official centre of London. The basis of the Knowledge is a booklet of routes known as the "Blue Book". In 1985 this was a little booklet with a pink cover. I don't think it was ever blue (it's now a glossy A5 booklet in corporate TfL branding). A trainee cab driver would be invited to a long series of oral examinations based on the Blue Book's list of 468 "Runs". A Run is a route between two "Points of Interest" (usually known simply as a "Point"). Once I'd learned all 468 Runs, plus countless Points, I could apply to be tested. The problem is that the Points asked during testing are unlikely to be the same ones as listed. The Runs are likely to be different too. You literally have to learn the Runs backwards. Sometimes the Runs would be reversed, so you would need to know all the one-way systems that could affect the route going the other way. In other words, if the Points and Runs tested bear little resemblance to the ones listed, they may as well be just plucked out the Knowledge Examiner's head on the day. I later learned that they often are. The Blue Book is little more than a guide to the sort of questions to expect. The examiners can, and do, ask anything they like. The idea is that you don't just learn 468 Runs and 936 Points, but you learn every important, and not so important, building in London within a six-mile radius of Charing Cross. They don't tell you the best way to connect up the two Points, you have to work that out yourself. The guidelines stipulate that it should be the shortest route.

You soon realise how big London is. The countryside doesn't start for about twenty miles east or west, and the outlying districts within the six-mile radius are barely suburban. The borders of the exclusion zone cover gritty urban areas such as East Acton, Harlesden, Stratford, Lewisham, Tooting and South Tottenham. These places are all full of heavy traffic day and night, and with nasty one-way systems that need to be internalised. They are hard places to learn and memorise.

Armed with the Blue Book I set about my task with a naïve enthusiasm. As I planned my first Run I laid a huge map on my bedroom floor and drew a piece of string from point A to point B. I was a motorcycle courier who knew how to get from one area of London to another, but I didn't know every one-way street, or every banned turn. And I'd never measured my route with a piece of string. I was reduced to tears before I'd even started my first Run.

These days there are internet chat rooms where Knowledge candidates provide support to each other and share the latest news on one-way systems, banned manoeuvres and roadworks. It's heady stuff. If a No Right Turn sign has blown down with the wind, a long online debate will run discussing whether it is now safe to turn right, or whether the sign's absence is temporary. Students know that their examiners might well be discussing the very same junction at their coffee break.

The 1980s Blue Book didn't list the Runs in a rational order. One Run might finish in South London and the next Run listed might start in North London. This wasn't useful if you were trying to learn two or more Runs a session. I purchased a whole set of pre-planned Runs from the Knowledge Point school in Islington. This fat wad of 468 pages of pink paper didn't necessarily list the Runs in official Blue Book order, but were arranged in a rational sequence, complete with suggested routes. They also suggested Points to look for near the start and end of each Run. This is standard practice now, but at the time it was a revelation. I saw a way forward and found a determination that I had rarely showed at school, or in my first few jobs.

It now costs several hundred pounds to apply to go on the Knowledge and to attend the required series of examinations. Back then, you needed to pay your doctor for a private medical, and a fee for your final badge and licence. As far as I remember, the rest was free of charge. Of course, you'd need maps and other essential materials, and you might want to subscribe to a school. You'd need to book some driving lessons in a cab towards the end of the process, in the unlikely event you got that far. Most people who start the Knowledge give up: the failure rate remains around 70%. The biggest expense would be transport and fuel in order to drive the routes. You'd also need to make sure you could take time off to be tested. Many Knowledge candidates combine the Knowledge with full-time work, sometimes going part-time towards the end when testing becomes more frequent.

Earlier generations learnt the Knowledge on cycles. You still see the occasional Knowledge Boy on a cycle, but by the 1980s, most people learnt by riding around London on a moped. Some people use a car, but it's expensive and not very flexible for "Point-Collecting". As a motorcycle courier I had the company's Honda VT 500 at my disposal, and as part of the mod revival I also had my own Vespa 200 scooter to use, complete with lots of chrome, lights, mirrors and a faux fur seat cover.

By the time I'd got going on the Knowledge I'd moved out of my mum's flat in Upminster, and into a bedsit in Sotheby Road, Highbury. Highbury was an up and coming area of inner-North London. It was exciting living in London proper, rather than in a genteel suburb twenty miles away. I drank in local pubs such as the Highbury Barn and the Bank of Friendship, and I could walk up to see bands at the George Robey pub in Finsbury Park. I found that they unlocked the gates at Arsenal Football Club in the second half. On a couple of occasions I stood on the North Bank and saw out the last ten minutes. Although I am a West Ham supporter I developed a soft spot for Arsenal (I'm getting over it now). Over several years I moved around Stoke Newington, Stamford Hill, Haringey and Wood Green. I started to consider myself a North Londoner.

I would complete several Runs at the weekend, and sometimes a few after work. Some things stuck, some didn't. Thirty years later I still couldn't remember all those crescents in Notting Hill, or those one-way streets running at funny angles in Pimlico – which were blocked off even back then. I'd sometimes ask these streets many years later as an examiner in the vain hope that I'd remember them myself. I've now resigned myself to the fact that some things just won't stick.

Some people enjoy doing the Knowledge, but I can't say I enjoyed riding around for hours jotting down the position of obscure buildings that I might need to know for the examiner but would never be asked for as a cab driver. I enjoyed exploring different areas of London though, and I got satisfaction from completing a Run. I'd hand-write the completed Runs up on A4 sheets and put them a file. I'd call over the Runs again and again. After thirty or so runs it became harder to recall them all as more were added to my file. I had to revise something every day in order to keep the plates spinning. Spinning plates were added at a modest rate of five to seven Runs per week. I took my file to Corfu on holiday, and I probably took a couple of maps too. Once the Knowledge takes grip, this is considered normal behaviour by those involved.

I was about half way through the list of Runs when I started to attend "Call Over" sessions at the Knowledge

Point School. The school is essentially the same. There are several tables spread around a room. On each table there is a large laminated map of London. Sat at each table is a group of men – and a few women these days – who take it in turns to "call" a specified Run.

Once the 468 prescribed Runs are internalised you can start learning new ones. You can devise your own, concentrating on areas you are weak on, and in the advanced stages you can test yourself on the Runs that Knowledge candidates were asked that day up at the Carriage Office. Knowledge Examiners have their favourite Runs known as "Bankers" and these come up again and again.

How do you know what Runs were called that day? The schools send people out with a clipboard to ask candidates what they were asked as they exit the building. On a busy day a scrum of people crowd around the dazed and confused Knowledge Boy. It's a bit like the television footage you see of people coming out of the Old Bailey to face the media – only Knowledge Boys don't take their solicitors with them for support. The Points Collectors ask what the candidate can remember about the experience: who examined him? What was he asked? Did he "drop" any Points? Later the same day, the schools publish a list of Runs asked by each examiner, and at what stage the candidate was on. Nowadays, that information is on websites within minutes.

Within my group at Knowledge Point we'd rarely waste time discussing anything unconnected to the Knowledge. You might not even know where the others lived, or what they did for a living. If you knew where they lived you'd only really be interested in it from a Knowledge point of view. It would be particularly interesting if it involved bridges and tunnels. To a Knowledge Boy, an A–Z map is as gripping as a good novel. You'd wonder what the best route home would be from the school in Islington, and you'd quite possibly dwell on it when you got home. There was pride in how single-minded and obsessed you were. There's still an almost pathological obsession with detail. Some taxi drivers are also keen historians who write books and articles with an astonishing forensic rigour. Most train-spotters are male, and road-spotting could be viewed as a similar endeavour. I'm convinced there's some degree of autism at work here.

We didn't socialise. If we met up away from school, it was to talk about roads, bridges, one-way systems and the precise location of thousands of buildings that we needed to internalise. Years later I played bass in two rock bands. It was the same there: you made little chit chat and you didn't ask what your colleagues did in the daytime. All you were interested in was what music they liked. And even that was problematic. I was possibly fired from my first band because I was the only Beatles enthusiast amongst us. I took consolation from the rumour that Glenn Matlock had been kicked out the Sex Pistols for the same reason. All my former band colleagues would be delighted to talk to you about Neil Young or Jimi Hendrix, but if you ever meet a cab driver at a party it's best not to reveal where you live. Not unless you relish a long discussion on river crossings and one-way systems.

If you ever find yourself looking at the adverts in the newsagent's window wondering what kind of sexual perversion a "Call Over Partner" is offering, I must disappoint you. For a while I used to visit the nearby home of a lady from Trinidad for the purposes of calling over. This involves reciting Knowledge Runs parrot fashion. I did warn you.

Manor House Station to Gibson Square

My fellow students at Knowledge Point would talk about their "Appearances" at nearby Penton Street. An Appearance is an oral examination on the Knowledge. An Appearance would typically last about twenty minutes, and you'd usually be asked four or five Runs. Run number one in the Blue Book is Manor House Station to Gibson Square. It's an easy one, running a couple of miles from the southern end of Haringey into a leafy square in the centre of Islington. You are required to state the shortest route. This Run would be typically called to the examiner thus:

Leave on the left, Green Lanes; right Islington New Park; left Highbury Grove; right St Paul's Road; comply Highbury Corner, leave by Upper Street; right Theberton Street. Gibson Square is on the right, Sir.

The "Sir/Madam" form of address was essential then as it is now. Female examiners are addressed as "Ma'am" like the Queen. You are "Mr" or "Miss". Your first name is never used.

Manor House to Gibson Square is one of the shortest and easiest Runs, though there is still more than one way to run it. I'm probably going to receive angry emails telling me I should have used Brownswood Road and Blackstock Road, but I like to keep things simple. So there. Throughout my cab driving career, I've never once been asked to take someone to or from Manor House Station – in fact I only drive past it every two years or so. I've been asked for Gibson Square once.

You are advised to drive around a quarter mile radius at the start and end of each Run, noting down any other useful roads and every important looking building: The idea is that once you've learnt the Blue Book thoroughly you have covered everything within the six mile radius. There aren't many Points of Interest around Manor House Station, but the area around Gibson Square is chock full of pubs and restaurants, a couple of theatres, and countless other places that an examiner might ask for. Imagine how many Points you'd need to collect in Westminster or Soho.

Needless to say, you need to develop a good grasp of geography. You need to know all the river crossings, one-way systems and cut-throughs. Learning one corner of the map at a time isn't enough. You need to learn how different areas relate to one another. You need a map covering the whole of London in order to learn how this giant jigsaw puzzle fits together. You'll also learn that the River Thames doesn't run straight and that the saying "South of the River" is more cultural construction than geographical fact.

At the school they'd tell us interesting little things that you could impress your future passengers with. For example, I remember learning that all the little ships on top of the lamp posts in the Mall have birds' nests in them. We were encouraged to look at the statue of Nelson outside the Old Admiralty Building. Nelson is doing something that no seafarer would ever do: he has his foot on a rope. I was intrigued by the story of Saint George the Martyr Church just south of London Bridge. On a tower sits a four-sided clock. The clock's faces are white apart from the clock facing east which is painted black. Apparently, this was a rebuke to the burghers of Bermondsey who were tight in donating to church funds. That's Millwall supporters for you.

When calling a Run in front of an examiner you need to be very precise. In order to remember Points we were encouraged to use mnemonics: patterns of letters or images serving as memory aids. There's a useful cut-through in Finsbury consisting of Skinner Street, Percival Street and Lever Street. So you don't get these three streets muddled up you could use a mnemonic and remember the simple phrase *Skin Percy's Liver*. I wasn't a particularly diligent Knowledge student, but I know the names of all the mansion blocks on Prince of Wales Drive in Battersea through my use of mnemonics. I'm sure there are former Knowledge Point students of my generation who remember the phrase *Place Your Primrose Over Cyril's Parked Connaught* (Overstrand Mansions, Cyril Mansions, Park Mansions, Connaught Mansions, &c.). I may not be 100% accurate, but my ability to remember the names of a string of flats in South London over thirty years later is testimony to the effectiveness of the memory aids I learnt at Knowledge Point.

At the school I'd listen in awe as my more experienced colleagues swapped tales of glorious battles with those who held their future career their hands. The examiners were feared but respected. They were mostly retired police officers in those days, but they knew how hard it was to complete the Knowledge. The whole set-up at the PCO was respected as being firm but fair-ish. You were forced to adhere to the most arcane rules imaginable but you kind of knew where you were with them. If you stepped out of line they'd be down on you like a ton of bricks. You couldn't answer back, or lodge an appeal. It was the days before customer feedback and accountability, and there was zero transparency. Everything about the PCO was shrouded in mystery. I called it the Kremlin. Cab drivers are all proud of their achievement, and most respected the PCO for upholding the good name of the London cab trade. I felt the examiners respected us too. It was said that they would be rude or difficult with you in order to test your character. This is certainly true in some cases. After all, if you become a cab driver you will be in a responsible job, dealing at close quarters with an unpredictable public. The examiners want to know you can handle it. The examiners also need to know you can handle the pressure of someone getting into your cab expecting you to set off immediately without thinking.

For their own twisted amusement, they might stop you in your tracks with an absurd Run. There are two exhibition centres at the Barbican, sat opposite each other on Golden Lane (I think they used to be separated by a concrete island, but I might have imagined that). At the time they were labelled Red and Blue. The rumour was that an examiner would ask you take them from one exhibition hall to the other, setting down on the left as protocol dictates. In the real world, the passenger would simply get in one door and exit the other, but on a Knowledge Run you have to set down right outside the door. You couldn't have your virtual passenger walking a few yards across the street, particularly if there was a concrete island in the way. Knowledge Boys would therefore learn this complicated run using several one-way streets, along with many more absurdities, just in case.

Let the Fun Begin

Eventually, it was my turn. I put in to be tested on the Blue Book and was duly called up for my first Appearance. I didn't have to worry too much about making my appointment on time. I was renting a room in Highbury, two miles from Penton Street. Some Knowledge candidates live well outside London and just getting there is an ordeal. I booked in at the window and was asked to take a seat in a sparse room at the end of the Corridor of Fear.

The Knowledge examination process is essentially a series of job interviews, resulting in a guaranteed job at the end of it. The saying goes that you can't fail the Knowledge, you can only give it up. Thereafter, unless you do something daft, you have a job for life. An Appearance always felt more formal than any job interview though. There would be few, if any, pleasantries. You wouldn't be asked how your journey was, and you wouldn't be offered a coffee. A handshake is traditionally only given on the day you complete the Knowledge. If you were lucky you'd get a smile, but you wouldn't expect anything else. You certainly wouldn't get a conversation about football or *Coronation Street* as you might get now if the examiner is running ahead of schedule and can spare the time. I was never asked what work I did, which is the question asked these days in order to break the ice. In those days the examiners liked the ice to remain intact as they sat in their igloo.

You'd sit in the waiting room in silence, soaking up the tension. You'd try to put to the back of your mind how important this moment is, as if you dwell on it you might go to pieces. You'd probably want to visit the toilet, but you'd be scared to go in case you are marked as missing in action. If you are not present when you are called you might lose your place and be sent home. Examiners stroll into the waiting room and call out your name. You'd solemnly follow your examiner to his office. You'd feel as if you were going to receive a thrashing by the headmaster. Demonstrating that they saw no point in having a dog and barking yourself, the examiners couldn't always be bothered with coming out of their office to call you and they'd simply ask the next candidate to send you in.

Things happen fast once in the examination room. You hand the examiner your appointment card, and as soon as your arse hit the seat you'd be asked the shortest route between two points of interest.

When the first question comes you hope that at least you'll know the two Points asked for, and what direction to set off in. If you don't know the Points you'll be offered alternatives, but you know you are losing marks and the tension mounts. You hope to be asked something you have learned so well that you can "see the line". It's a good feeling when you can see every road in the line, played out in your mind like a speeded up film.

I was called in to see Mr Fryer. I knew better than to sit down before I was invited to, as anyone who's seen *The Knowledge* knows you shouldn't move the chair without explicit permission. You'd sit opposite your examiner in a small office, but it felt like you were sat half a mile away. He'd have a map on a large board tilted in front of him (in later years there would also be a computer). The personal knick-knacks that you'd find on a normal office desk were rare. There was nothing normal about the PCO or the Knowledge process. I can vaguely remember what Mr Fryer looked like, but I can't remember what he asked me. I was quite well prepared though, and I know I didn't disgrace myself.

That day I felt I'd left home a boy and returned a man. I had jumped my first major hurdle, and with reasonable success. I could now relate my own tales of wartime skirmishes back at the school.

You never knew when you might graduate to the next stage, from being seen every eighty-four days to every fifty-six days, &c. You just had to study hard and bide your time. When the examiners felt you'd proved yourself they'd move you up. It's different now, but in those days you were expected to have learnt all 468 runs before you could apply to be examined. You might have spent two years on the Knowledge before you met an examiner, and you wouldn't have had any formal feedback on how you were progressing.

My subsequent Appearances were satisfactory and I continued to make steady progress. The examiners said very little, though I was once told that I'd been through a period of "treading water". I took this to indicate mid-table mediocrity.

Today's client-focussed approach requires that you leave the examination room with a piece of paper outlining how you'd performed. Marks are ascribed to each of the four questions asked. In the 1980s, you might have been asked four Runs, or you might have got six. You weren't usually told whether you'd done well or not, and you wouldn't have dared ask. You wouldn't have been allowed to see your file under the Data Protection Act in the 1980s. Thirty years later I found out the examiners used a marking system involving drawing smiley faces on your file.

The whole thing took about twenty minutes. You were then sent out with your appointment card to book your next

Appearance, with the next examiners initials pencilled on the corner of the card.

Some candidates appear cool and in control. Some go to pieces. Most are in between. I felt pretty much in between throughout the process. I was about as nervous as I am at regular job interviews: nervous, sweaty and painfully self-conscious. Although I was never so nervous that I froze, unable to speak, I sometimes took a lot of thinking time before I could see the line and begin calling the Run. When the cogs of your brain are whirring but nothing comes out of your mouth, the silence is deafening. Interviewing people years later as a Careers Adviser I learned to be comfortable with the silence. In the examination room you lose marks for hesitancy, but I'm a believer in taking a bit of thinking time in order to get things right. You should only speak when you're ready, and you mustn't panic at the noise in your head telling you to say something. Anything.

Through my school sessions I knew the names of the examiners and their supposed specialities, but it was rather like being at school in the 1970s. You didn't know their first names, and if you did, you'd never address them with such a brazen familiarity. The examiner I remember best was Mr Lippit. This white-haired man came over as a kindly chap. He always smiled and once or twice he gave me a few brief words of encouragement. He wasn't known for trying to catch people out with particularly difficult Runs or obscure Points – not that any examiner did that with me anyway. He was regarded as a gentleman by everybody. When I became an examiner myself I had Mr Lippit in my mind.

Once you got onto fourteen-day Appearances you were nearly there. You were within touching distance of your

"Req". I wish I could tell you all about the glorious day when I passed the Knowledge of London, but I remember virtually nothing. It wasn't Mr Lippit who gave me my Requisition to indicate that I had successfully passed the Knowledge of London, but I don't remember for sure – it was possibly Mr Miller. I vaguely remember feeling warmly relieved and calm.

The Knowledge process wasn't quite over yet, though. I still had to learn the suburbs. You're not expected to physically drive the suburban routes, but you still need to demonstrate an acceptable knowledge of the main routes around Greater London. After three years spent intimately learning everything within six-miles of Charing Cross, the suburbs are comparatively easy. Like myself, most people just need one suburban Appearance to convince the examiner that they are ready to be let loose on the general public. You'll rarely visit the areas learnt on the suburb test, particularly if you're a day man. I've yet to physically visit such mysterious suburbs as Foots Cray or Pratt's Bottom. I'd forgotten where they were a fortnight after my final test anyway.

The Drive

I passed my regular driving test at the second attempt, nine months after I started the Knowledge. I was then able to drive an Escort van alongside the company motorbike. I later became a self-employed motorcycle courier at Hornets in the West End.

Towards the end of my time on the Knowledge I had the idea to buy a retired taxi to practice on and to use for courier work. I took £1000 in cash down to a cab garage in Bonny

Street, Camden Town, and drove away with an old FX4. This was like the cabs I used to ride in with my mum after shopping in Romford.

It was easier being a passenger than a driver of an FX4. There was no power steering or braking, and a long metal pole operated the manual gearbox. It was like driving a gymnasium. Water leaked in from various orifices, and there was a hole in the floor through which you could see the road. Sometimes the driver's compartment would fill up with smoke. There was little sound insulation, which made the engine sound even noisier than it should. It also felt very big, particularly as you sit up much higher than you do in a regular car. Overall, it was a slow, noisy, smelly old vehicle that would be best off in a museum. This was my first car.

The final hurdle to becoming a London cab driver was "The Drive". The Metropolitan Police driving test was more stringent than the standard driving test (these days the test includes disability awareness and how to load wheelchairs safely). I had my own retired taxi to practice on, but tuition on what to expect on the test was essential. Knowledge Point sold me a package of tuition and loan of a cab for the test. You'd go out on the road with your tutor in the back, and you'd practice reversing in the school's car park. During my first lesson I was persuaded to take my test in an automatic. I wasn't sure at first, as if you were licensed for an automatic you couldn't switch to manual later. I didn't realise at the time that almost all London cabs were automatic, so figuring it unlikely I'd ever want to drive a manual I made the switch. I found driving an automatic easier and never looked back. I still don't know why people drive manual cars in this country.

These days, you take the Drive when you are at an advanced stage on the Knowledge. Back then, the driving test was the final hurdle after all Knowledge formalities had been completed. You would therefore have a gap between finishing the Knowledge and gaining your badge, especially if you failed the test. The driving test centre was in Southgate Road, Islington (predictably converted into a block of flats many years ago). As I drove out of the gate with the examiner in the back, a man stopped me to ask for directions. This threw me, and I ended up making mistakes and failing the test.

I failed the next one too. Reversing around cones evidently wasn't my strong point. I was also told off for driving above thirty miles per hour on what the examiner called the "Turkish Sector" of Green Lanes in Haringey. I'd apparently run a red light to boot. I swear it was amber guv.

I'd given up my courier work after the Knowledge and was penniless. It was with enormous relief that I passed on my third attempt. I returned the cab to Knowledge Point and bought some essential equipment for my new career: a badge holder, coin dispenser, maps, and a not-yet compulsory *Thank You for Not Smoking* sticker. I was asked to return to the Public Carriage Office later that afternoon to collect my badge and licence. I celebrated with a pint on my own at the Flounder and Firkin on Holloway Road. On my way back to the PCO I bought some Christmas tinsel from Chapel Market to decorate my cab with.

These days there's a graduation ceremony at TfL's Palestra building, where the Director of Taxi & Private Hire gives an inspirational speech, and poses for photos as he hands you your badge. Your proud loved ones record everything on camera, and you can laugh and joke with your old examiners as equals. It's a happy occasion. There were no such festivities welcoming me to the trade back in 1988. I just walked up to the Booking Out window on my own, paid my licence fee, and collected my licence, copy licence and green enamel badge. That was it; I was a London Cab Driver. Welcome aboard, son.

2

Butter Boy

My next job that afternoon was to acquire a working cab. I sold my old decommissioned manual cab to a local taxi garage and drove off with a rented seven-year-old automatic. A business start-up in the cab trade is easy: on the day you're licensed you arrange to rent a taxi, learn how to stop and start the meter, and away you go. So, armed with a licensed cab with meter, and a working knowledge of the mansion blocks on Prince of Wales Drive I gradually eased my way into my new career by working my first few hours on Saturday December 9th 1988.

A new cab driver is called a Butter Boy. No one knows for sure why. I've heard two plausible explanations. One is that the term means "But a Boy". Another refers to the feeling that the new driver is taking the butter out of the older driver's mouth. New male drivers are known as Butter Boys regardless of age. I assume new female drivers are called Butter Girls. I've not heard them referred to as such but I don't yet think there's a gender-neutral term for a newbie.

How long does one remain a Butter Boy? I'd say until they have experienced the different phases of the first yearly cycle: the depressingly slow New Year period, the pleasant spring and summer seasons, the busy autumn months, and the fraught and frenetic Christmas period. The different seasons bring different joys and fears. First, we have to get through the deadly slow New Year Kipper Season. This is another term shrouded in mystery. It's possible that in earlier times cab drivers would choose the cheapest meal on the café menu, which was kippers. Or it could just mean that the trade is as flat as a kipper. In recent years, the Kipper Season has lasted well into March. It's depressing driving on dark winter evenings, but my mood lifts when spring shows its head and things get lighter and warmer.

The Knowledge was the most challenging learning task I'd ever completed, and it remains so today. I'd proved myself, and I had the confidence to find my way around London. London's cab trade is unique in that you are expected to know much of it before you start. You don't learn it as you go along as in other cities around the world. The Knowledge forms a good basis on which to build, but you still need to work at it and keep it topped up. London is vast and there's still a lot to learn once you've earned your green badge. You learn something new every day, but you will never know it all. There is some truth in the saying that your Knowledge is never as good as it is when you've just qualified. A new cab driver may have a better grasp of the suburbs than a more experienced driver, as there are some parts of London that cab drivers are rarely asked to go to, particularly in the day time. A day driver will rarely be asked to go to Tooting or Lewisham. I've heard experienced drivers complaining about being asked to go to Hackney Wick Station. It was if they'd been asked to find the source of the Nile. I can understand that. I was asked to go there in 2018 and I was well out of my comfort zone, as I hadn't been there since doing the Knowledge thirty years ago. The experienced driver will certainly have a more intimate relationship with inner London though, as that's where you're likely to spend most of your time.

Cabs and Cabmen

I rented various FX4s. This is the cab with the "iconic" body shape that reigned supreme for several decades. The engines and interiors changed over time, but the body shape had remained the same since 1958. The cab had an instrument panel like you'd expect to find on a military vehicle from the Second World War, and a steering wheel the size of a cartwheel that left black marks on your trousers. Various engines were used, mostly woefully underpowered. Driving up steep hills you'd be crawling along belching out black smoke while faster vehicles queued behind you. Almost all London cabs were diesel automatics, and by the time I started, most had power assisted brakes and steering. The cabs I drove were either poorly maintained by the garages, or they weren't very good vehicles to start with. I think it was a bit of both. Today's cabs are extensively tested in freezing arctic conditions and in hot desert climates. I don't think the cabs of the 80s were even tested in London. They would fail to start in the winter, and overheat in the summer. It would often be necessary to squirt some Easy Start up the air filter tube to get the cab going in the morning. A garage would leave a gallon of water and some top-up oil in the boot, as radiators and engines would regularly leak fluid. Broken down cabs and buses issuing steam from radiators were a common sight in the summers of the 1980s and 1990s.

Separating the driver's compartment from the passenger cabin was a transparent glass partition (it's now made of plastic). By Carriage Office law, you could only have a gap in your partition of 4½ inches. Many drivers removed the wooden block from the partition groove and opened the partition fully. When the noisy rumble of a loud diesel engine combined with the soundtrack of London you could barely hear the customers. If you meet taxi drivers away from work you will notice that they tend to shout, even when you're not speaking to their back through a 4½-inch gap. The partition gap is now fixed, and even with quieter cabs and intercoms, communication is difficult. It's not surprising that most complaints received at the PCO are put down to a lack of communication.

After a year or so I bought a new Fairway taxi. This model essentially retained the FX4 body shape, but came with a powerful 2.7 litre Nissan engine and many modern modifications. The switches and dashboard made the interior feel a bit more like a modern car of the time. You could have a dash-mounted stereo radio and cassette player – luxury! It wasn't long ago that radios were banned from London taxis altogether, and before the Fairway they were hidden away under the roof. You could also have electric windows and air-conditioning if you were particularly flash.

The Fairway was more modern and comfortable, but it was unmistakably still a taxi. I've never wanted a taxi to look and feel like a car – where's the fun in that? It has to be unique. The Fairway proved itself reliable, and drivers had a lot of affection for the model. The last Fairways in London were retired in 2014, but taxi aficionados can still find a few working in the provinces.

The trade has ridden on a nice wave of publicity ever since scientific researchers at University College London found that cab drivers had bigger brains than everyone else. Kind of. Apparently, the hippocampus; the part of the brain that's associated with memory in birds and animals is enlarged in the brain of a cab driver in comparison to other people. It also grows with use.

I don't think it makes you talk more, but regular cab customers know that conversation is attempted by many lonely souls deprived of basic human contact. The stereotype of the garrulous cabbie doesn't really hold up though. Most respect your privacy and don't speak until spoken to. Be warned though, once they have the green light to talk you might not be able to stop them. You don't need diversity awareness training or political correctness workshops to do this job. There's no manager supervising your work and making sure you project the right corporate image. Many drivers are listening to talk radio for twelve hours a day and are never short of opinions on current affairs. Advice and opinion comes unfiltered straight from the tap. Cab drivers dominate talk radio phone-ins such as LBC, and politicians wanting the real feelings on the street regularly canvass the opinions of cab drivers.

The advent of smartphones spoilt things a bit when drivers found they could record conversations. In 2014, a cab driver picked up David Mellor. He found the former Conservative Party Minister in a foul mood and they argued over the route taken. Mellor called the driver a "stupid, sweaty little shit" and told him to "fuck off." In an almost unbelievable show of arrogance he added: "You've been driving a cab for 10 years, I've been in the cabinet, I'm an award-winning broadcaster, I'm a Queen's Counsel. You think that your experiences are anything compared to mine?" The driver recorded the exchange and it made the national media. Mellor apologised later, but I'm sure he would've found it hard to get a cab for a while afterwards. Generally though, I consider it bad form to record someone. What happens in the cab should stay in the cab.

If some cab drivers are considered too nosey and opinionated, others could be viewed as grumpy. I try to avoid grumpiness, but please bear in mind that considerable concentration is required to steer a cab safely around congested streets full of other cabs, buses, cycles and pop-up pedestrians. Drivers can't always give you their full attention when things are busy on the roads.

All cab drivers join the trade as part of a career change. They aren't school-leavers: they're hairy-armed blokes who have been doing proper man's jobs for years; plus an increasing number of women who have been doing sensible work for a good while. Cab driving is not something you think of doing while at school, and you can't take a course in Cab Studies at your local further education college. The cab trade is rather like the French Foreign Legion, in that it provides a sanctuary for misfits and freaks from around the world: people not suited to conventional employment. You join to forget your past. It doesn't involve teamwork, though, and there's no boss telling you what to do. The trade best suits those who are happy working alone and are left to do their own thing their own way. The only authorities we need to worry about are the police and the Carriage Office if we step out of line; and the parking wallahs when we nip into a café for a coffee.

Cab driving is widely regarded to be the best part-time job you can have. Many drivers combine it with other work as it offers so much flexibility, and when things are running well it can provide a decent income. For many, cab driving is not their main job, or their main talent. Many cab drivers are involved in music and acting; two occupations that involve working strange hours with plenty of downtime. I remember stopping at the Paddington tea stall and being surprised to see a bloke in the cab parked next to me blowing into a saxophone. He had the interior light on, his door open, and he was following his notes from a sheet on a music stand. If you ever go to a West End musical there's a fair chance that someone on stage will be driving a cab the next morning. Some cab drivers combine it with what are considered good conventional jobs. The man who I rented my cab from said I was about the only driver at the garage who wasn't a teacher. The cab trade often provides a home for ex-professional sportsmen. Knowledge Examiners have seen some well-known footballers pass through the system. The first person to buy one of the new electric cabs in 2018 was ex-professional tennis player, David Harris.

Many drivers are kind and generous. As a Knowledge Boy up at Penton Street, a cab driver took me over the road for a coffee before my Appearance. One drove me home as a customer to Highbury from the West End. He sat for a while talking about the Knowledge. His advice was to "drop people off where you want to drop them." That's good advice. I often agonise whether to go to the proper set down at Paddington, or drop in Praed Street. Both options are right, so if the customer doesn't express a preference, I'll drop off at the most convenient spot for me.

Various cab charities run excursions for underprivileged children or war veterans. On the road, a cab driver will often help to assist someone whose vehicle has broken down; either a fellow cab driver or a civilian. In my experience, cab drivers know little more about cars than a regular car driver, and we are at the mercy of the breakdown services and garages as much as everyone else. I don't know one end of an engine from another, but I could write a passable short story about one. Twelve hundred words on bushes and wishbones by Monday, no problem.

If you're ever visited London, you've probably walked by a cab shelter. Perhaps you've thought these mysterious green wooden huts were used to store gardening equipment for the Royal Parks. Or were flower stalls. The chimney gives a clue to their true function. They are little cafes exclusively for cab drivers, containing little but rows of bench seating. They were started as a philanthropic move to provide cab men shelter from inclement weather in the nineteenth century – and to keep them out of the grog shop. Between 1875 and 1950, forty-seven shelters were set up by influential people as a form of charity. They are fewer in number these days, but several still exist. Oh, the green hut in the middle of New Bond Street *is* a flower stall.

One of the first things I did early on in my new career was to have a coffee in a cab shelter. It's something of a tradition for veteran cab drivers to tell newcomers and Knowledge Boys that "the game's dead." On my first visit to the Aldwych shelter, another cab driver asked me how long it took me to complete the Knowledge. On replying that it took me three and a half years, the driver helpfully told me it would take me "longer than that to get out of it." As it happened he wasn't far wrong, but at the time I was young and keen to work. I didn't pay attention to some silly old man and his negative "the game's dead" attitude.

Veteran cab drivers like to remind newcomers of their seniority. I had one driver pretend to polish his badge to remind me that mine was still green and shiny. Actually, they remain green and shiny if you leave them be. The old boys with something to prove make them look old on purpose. They probably spend hours rubbing away the enamel to give it that distressed look. Drivers now have to display an identifier in the back window of their cab with their badge number on it. Drivers who lose their badges get a new licence number and identifier when TfL replace their badge. In order not to be mistaken for a Butter Boy, some of them write their original licence number underneath the new one (sigh).

Cab Women

Over the years, women have been disgracefully held back by the Public Carriage Office, the unions and the government. Thankfully things have now changed. The cab trade is now proudly democratic, and completely free from gender inequality, or pay gap.

In the earliest days of the cab trade, a widow could inherit her husband's hackney carriage. A list from 1664 lists nineteen women who had inherited licences. Females would have found it hard going though, in such a male-dominated world.

In the supposedly more enlightened twentieth century there was still considerable resistance to women driving cabs, and despite the Sex Disqualification (Removal) Act of 1919, women were still discriminated against. It seems unbelievable now, but in 1922 the London and Provincial Union of Licensed Vehicle Workers balloted its members on strike action should a woman appear on the road as a cab driver. Women were held back on the Knowledge, and in the unlikely event they should they succeed in gaining a licence they would have found it difficult to find a cab to drive. The situation remained very difficult for females until at least 1946; despite women's valiant work building planes, tanks, shells and guns for the war effort.

It was the usual fears over women taking over men's jobs. This attitude wasn't of course confined to the cab trade, and I'm not sure how much resentment was down to the actual drivers.

There were few female cab drivers when I started out, and it's good to see a lot more nowadays. It's an intimidating, macho, world out there on the streets of London, and I respect and admire the women who have taken on the challenge. God bless 'em. Female cab drivers don't tend to be shrinking violets. They aren't necessarily accomplished at embroidery and on the piano forte but they are skilled in employing a range of put-downs should any chauvinistic dinosaur tell her she should be at home making her old man's tea.

Making a Start

My first job was to take a young lady from Theobald's Road, Holborn, to Victoria Station. Nothing too complicated. By tradition, cab drivers give their first ride free of charge. Either I didn't know about the tradition at the time, or I was so worried about the debts I'd built up on the Knowledge, that I charged her as normal. I really don't remember. Many years later I read that it was acceptable to donate the fare to charity, so I added on twenty-five years worth of interest and did just that. It was a belated attempt to claw back some good fortune, but it made me feel a bit better.

I found my first few days mentally exhausting and tended to go home after a few hours. My strategy was to build my hours up gradually. I soon settled into a routine. I'd set out from my home in Highbury at 2.30 pm and stop at about 7 pm for an hour's dinner break. There were four private taxi cafes in Central London I used to frequent, complete with toilet and parking facilities. Here you would experience the vast range of personalities that make up the London cab trade. Many sit in groups, but many others sit alone keeping themselves to themselves. Did you notice that quiet bloke reading his book or writing out notes? That's me. Sometimes I'd park semi-legally on a rank near Piccadilly Circus and visit the New Piccadilly Café in Denman Street. This legendary Italian eatery sadly closed down several years ago. As now, my meal stops were largely determined by the availability of parking and toilet facilities. I'd have another half hour coffee break later in the evening. I'd work five days per week. The great thing about the job is that it's so flexible. You can use the twenty-four hour clock to arrange your work hours. I'd work a bit at the weekends but made sure I had Mondays off as my fun day.

Speeding traps and speed bumps were in their infancy back then. Traffic systems were less complicated and things flowed easier. Parking up to get a meal or a coffee wasn't as risky as it is now. I remember parking in Brompton Road and on Kensington High Street to go on brief shopping trips. The traffic was lighter and there were no cameras.

I found my way around all right, and had the opportunity to top up my knowledge of the suburbs by regularly driving people home to the Blue Book's six-mile limit and beyond. I'd frequently get out to Clapham and Balham; places on the

Northern Line that the locals were scared to travel back to at night on the underground. Trips out west were common, as were fares going north. I'd often drive Japanese businessmen home to suburbs such as Finchley. It was a nice eight-mile jaunt, and one that I was delighted to undertake when I was thinking of home and living in North London. I don't know where the Japanese have gone to, but I miss them.

The eight until ten period was quite pleasant: things were nice and relaxed and there was little traffic. Initially, I'd work until about midnight, but I soon found that the nature of the job changed from about ten o'clock. Once the theatre burst had cleared you had to be on your guard for boozers and weirdos. You learn early on to stop some yards beyond a potential customer to see if they can walk straight. You learn never to pick anyone up who is being physically supported by friends.

I generally found customers nicer than I imagined they'd be. Most people are relaxed when they are going home, and some customers are very generous of spirit. In my early days working late, one or two people invited me into their homes for a Christmas drink – which I declined. One person gave me a bottle of champagne as a Christmas tip. Past ten o'clock many people have had too much to drink. Most cab customers who've had a few drinks and are being loud wouldn't attract attention in a crowded pub, but in the confined space of a taxi they can make a hell of a noise, and can be intimidating. I found this aspect of the work difficult. I could shrug off the comments that my services were expensive as I don't set the fares, but I was angered by any perceived lack of respect and boorish behaviour. In those days I lacked the confidence to attempt to stop any bad behaviour. Knowing you can't reason with drunks anyway, I became nervous working beyond ten o'clock, and I cut my hours. I also became lazy.

Gangsters, prostitutes, Essex girls who've had too much to drink: who's most likely to give trouble? You got it; it's the drinker every time. Certain groups of people have a particular presence about them. You can tell actors, gangsters and prostitutes by a bearing unique to their profession. I like to think I can identify actors by their confidence and their loud, clear, voices. Some people just look familiar from TV. Sex workers are of course actors of sorts. They are always friendly. Members of these three groups tend to be polite and respectful, charming even. They are respectful of others doing unconventional work at unconventional hours and don't give trouble. They're not squeamish about money and have a pragmatic approach to business. Early in my career a prostitute asked me matter-of-factly to take her to the "red light beat" of Stamford Hill. Another cheerful lady who I was driving to City Airport told me how she was being flown out to Paris to meet a client. All our customers have a story to tell.

Despite having a new cab and enjoying the status as owner-driver, I became disillusioned. Once the honeymoon period was over I became complacent. Living in rented bedsitters I had few responsibilities. I had a disposable income far larger than I have now, and much of it went on foreign holidays, and days off. I'd put money away for my tax, and I even paid into a private pension plan for a while when times were good. I proudly told my landlord that I only went to work when I needed the money. Arrogant, but pretty true.

Notwithstanding the reduced hours, I noticed a reduction in business. I didn't know it at the time, but a major recession had started following the big financial crash of 1987. I used to circuit the St James and Mayfair areas looking for work on the street. These places used to be buzzing with people. After a few months the place was deserted. Rather than stay out longer in order to maintain my income levels, I took the opposite approach and took more time off. I started to find the job demoralising and I figured my time would be better spent in West End cinemas when the work dried up.

I admit to having an inferiority complex at the time. My brother, Andrew, had gained a PhD and was forging a successful career in cancer research. My Turkish girlfriend, Nilüfer, was about to graduate as a teacher in Ankara. What were my qualifications? I knew about bridges and one-way systems. I now know that to be a daft thing to think, but dissatisfaction with my chosen career led me to look for an early exit and to a field where I perceived the grass to be greener.

3

My Personal Revolution

At a family meal in Blackheath I announced to my family my intention to go to university. No one laughed. I was going to change my career whatever it took, but having the support of my family helped me on my journey. I call this period My Personal Revolution.

My initial idea involved moving to Turkey to live with my girlfriend, Nilüfer. I researched teaching English as a foreign language, but found I'd need a degree to do it properly. Going to university was an interesting idea, but there was the little matter of A-levels. My secondary school career was lamentable and I left without qualifications. I didn't even take O-levels at sixteen, so it was highly unlikely I'd get anywhere near an institute of higher learning. The idea was a non-starter, unless I spent years studying at night school. My determination was such that I decided to find out about courses to start ASAP.

I discovered courses that allow you to achieve equivalent qualifications to A-levels. Interestingly, these access courses for adults are sometimes run by residential colleges. Even better, you could apply for a grant. This option excited me, and before long I found myself on a train bound for West Wales for an interview at Coleg Harlech.

I vaguely remember changing trains at Wolverhampton, then again at a town in Wales that I'm not going to attempt to spell here. Suffice to say it had a long name containing a lot of Ls. A smaller train took me slowly across a not unattractive, but alien landscape of marshes and estuaries, before pulling in at Harlech. It was a small town with a long sweeping sandy beach and a remote feel. This place would suit me fine.

The first thing I do on arrival in any new town is check out the pub action. I had one beer in a town centre pub before returning to the bar at college. It was as quiet as the pub I'd just visited.

I then noticed a commotion at the other end of the room. I thought, perchance, a chapter of Hell's Angels had burst in and were about to kick over some tables – and perhaps look for some English people to harass. This gang of noise-merchants turned out to be the very students charged with looking after me for the night. They duly took me under their wing. I don't know what time I got to bed, but there was a fair bit of drinking and herb-burning in one of their rooms. I told one chap he had the air of a union leader. He was thrilled with my description, as that was exactly the image he wanted to project. They were yobbos turned born-again intellectuals. I could identify with that, and I felt it was something to aspire too. I'd meet plenty more people like this over the next few years.

I was interviewed the following day, but they didn't feel I was quite ready for the Harlech experience. I was given a booklist and encouraged to apply the following year. I read most of the books on the list in the months that followed, and I still occasionally read my favourite ones. In order to strengthen my application I took a short A Taste of English distance learning course with the National Extension College. I found it easy, so signed up for a more ambitious A-level in English Language & Literature. Again, I didn't find it particularly difficult, just interesting and a lot of fun. My tutor said I could have gained an A or B grade, but by the time of the exam I had a college offer in the bag. I still regret not sitting the exam to see how I would have done.

I didn't reapply to Coleg Harlech though. I was offered a place on a similar course at Fircroft College of Adult Education in Birmingham. As I had friends in Birmingham I took it. In September 1993 I drove up to Birmingham in a rented cab, nearly demolished a college wall by reversing into it, and unloaded several boxes of CDs into my little college room on the first floor. I drove the cab back to the garage in Hackney and left it there until the next college vacation. The long-distance romance with Nilüfer in Turkey didn't survive, so I started the course with a need to rebuild my self-esteem. I had no distractions and a hunger to succeed.

Birmingham

As I entered the door of Fircroft College I felt I'd come home. For nine months I was to live and work with like-minded men and women; people who were keen to learn, but were yet to reach their potential. We had underachieved in our respective ways and were now ready to prove ourselves.

I enjoyed the study, and I did other things that I'd never attempted before. Jason Hudson and I volunteered to write the college newsletter/scandal sheet, under the fatherly eye of inspirational tutor, Dave Turner. I played around with a bit of ham acting, did a parachute jump for charity, and

Dave Gregory and I performed Monty Python's "Argument Sketch" for the end of year revue. I also got myself fit by running around the sports field at the back of the college.

Most students went on to apply to university, and it was an exciting time making applications towards the end of the year. By the time the course finished I was holding unconditional places at a couple of universities without being interviewed, and I later attended a few admissions interviews at other universities I'd applied to. I didn't apply to any universities in London as I wanted a completely new cultural experience. I certainly got that at Bradford.

Bradford

The University of Bradford is a small, down-to-earth, university in a working class industrial city. Bradford was palpably poor compared with London, and quite run down. You knew you were in the north. You could go to a trendy wine bar in Leeds or Manchester and pretend you were in the south, but there were no such pretensions here. Bradford was racially divided, with a Pakistani inner city, and just a few suburbs left for those who hadn't joined the white flight out to other towns and villages. It was an odd place to be sure: rough as hell, but generally friendly and welcoming.

I was sold on Bradford because of its reputation as a curry capital, and because it was a relatively inexpensive place in which to live. It's also a good town for real ale. Naturally, I explored two or three pubs on my interview day. The university's Steve Biko Bar was the only university bar listed in the *Good Beer Guide*. I was very impressed.

Many students were nervous about going into the city centre during the hours of darkness. Per capita, there are probably as many freaks and weirdos in Bradford as there are in London. Not to mention hard geezers. You certainly had to be on your guard: Bradford's a tough working class city, and students are seen as a soft touch. At thirty-two, I wouldn't have looked like an obvious student, but I looked and sounded like I came from the soft south.

I was a smaller fish in a bigger pond at university. It didn't have the intimacy of Fircroft College, but my Interdisciplinary Human Studies Department (IHS) was sited in a terraced house opposite the main university, and we had a bit of a community thing going on there.

IHS looked at humanity through the study of logic, literature, sociology, philosophy and psychology. In a university geared to serious vocational subjects like science and engineering, IHS was widely regarded as a woolly arts subject for dilettantes and southern poufdahs. Buoyed by my rebirth as an intellectual I happily embraced the image of a southern arty type, complete with a philosophy book sticking out the pocket of my suede jacket. I probably convey a similarly effete image at the cab cafes today.

I was older than most of my colleagues, but I was comfortable with this situation and I enjoyed playing it up. Whenever students mentioned certain bands I would say I'd never heard of them, like that high court judge did when someone mentioned the Beatles in court. I could talk about actually seeing The Jam and The Clash play live back in the day. And I'd chatted to Robert Plant of Led Zeppelin in my cab. That kind of thing gains a man respect. Gathered around for a seminar the others were talking about their gap year. I proudly said that I'd taken sixteen years out. My comment raised a laugh, which pleased me. I should be on the stage.

I somehow got myself on to the *University Challenge* team. We weren't like the nerdy Oxbridge teams you see on TV; more like the Scumbag College team on *The Young Ones*. We knew little about classical music or art. We'd have a fair stab on questions about beer, bands and football, but that's not really what *University Challenge* is all about. We were called to Leeds to have a chat with researchers, but we weren't chosen to take part in the TV show.

Early on in the year, a colleague told me they were interviewing students interested in spending their middle year abroad. I hurriedly applied and was interviewed. I was delighted to find I'd won a competitive place to spend the following year at Louisiana State University.

Louisiana

Louisiana State University sits on the banks of the Mississippi River in the sprawling southern suburbs of Baton Rouge. It felt rich and confident, with beautiful buildings, and students with good dentistry.

American Football was taken seriously. The Tigers football stadium housed 80,000 spectators and they regularly filled it. When REM played at the university they were put in the basketball arena rather than on the hallowed turf of Tiger Stadium. Thanks to American punctuality I only caught the last five minutes of the support band's set: an up and coming British outfit called Radiohead. I still regret turning up late for that one.

It was a world away from Bradford. Even the weather was alien. I arrived on the LSU Campus on a boiling hot August day. It was like walking through treacle. I'd never known heat and humidity like it. It was hot most of the year, but during a brief run of chilly weather around Christmas, they closed the place down. They need to spend a winter in Yorkshire some time and toughen up a bit!

At Christmas I went travelling to even sunnier climes anyway. Finnish Erik and I got a Greyhound bus down to San Antonio, Texas, for a night; then made for the Mexican border the following day. In the UK you can drive from Cornwall to Scotland in a day. It's easy to underestimate the size of the USA. Distances between cities can be huge, especially in Texas. We spent several hours gazing at the same dull scenery. I sometimes imagine using a sat nav in Texas: "Continue for 400 miles…" We spent Christmas in Mexico City and visited a couple of smaller towns before booking a Mexican coach back to Louisiana from a border town. We paid $50 each and the driver dropped us off right on the LSU campus.

In a British university you take one main subject, with perhaps one or two minor courses. In the US you can mix and match anything. Despite my eventual degree title, I had free rein to pick whatever courses I wanted to take. I took courses such as The Western and French, alongside the sort of courses I'd been studying at Bradford.

They might speak a kind of English in the USA, but it is definitely a foreign country. There wasn't much of a city centre in Baton Rouge, and it certainly wasn't like the vibrant cities we are used to in Britain. Bradford might have been a bit down-at-heel, but it had some life to it. Downtown Baton Rouge was like a ghost town, with an eerily hushed atmosphere. There were just a handful of bars, restaurants and shops, catering for the few office workers who ventured out at lunchtime. Public transport was almost non-existent, and it was frustrating not being able to get around. There were very few buses, and the train station was a train museum.

There were fewer older students than there were at Bradford. It didn't worry me unduly, but it added to the culture shock. Most students were from small towns or from suburbs of bigger towns, usually in the southern states. They tended to be more conservative than British students. I tried fighting against the aspects of American culture that I didn't agree with, and I sometimes found the early days a bit difficult. There were times that if I saw a 38 bus going to Clapham Junction I would have got on it. I eventually realised I couldn't change things and settled in.

I made friends with some American students, and there were many international students to associate with too. There were several British students on exchange programmes such as myself, plus others from around the world. I took a trip out to the alligator bayous of South Louisiana with American, British, French, German and Dutch students.

The British students were housed in the same halls of residence – women's halls were separate (a local student said mixed dorms would never happen in the South). We formed a happy band, visiting the bars within walking distance of the campus. Many American students had cars and could drive out to other places. There were no bars on campus as you had to be twenty-one to drink alcohol, and most students were underage. Local bars were strict and asked for ID. I was asked for ID a few times and I was thirty-two. The international students tended to be older. The British and Irish contingent formed good relationships with students of different nationalities, particularly the exchange students from the former Soviet Union who were accommodated in our halls. The Asian students were more work-focussed and didn't tend to socialise in bars. Some Indian students talked about playing cricket, but I don't know if anything came of it. That would've freaked the locals out.

You learned to take what the Americans said with a pinch of salt: if they said you couldn't walk to a certain bar because it was too far away I took it as a challenge. I found one or two new places that way. One evening a big group of British and Mexican students walked up to a bar in the "ghetto" on Highland Road. The Americans considered Highland Road a no-go area for white folks – another challenge to put to the test. With an erratic bus service I'd walked up Highland Road to the downtown area a few times. It was certainly all right in the daytime. There wasn't a lot going on downtown, so there was little need to visit at night anyway. My English compatriot, Darrel, told of stopping at a convenience store on Highland Road and drawing a crowd of locals marvelling at his Birmingham accent.

There was something of a de facto segregation thing going on around the campus, with black and white students sitting apart. They'd sit in their own groups around campus and in the dining halls. I don't think there was any bad feeling, but I got the impression that many of the white students' experience of black people was having their parents' homes cleaned. I went to several LSU Tigers football games. It was a great experience, but even there I noticed that groups of black students sat apart in Tiger Stadium. I wrote about my observations in a letter to the university newsletter. When word got around who wrote the letter I was briefly feted as a black hero. The black students seemed to know more about the real world and were definitely the coolest people on campus.

LSU students could also take courses as part of an agreement with Southern University, also in Baton Rouge. Southern was smaller, less affluent; and was essentially a black university. Southern was one of the few places you could get to on public transport, so I caught the free shuttle bus up from LSU. I was interested in taking a race relations course and relished the interesting dynamic of being the only white person in class. Sadly, the class only ran in the evening. The bus didn't.

I'd plodded along happily at both universities without exerting myself, so back in Bradford I had to work hard on my final year dissertation to turn things around. I scraped a 2:1 degree on the strength of my dissertation on the concepts of Englishness.

Hey Teacher!

I took to being a student straight away. Loved it. The work wasn't too challenging. The living was easy. I was privileged to be one of the last cohorts to get a full tuition and maintenance grant. I feel sorry for today's students who have to take on part-time jobs to survive, and then leave with a huge bill that'll take years to pay off.

In my final year at Bradford I took part in a student tutoring programme, spending time in a girls' secondary school helping out in the classroom. I enjoyed my afternoons at school and thought I might like to be a teacher. I'd been thinking about becoming a university lecturer but was put off when I realised how competitive it was. I was now confident I could be a good teacher and applied for courses. I was delighted to be offered a place on a Postgraduate Certificate in Education (PGCE) course at the University of Birmingham. I was to train to teach Secondary English.

Throughout my academic career I'd rented a cab out in vacations. After graduating I spent a happy few months staying with my mum and stepfather in Blackheath. The cab trade had improved after the recession, I had a degree, and I was going back to university in September. I was to stay with my friend, Adam, in Birmingham, when my teaching course started. Things were looking good.

I met up again with Darrel from Birmingham that summer. We were friends at LSU, and I bumped into him in the street in Birmingham when I was on a visit there. I told him about a voluntary project I'd heard about, and we both signed up. We spent a month living with families in Olsztynek in Eastern Poland teaching them English. The Sternik family's English was already pretty good so it was largely a matter of spending evenings in a local bar and conversing. If any local females wanted to join in, that was great.

Before I went up to Birmingham to start my teaching course I had to spend a week or two observing at a primary school. I enjoyed myself at a school in Blackheath and was still convinced this teaching lark was for me. Oh the idealism of it.

My placement ended at the end of the school term. I joined the teachers in a local pub and curry house on the last day. These female primary school teachers were the biggest bunch of boozers I've ever had the pleasure to meet. After a while one teacher asked me how many beers I'd had. When I replied I'd had three pints she told me I'd have to do better. I'd have to up my game by way of drinking, but I was excited about my fledgling teaching career.

At the University of Birmingham I enjoyed the university-based study, but wasn't prepared for the practical placement.

I was allocated a girls' school in workaday East Birmingham. On placement you are for all intents and purposes a proper teacher, albeit with a reduced workload. I had to plan lessons and schemes of work, deliver lessons, and take books away to be marked (usually undertaken at the New Inn, Harborne). My brief experience as a student tutor in Bradford had lulled me into a false sense of security. School discipline was poor, and staff morale was low. The pupil intake was 80% Muslim and the school felt as if it was run by the Taliban. It was oppressive. A member of senior management told me the school was known as a "Paki school", and it played this up in fine style. Eid was a big occasion, but I was told the school didn't celebrate Christmas or Easter. I couldn't imagine this place being much fun for the Christian minority.

Girls would disappear for months, but their absence wasn't treated as anything unusual. I believe they were being sent to Pakistan to get married. I found the whole set-up abhorrent, but what could I do? I was just a student teacher, struggling to make sense of it all and keep out of trouble. Even back then I knew not to question cultural practices.

I'd like to blame my failure to see the course out on the oppressive Christmas tree-less environment of the school, but I can't. I'd like to tell you that I had the no-nonsense hard man demeanour of one of Ray Winstone's film characters, but I can't. I had no stage presence. My nervousness probably showed, and the absurdity of my situation played on me. Well, I would have laughed if someone told me in the 1970s that I'd be a teacher.

However stressful it is pushing a cab down Oxford Street, it's nothing like waiting for that school bell to go. When thirty teenaged girls run riot they are a match for anybody, and I found it difficult to assert my authority without being heavy-handed and threatening whole-class detentions. Things could be unruly at my Hornchurch comprehensive in the 70s, but at least there was some discipline. The principal sanction here was a black stamp in the girls' exercise book.

I also thought it would be an eight-to-four job, with a bit of marking in the evenings. I'm quite a disciplined person. In the cab I have exactly an hour for lunch and exactly thirty minutes for coffee. In teaching, you're working to bells, but your work duties are flexible and are frequently changed at a moment's notice. If you have any free time they'll find you something to do. And if you have no free time, they'll still find you something extra to do. Your lunch break could be taken up with playground duty, and you could be running any number of little projects before and after school hours. Once they found out I was a cab driver they'd surely have me driving the school bus. I could see the way it was going and I couldn't live my life like that.

A fair few students on my course had already left. I never thought I'd do the same, but soon after New Year in 1998 I left before I was pushed. I returned to London with my tail between my legs and to my mum in Blackheath.

Back to London

I needed to find a place to rent. One evening I went to see West Ham play at Crystal Palace. In a strange twist, the very next day I ended up renting a flat right by the stadium in Holmesdale Road. I called my house the Holmesdale Road End.

I was a full time cab driver again, but dissatisfied how my career had panned out. I visited the Job Centre. There were no openings for trainee philosophers in South Norwood, so I revisited earlier ideas about making my way back to university and staying there. I signed up for an MA course in Popular Culture. The course was with the Open University, so I could stay in London and work around the course. At Masters' level there isn't much supervision; I just had occasional seminars to attend. You need a lot of self-discipline to study this way, but I showed the same level of determination I showed ten years ago on the Knowledge.

I always smile when cab drivers claim the Knowledge is the equivalent of two or three A-levels. Nonsense. The Knowledge is much harder than that. I wouldn't say there was anything particularly hard about either of my degree courses. The formal academic process just helps you to think critically and to write essays. Many people have the ability to think critically: the skill is getting it all down on paper, succinctly and without waffle. Once you learn how to write essays you gain a degree by working steadily and producing coherent works on things you've read in books. In my first year at Bradford my Department Head told us straight how to score in a philosophy essay: "tell me what Plato thinks, tell me what Descartes thinks, and then tell me what *you* think." That advice kept me in good stead.

I used to spend a lot of time in libraries consulting the huge *Occupations* book and researching possible careers. After much soul-searching I signed up for a one-year Diploma in Careers Guidance at the University of Central England in Birmingham. I reckoned it would be less high-powered and less stressful than teaching. I suppose it was natural for someone who didn't know what to do with his life to become a Careers Adviser. Having said that, I'm now fifty-six and I still don't know what to do when I grow up.

Ironically, as part of the course I had to buy a copy of the Career Advisers' bible, *Occupations,* the weighty encyclopaedia of jobs that I'd spent so much time consulting in public libraries. In anticipation of my new professional career I made a terrible mistake: I decided not to renew my cab licence.

Careers Adviser, Advise Thyself

Back in Birmingham, I once again enjoyed being part of a close-knit group of students on a speciality course; this time at UCE's Westbourne Campus in Edgbaston.

We had to undertake three practical placements. I was happy to take a long-distance placement at Bradford Careers. It cost me quite a lot of money, but I enjoyed being back in Bradford. I lived in a room at the New Beehive Inn for two weeks. I'd pop down to the bar for a pint, and I had ten consecutive curry dinners, just to see if I could do it. Experiment complete, my findings concluded that I never get sick of curry, or beer.

My second placement was two bus rides away at Solihull Sixth Form College. I sat with the college's sole Careers Adviser and soaked up his experience. I still wasn't ready to impart careers advice at this stage, but I observed interviews and chipped in a bit. The college's adviser worked on his own most of the time. When he got bored he could walk around and talk to other members of staff or students. The students were bright sixteen and seventeen year olds so you could talk to them as adults and have proper discussions. If a student appeared to like his music I could witter on about going to see The Clash at the Lyceum. I could imagine myself ensconced happily in this kind of environment; supervising my own work and going walkabout when I wanted someone to chat to. It all appeared pleasant and easy-going, just what I wanted.

My third placement was at a boys' school in Birmingham. The kids might have sometimes made a noise and played up, but I got on with my teacher-mentor, and I rose to the challenge. Back at university though, I was still daydreaming in class and not taking everything in (ADHD? More about that later…). After failing the practical interviewing assessments I had to return to take them after the course had officially ended.

Towards the end of the academic year we'd start to look for jobs. Some people had jobs lined up before we left. I'm good on paper, but poor in interviews. I travelled as far south as Enfield and as far north as Whitehaven in Cumbria. I had eleven job interviews before I got lucky and was taken on by Career Path in Northamptonshire.

Careers advice isn't taken as seriously as it should be in schools. In 2000, careers education was something of a frivolous add-on to the curriculum, and it was to get even worse. A teacher would be allocated to take on the responsibilities of a Careers Coordinator. The Careers Coordinator wasn't qualified in careers advice and was prone to promote the school's own post-sixteen options. Schools were obliged to additionally enlist the services of visiting Careers Advisers, which is where I came in. Qualified and impartial advisers would visit the school maybe once a week and run group sessions and offer individual careers interviews. Visiting Careers Advisers weren't always treated with the respect they deserved. The school might book all your target pupils out for a trip without telling you, or they would just forget you were coming. On my first day in a Daventry school I was alarmed at being shown into a storeroom in which to conduct my interviews.

Later on at Mereway School in Northampton I was called in to the Headmaster's office. Being summoned to see the Headmaster reminded me of my canings back in the 70s and I fell decidedly ill at ease. He told me he was trying to build up his sixth form and he didn't want me promoting the competition. "The colleges can do their own promotion," he said. He didn't want to see any college prospectuses around. It was an astonishing and arrogant outburst, and one that clearly flies in the face of impartiality. I was a wet behind the ears probationer and didn't know how to react. I said little, but reported it to my supervisor back at Career Path. I don't know if anything was said to this twat of a Headmaster, but I could see that the world of career advice wasn't as cuddly as I thought it would be.

My motivation nosedived further when the whole school-based careers service was subsumed into the new Connexions initiative. Careers Advisers were de-professionalised overnight and unqualified people were sent out to deliver advice in schools. You no longer needed a Diploma in Careers Advice: if you had other experience working with teenagers you could essentially do the work of a Careers Adviser. The obvious cab trade parallel is licensing many thousands of private hire drivers to act as taxi drivers but with fewer rules and regulations.

I completed Part Two of my Diploma and was now a fully qualified Careers Adviser. I gained my MA at about the same time. The highpoint of my self-esteem was being interviewed by the Open University for the role of Associate Lecturer. I would have taught degree level courses in social history. I wasn't successful, but being given serious consideration was an achievement in itself. I'd covered a lot of ground in the last ten years. I firmly believe that passing the Knowledge of London gave me the confidence to believe I could succeed in anything I put my mind to.

However, I wasn't successful in securing a position as a Careers Adviser on Guernsey either. Several hopefuls were flown out for an overnight stay and interview, and I was bitterly disappointed not to be offered the job. Guernsey is my favourite place in the world and it would have been a dream come true. Feedback suggested I didn't get the job because I hadn't been trained to administer psychometric testing. Personality tests went out of the window when Connexions came in and Careers Advisers were pushed into being unqualified social workers. Thanks, Connexions.

Under the Connexions regime the focus was on the disaffected. They had a snappy acronym: NEET (Not in Education, Employment or Training). Those who were doing well in school were side-lined. The thinking was the more able could handle their own futures. It was those "At Risk" who were targeted. Most of us worked with kids with special needs and that's fair enough; but low attaining kids, or any kids with attendance problems or behavioural issues, were going to be pulled out for interview by your caring sharing Connexions personal adviser. In a charming piece of profiling, anyone from an ethnic minority background was labelled "At Risk". I would have found it objectionable to be labelled At Risk had I been black or Asian. Thankfully, the practice was eventually airbrushed out of history.

For a while I gave careers advice in St Andrew's Hospital, a medium security psychiatric institution. The teenagers I interviewed might well have been sectioned for murdering their siblings, but they were no more off the wall than those in mainstream schools.

The specialist institutions were better to work in. I spent a fair while at Gateway School. All the kids had been expelled from mainstream schools and had Statements of Educational Need. Many were diagnosed with Attention Deficit Hypersensitivity Disorder (ADHD) and were prescribed Ritalin to keep them calm. I wasn't even convinced such a disorder existed. In my day it was called being a little shit, and I probably suffered from it in the 70s (out of curiosity I recently took an online assessment to see if I had ADHD. No, I haven't got it, but I suspect my cat does).

The school's Careers Coordinator said our job was to keep the kids out of prison: "they inhabit a world I don't understand." I didn't understand it either. In many cases, the kids came from chaotic backgrounds with no boundaries. Often, the parents wouldn't turn up for their statement reviews, though the situation wasn't much better in mainstream schools, such is parental apathy these days. Notwithstanding inadequate parenting, Gateway School was well run and supportive of the children. Some kids certainly had the mind-set to succeed once let loose in the adult world.

A surprising number of children don't attend school at all. One little scam is home tuition. If a pupil is disruptive, the school will agree to allow the little cherub to be educated at home. This is good for the school as its league tables won't be brought down by a poorly performing pupil. The school will arrange for homework to be sent home, but most home educated pupils have parents who are unlikely to facilitate any meaningful study. Even the families that enter into the spirit of home education are doing little for their kids by way of socialisation.

My attitude hardened and I started to resent my job. I wasn't happy the way Careers Advisers were treated in schools, and I wasn't happy that Connexions had de-professionalised my job. I found it hard to relate to the kids I was interviewing. I didn't always see how I was helping people who wouldn't listen, or didn't have the capacity to make anything of their lives. Many youngsters lived in their own small world. In my world growing up in the 1970s, a sixteen-year-old would be expected to travel twenty miles across London to find work. Many of the teenagers I saw only knew their local area and would travel no further than the town centre. We could no longer be prescriptive in today's client-centred world of choice and personal ownership.

I started to play up. We were all issued with mobile phones. I took mine out of the box, but never charged it up. I saw it for what it was; an electrical leash. I'd enjoy the respite of a beer and burger lunch at Wetherspoons and I wouldn't always hurry back to the office.

I was put on a couple of disciplinary charges and was put on the At Risk register myself. I looked for a way out. I think my discipline problem was an unconscious move towards the exit. The company had funding issues and staffing was cut. I'd spent ten years as a Careers Adviser/Connexions personal adviser, and I was disillusioned with the professional world.

In moments of weakness I'd think about my old job as a cab driver. Was it that bad? I had my freedom back then, and I was my own man. More staffing cuts looked imminent. Even had I wanted to settle down, straighten out, and fly right; I didn't fancy my chances should the personal adviser team be downsized and I'd have to re-apply for my job. Although I was living seventy miles from London and hadn't driven a cab for eleven years, I applied to go back on the Knowledge.

4

Back on the Cab

I chose to become self-employed again because I was disillusioned with the so-called professional world. I had my name on a plastic badge to make myself look important, but from the outset I realised it was a sham. Driving a cab was in many ways more honest and pure. There was no pretence or politics. It had taken me several years to truly appreciate that.

I was the captain of my own ship again. I would look after my own discipline, and handle my own appraisals. Looking around the cab café months later, I wondered how my colleagues would take to supervision from a woman thirty years their junior. How might they justify their Performance Indicators over the past three months, and how they might improve their performance in the next quarter?

I was accepted back on to the Knowledge and prepared my plan of attack. After eleven years out of the trade, and out of London, I had forgotten so much. I could pinpoint geographical areas on a map of London, but I couldn't remember the names of the roads or how they linked up. I didn't join a Knowledge school, but I did purchase a sophisticated list of Runs from the Knowledge Point School. I thought if I physically ran a third, or a half, of the 320 prescribed Knowledge Runs it might take me a year; then maybe another year to complete the whole examination process.

I started the Knowledge all over again from the start, as any Knowledge Boy would: from Manor House Station to Gibson Square. I did this in a car, driving down to London from Northampton for a few hours at the weekend. I quite enjoyed reacquainting myself with the geography of London, though I didn't spend so much time chasing Points of Interest. I never did really.

I was to gain a new green badge sooner than I anticipated. After four months I received a letter from Transport for London. I was surprised to be invited to take a Knowledge Re-test. I didn't know re-tests existed (I think they'd only recently been brought in).

Had I thought about it more I might have been paralysed with fear, but I'd been given an Appearance many months before I expected. I felt I had little to lose. I would do well to convince the examiner that I was at the required standard to be relicensed, but if I didn't do it at the first go, I'd be asked to return in a few weeks time. I'm not sure how many times I'd have to reappear, but I'd still be ahead of the two-year schedule I had in my mind.

Transport for London had taken on responsibility for taxi licensing from the Metropolitan Police ten years previously, and had recently moved out of Penton Street into a very different environment of steel and glass.

On a hot summer's day, in July 2010, I found myself sitting in the waiting area of the Palestra building. I was called in by an examiner. He was cheery, and less formal than the examiners I experienced twenty-two years previously. He put me at ease. At the time I didn't knew who the examiners were, but I later found out him to be John Wilkin. What followed was the longest Appearance I'd ever experienced. Regular Appearances last fifteen or twenty minutes, and involve four questions. Mine was much longer. It felt like I was sat there for an hour, though it was almost certainly less. I was asked the type of Runs a regular Knowledge Boy would be asked, as well as some questions I wasn't expecting, such as suburban routes. I hadn't learnt any of the main routes out of Central London because I wasn't expected to be asked for them. I was also hit with a quick-fire round of Points of Interest. All in all I may have answered 40% of the questions well. Eventually, Mr Wilkin asked if I thought I'd "had enough?" I replied in the affirmative. To my surprise he said he was impressed with what I had shown, and invited me to get a coffee from the kitchen area while they prepare my badge and licence. Some minutes later, I handed over £200 and walked out with a shiny green badge.

Walking on air, I crossed Blackfriars Bridge aiming for the first pub I came to. I was almost there when a young woman asked if I knew where Blackfriars Lane was. I had to admit I wasn't sure. I was no longer capable of answering geography questions after my ordeal with Mr Wilkin. My brain had turned to mush, and only a pint or two of British ale would get it going again. In celebratory mood after my pint at The Blackfriar, I fittingly treated myself to a cab to Euston to catch my train home to Northampton.

When I got home I couldn't sit still. I phoned a friend and I walked up to meet her in the garden of a country pub. Surbjit was a work colleague at Connexions, and what she told me sent me into space. She said Connexions were looking for Careers Advisers interested in taking voluntary redundancy. My next pint didn't touch the sides. I hoped Connexions wouldn't change their minds before I could get my redundancy application in on Monday.

I was on a high, but I had serious matters to deal with: namely a radical change of career. Connexions accepted my offer of voluntary redundancy – no surprise there, considering my disciplinary record. I was delighted to be given some redundancy money too. I decided to buy a taxi on finance, and in the next couple of days went down to London to sort something out.

With a couple of thousand pounds redundancy money to use as a deposit on a taxi I went along to the London Taxi Company to see what they had on offer. I should have bought the latest model, a TX4, but I figured an older model cab would save me a bit of money. I picked out a TX2, largely because I liked its racing green colour. I had to wait a week or two while the cab was serviced and presented for licensing.

Once the cab had been passed and plated, I returned to London to pick it up. I drove it straight home to show the wife. She probably heard me turning off the M1 anyway, it was so freaking noisy.

After driving a regular car for several years, the driving position felt unnaturally high. It was slow and noisy, and I could barely hear the radio – or my future passengers. Evidently, cab technology hadn't progressed much in the eleven years I'd been away. With the new model TX4 it had progressed a bit, but the TX2 hadn't progressed at all. The model housed an engine used in the Ford Transit van and was underpowered for such a heavy vehicle as a London taxi. The much earlier Fairway had a better engine, but that was a very old cab by now. Anyway, my TX2 came with air-conditioning, which was nice. When I last drove a cab, air-conditioning usually meant opening the windows. I don't know how we survived without air-con: not that it was very effective on this particular model.

I found an unusual design feature: a gap next to the automatic gearshift that sucks banknotes down into the dark recesses of the gear mechanism. Perfect for when that chap gives you a £50 note at Harrods, and you throw it down before speeding off with a coach behind you.

I hadn't driven a cab for eleven years, and I was rusty to say the least. I felt nervous; almost as if I was a Butter Boy again going out on my first day in 1988. I took it slowly at first. I'd just work a few hours, then go home when I got tired.

Cab drivers often expressed surprise when I said I lived seventy miles out in Northampton, but I figured that once you get to the M1 at Brent Cross, what does it matter if you drive another hour on the motorway? As if driving in and out of Essex is any better. It was expensive though, with my daily diesel costing me £30 before I'd even picked anybody up.

New Road Systems

The Central London Congestion Charge had come in while I'd been away. I didn't think traffic levels would be much higher than they were when I left the trade, as I thought few private motorists would pay £8 a day to drive in the Congestion Zone. I was wrong, and I was shocked at how heavy the traffic was in the daytime. I now know that people will pay almost anything to drive in Central London.

Work levels were lower than they were when I last drove a cab in 1999. I saw the cabs queuing from Harrow Road to get on the Paddington Station rank and I thought it was a drive-in demo. Caught in Walthamstow on a Sunday afternoon I wondered if there was a bus convention on. I still find myself wondering where everyone goes to on a Sunday (you always end up sounding like your parents eventually). I know I'm part of the problem by working on Sundays, but we've lost something: the one day of the week when everything was quiet and peaceful.

It had become more difficult to navigate through London. As a professional driver, the route you chose is analysed using current geographical knowledge coupled with past experience. You know which roads are likely to be most congested, and when. These variables change throughout the day. The default routes you choose need constant updating to take into account changing road systems. Twenty years ago, everything from Mayfair going north went up Park Street. People would complain if you used Park Lane, Marble Arch and Edgware Road. Park Street now means joining a queue, and Edgware Road is often the best bet. You're still swerving around Arab families with pushchairs, but it saves waiting to get across Oxford Street, and into a chicane caused by the siting of a bus stop just after the junction.

There had been other changes in the time I'd had away. One of my weak spots had been the inner-London district of Shoreditch. I never fully got my head around its complicated one-way system and maze of dead end streets. In the time I'd been out of London, they'd reversed some of the one-way workings and had closed off important roads. Long-established Points of Interest had changed all over London. I was amazed to learn that the London Stock Exchange had moved a mile down the road. St Pancras had replaced

Waterloo as the new hub for Eurostar trains to France and Belgium. In the modern way of things, St Pancras International had become a shopping mall, with a train station attached to it. Before boarding a train to Paris you could enjoy this exciting retail and leisure experience, and consume cake and fine wine until you explode.

When I was driving a cab the first time around there were still regular bomb threats from the IRA. The City of London brought in a "Ring of Steel" to protect the financial district. Many roads were sealed off, and police checkpoints were installed at various locations, complete with chicanes and inspection booths. The polizia still sometimes stop vehicles at the checkpoints when they've got nothing better to do, but the booths are now largely used as mobile phone shelters for builders.

Out west, the A40(M) Westway snakes out of the West End towards Shepherd's Bush. It was always a joy to drive above a few miles of West London sprawl on this elevated urban motorway, but it had somehow lost its motorway status. It was now just the A40, with a 40 mph speed limit. Average speed cameras were later added.

One of my favourite cut-throughs; Skinner Street, Percival Street and Lever Street (Skin Percy's Liver – remember?) now had speed bumps, and had been narrowed to one lane with a cycle lane on the left. The London Borough of Islington had become Speed Bump Central, and accompanying the traffic calming bumps came a blanket 20 mph speed limit, and more cycle lanes. Lots of them. This sort of thing was repeated all over London.

The traffic was being slowed down artificially, and this was something that was going to get much, much, worse in the coming years. The IRA were no longer considered a terrorist threat, but the closed streets were never reopened. It's now almost impossible to get on to Southwark Bridge from the west, and options are severely limited for access to Upper or Lower Thames Streets – now part of the controversial Cycle Superhighway.

Former London Mayor, "Red" Ken Livingstone, brought in a new law: taxi drivers could no longer refuse a trip of less than twelve miles – previously it was six. Ken also closed Trafalgar Square to traffic, and had the pigeons shot (allegedly). The northern side of the square was pedestrianised and became a tourist wonderland of human statues, freaks and pickpockets: a microcosm of London right outside the National Gallery. An ugly pile of concrete blocks still sits on the north-west side of the square. I don't know whether they've been dumped there by builders, or whether it's some kind of homage to modern art.

New Cab

Despite local authorities conspiring against me, I got into a groove and built up my hours to about seven a day. Then the cab started playing up. The starter motor went, the battery failed. It seemed like every few weeks something went wrong. One night I drove home and as I approached Northampton town centre the machine ground to a halt. The cab spent ten days off the road. I'm not sure exactly what happened but the insides seem to have exploded. The cab was under warranty, but I'd lost several days work.

In addition to the expense and frustrations over mechanical breakdowns, I was quite able to bring on disaster by my own volition. One morning I set out for London and stopped at my usual fuel station to fill up. The pump I usually used was out of service so I swung the cab around and used another pump. After a while I realised I'd been pumping petrol into my diesel engine. Apparently, you can't attempt to move a vehicle if it contains the wrong fuel; you have to have it pumped out immediately. When the rescue van came it might as well have had "Helping Dick-heads Who've Put the Wrong Fuel In" plastered on the sides. They pumped out a tenner's worth of petrol before I could buy another tank of diesel. It cost a lot of money to put right.

I put up with the cab for eight months. When you go out to work expecting something to go wrong you know something has to change. I bought a new TX4. This cab was faster, quieter, and better in every way than my old TX2. It wasn't without its problems, but it was a lot more reliable than the heap I'd got shot of.

5

How it all Works

Cab driving is one of the most democratic occupations known to man. How many other occupations allow you to start training with no qualifications, and then offer a job for life? You're not asked to provide a CV or your academic record when you apply for a London taxi licence. You don't need to sweat while your application is pondered over by a college admissions tutor, and you don't have to convince anyone of your cleverness before acceptance. The entry requirements are a good brain and above-average staying power. As the fictional examiner, Mr Burgess, says in *The Knowledge*, it's not about *who* you know, it's about *what* you know. It doesn't help if you know the examiners. Your parents can't arrange an internship through a friend of a friend, or through a chum from the golf club. Every applicant is on an equal footing, whether you start the Knowledge with a degree under your belt, or whether you earned a dishonourable discharge from a sink comprehensive.

Commitment is what separates the successful applicants from the 70%–80% majority who give up. You have entered a world of pain, but you know that as long as you keep going you'll get there eventually. The Knowledge is extremely hard work, but unlike many other courses of study, it doesn't have to be fitted into a set period of time like a degree course.

You're on a self-directed training plan, and you can take as long as you want.

The qualification gained on entry provides a minimum competence to do the job. We know we don't know it all when we gain our licence, but we have a sound basis on which to build our competence. Everyone who has passed the Knowledge can show a truly awesome grasp of geography. Those who have been through the system have proven analytical skills, which need to be worked on continuously throughout your career. The Knowledge is very hard to learn, but very easy to forget. It needs to be topped up constantly.

Starting Out

These days, most people buy their own cabs after a period of time. It's a big financial commitment though, so it's best to rent a cab to start with. Some people devote three years of their life learning the Knowledge only to find they can't stand driving a cab. Also, if you're driving skills aren't up to standard, you'll be soon found out. Better to put a dent in a rented cab than your own.

I try to drive the newest cab possible. Cabs are built to last many years, but a cab's mileage is likely to be high in relation to its age. You need to rent a cab from a garage that services its cabs regularly and tries to prevent problems before they arise.

Cab driving doesn't suit everyone. It's a lonely existence, and you need to be comfortable with your own company – or the company of strangers every thirty minutes. You have no work colleagues to speak of; just fleeting meetings with other cab drivers in the cafes or on taxi ranks. This doesn't suit some people, particularly those who have come from a more sociable career. I've spent most of my life avoiding other people, so it suits me fine to work alone. On the downside, I'm not keen on responsibility, and this is a job that comes with a lot of it: driving around London all day is fraught with risks, hazards and responsibilities. You are the boss, and if something goes wrong, it's down to you to sort out.

Before gaining your licence you will have had training on how to load wheelchairs. One reason your cab is so expensive is because of all the extra modifications and all the specialist equipment we need to carry. On my TX4 there's a pull-out ramp for wheelchairs, and in the boot there's another ramp that can be fitted to provide a step for passengers who find access difficult. Wheelchair harnesses are also provided, and must be carried at all times. All the internal handles are coloured bright yellow to help those with limited sight, and there's a hearing loop.

Running Costs

It's nice to own your own cab, but they are expensive to buy, and to run. Living thirty-five miles from London, I spend £20 per day on diesel just travelling to and from work. Garage bills are invariably high: parts wear out and damage has to be repaired. It's not uncommon to have to spend £1000 at a taxi garage, particularly if several parts wear out at the same time.

Renting a cab is expensive, but some drivers are happy to pay for the peace of mind. If anything goes wrong, the garage will take care of it and lend you spare cab. It'll cost around £250 a week to rent a decent cab, and that's more than it would cost to buy a similar cab on finance. It's dead money too, as you'll never have a cab to sell on or part-exchange.

If you buy your own cab you'll have to spend maybe £2000 on your annual comprehensive insurance policy, and your vehicle excise duty. You'll need to rent a meter for around £200 annually. The meter is checked and certified every year prior to the cab's annual licensing inspection. You need to present your cab for re-licensing every year and pay for a new licence for your vehicle. Your cab driver's licence is separate. It's renewed every three years and costs around £200. Your cab needs to pass two Ministry of Transport (MOT) inspections each year, in addition to the official licensing inspection. Once all that's paid for, we have our biannual income tax and National Insurance bill to pay. Most of us see an accountant once a year and they arrange that for us. We don't pay as much tax or National Insurance as a regular employee as our running costs are taken into account when assessing our taxable profit.

As self-employed workers we get no holiday pay, sick pay or pension. The decision to take days off isn't taken lightly. In an occupation where you have the opportunity to work twenty-four hours per day, you can feel guilty for taking time off, however deserved it might be. Days off for hangovers are expensive, and it's something I never do. You have to be in tip-top condition to spend a day driving a cab, so boozing the night before is not a good idea. Taking thirty days holiday a year as an employee would, is a luxury many of us can't afford. A lengthy bout of illness could ruin us when margins are tight and we haven't been able to build up any financial fat for unforeseen events.

Some drivers subscribe to a computerised booking circuit, or use mobile phone apps, sometimes both. Credit card acceptance was made was made compulsory in 2016.

Before then, the London taxi trade was run mostly on cash. Before you start, you have to decide which credit card system to subscribe to. It's a controversial subject, but even accepting payment costs us money these days. You'll need plenty of banknotes and coins to use as a change float. Plenty of customers still pay with cash, and I guarantee your first passenger is going to pay using a fifty pound note.

Nice & Clean

You'll need to make sure your cab is clean and tidy. Many cabs have a lived-in look, but there's no need to keep a dirty vehicle. To keep the air fresh and to deter germs I open the windows and give the cab a blast of air every day on my drive into London. A hanging air freshener helps to keep the freshness going during the working day. I favour those fresheners shaped like trees, but if you are lucky enough to pick up a gaggle of Arab girls who have spent the morning on Selfridges cosmetics floor, that does the trick too.

Smoke, Stairway, Paranoid

You'll be spending several hours in the cab, so you'll have to make your own entertainment in between customers. I daresay some drivers listen to music on their mobile telephones. I prefer the traditional approach.

The stereo supplied with the cab isn't quite the apex in sonic technology, but a high-end system would be wasted on a vehicle with a noisy diesel engine and the aerodynamics of a cathedral. The holy trinity of Deep Purple, Led Zeppelin and Black Sabbath sound OK on CD, but even the nuanced dynamics of Zeppelin's quieter passages can be hard to follow with the engine and wind noise of a motorway drive. Heavy metal and punk rock cuts through pretty well: you're fine with Motorhead, Metallica, Maiden, The Clash or the Sex Pistols. Folk and country-type stuff can go either way: Dylan sounds good, less so Neil Young. Jazz and classical is too subtle for motorway use. I'm a big fan of Herr Beethoven. You might get away with Ludwig Van's noisier symphonies, but a piano concerto is wasted on a cab stereo at high speed. Horn-led jazz can be OK, but you won't hear the bass properly. Any difficult jazz is a distraction anyway, especially when Coltrane goes off on one. I've got to say though, you can't beat the calm ambiance jazz or classical has on a busy night when there's madness on the streets all around you. It's great for the theatre burst. OK, let's nail it once and for all: punk and metal for the motorway, jazz and classical for urban work.

You need to be careful with what music you play if you have passengers on board. My friend, Paul, had a customer threatening to withhold payment after he assaulted a passenger's ears with Tangerine Dream. My Fall CDs would probably have the same affect, so I only play music when I'm on my way home. So, if your tastes run to difficult krautrock such as Tangerine Dream, best keep it to yourself. Or listen to talk radio like a proper London cab driver.

Football and the Cab Driver

It's in the cab driver's nature to view the glass as half empty. Most of us come at it from an angle of scepticism. If you support West Ham, Crystal Palace, Millwall, Charlton Athletic, Barnet, Brentford, Leyton Orient or Dagenham & Redbridge you'll make a fine cab driver. This is because your aims are realistic. Arsenal, Tottenham, or modern-day Chelsea fans aren't always the best disposed towards a cab driving philosophy because they are accustomed to success. If you expect success in the cab trade you are setting yourself up for failure. You might enjoy a bit of a cup run, but you'll never make the Champions League.

I've enjoyed a little sport with supporters of Millwall Football Club in these pages, but it's done with affection. You see, inside every cab driver there's a Millwall supporter trying to get out. OK, not an actual Millwall fan, but an individual harbouring a similar fatalistic philosophy. Cab drivers hope for the best, but expect the worst. We want to earn good money, but we rarely do. We want to be liked. But if we are not liked or respected we are thick-skinned enough to be able to take it. "No one likes us, we don't care" is Millwall's most famous song – brilliant! It perfectly encapsulates the inner-Millwall supporter inside us. We are everything that the young, ambitious, corporate wage-slave isn't. We play poorly as a team. We constantly fail to meet targets. We set goals that we cannot reach.

And if you ever see a group of cab drivers converge on a café, it's like a mob of Millwall fans turning up at your boozer. That's your quiet Sunday lunch with the family gone…

One last thing: should you be tempted to show your football allegiance by displaying an appropriate air freshener or sticker, you are setting yourself up for all sorts of problems. Other cab drivers love commenting on your team's humiliating defeat after the day's results have come through: "I see West Ham lost again at home, heh!" Even if they have won I don't like being told the result. I rarely attend matches and I don't watch live football on TV or listen to it on the radio. In traditional fashion I wait until I get home on a Saturday to watch *Match of the Day* with the wife.

Many passengers are up for a chat about football if they know you are a fan. I like football, but I don't understand it. I'm happy to talk about the general aspects of being a supporter, but things can get technical. Once someone wants to discuss the nuances of England's midfield engine room I change the subject to flower arranging or something.

Where and When

Your daily objective is to earn as much money as possible in the shortest period of time, with the minimum amount of aggravation. I highly value a stress-free day with satisfied customers, even if it's at a detriment to my earnings. Some drivers have a set daily earnings figure in mind, and won't go home until they reach it. Others work a set amount of hours.

Gross takings don't mean much on their own. You have to take into consideration your individual outgoings: for example, if you're running a new cab on finance, or renting from a garage, you're going to have to earn between £800 and £1200 per month more than someone whose cab finance is paid off. A driver who owns his own cab is called a "Musher".

I aim to work between seven and eight hours – not including breaks. If I get a job going in my direction home after six hours, I'll probably call it a day. If I'm still feeling fresh I might sit it out for an account job going north. Most drivers work longer hours than I do. There's often the guilty feeling that you should work more hours; but the fact is you get tired. When you get tired driving becomes a pain and you become bad-tempered. If you push on through the pain barrier it can become dangerous, particularly if you have a long drive home.

An All-London green badge driver can work anywhere in Greater London, and you can use the twenty-four-hour clock to plan your working day. You can cruise the streets looking for a hand to go up in the traditional way; you can queue on a taxi rank; or you can choose to subscribe to a radio circuit or use a taxi-app to find work. You have the freedom to use all three methods throughout the day.

The majority of drivers are most familiar with Central London and gravitate towards the densely packed streets of St James, Mayfair and the City. Others have as little to do with Central London as possible and only rank up at Heathrow Airport. A minority prefer to base themselves just outside the centre. Those with good local knowledge look for customers in wealthy areas such as Chelsea, Kensington and Hampstead.

Some people prefer to work nights. The meter runs faster at night and there's less traffic to hold you up. You're likely to get longer, more lucrative, rides. I've never been one to work unsociable hours and I've rarely worked past midnight. It's a hard slog in the daytime, but I like some quality of life and to see some daylight.

The Burbs

Some London cab drivers only apply for a licence to work in the suburbs. Suburban drivers have the same running costs as All-London green badge drivers, but can only pick up in their particular sector.

One current concern is cross-border hiring. Sometimes a taxi or minicab driver applies to be licensed in an area where regulations are slack, with the intention of working in another licensing area. It's still a grey area whether this is legal. We mostly associate cross-border hiring with Uber drivers, but in the past there were problems with Suburban London taxi drivers plying for hire in Central London. With taxi licensing plates identical, TfL now stipulates that every taxi must carry a colour-coded identifier with the driver's licence number on it. The identification cards are either green or yellow. All-London green badge drivers don't take kindly to yellow Suburban drivers illegally working in Central London, though they appreciate times have been particularly hard in the suburbs for several years.

I was responsible for a bit of cross-border hiring myself when I lived in Northampton. I noticed a woman trying to hail a cab close to my home as I made my way to London in the morning. After seeing her a few times I decided to stop for her one day. I figured she'd be going into the town centre or the train station. It would be an easy enough job for me to do and I wouldn't be depriving a local driver of work. There are plenty of cabs in the town centre, but there are fewer cabs passing through the suburbs, and there are no ranks. She appeared to be making her way to the bus stop when she saw me.

I explained I was a London-licensed driver, but that I was willing to convey her to her destination. I further explained that my meter was set for London fares, but she could pay whatever she normally pays – or two-thirds of the meter. I was a bit surprised to learn she was heading north to an out of town business park. It took fifteen minutes to get to Moulton Park and back to the pick-up point in Kingsthorpe. I earnt £6, so it was worth doing. It felt strange working as a cab driver in my own town though.

I stopped for her a few more times. On one occasion she changed her destination to St Crispin's Hospital in the west of town and she had to direct me. I picked her up a few more times before I stopped seeing her.

London Driving

I've lived in many different places and have experienced many different driving cultures. You have to drive assertively in London or you won't get anywhere. You must always expect the unexpected as the unexpected happens all the time. Moving from London to Birmingham I was taken by the quaint custom of giving way at roundabouts. Moving from Birmingham to smaller towns the driving culture changed again. In small town Bedfordshire you have to be prepared for someone to stop unexpectedly to let someone cross an empty road. This generally doesn't happen in London, though the pedestrian stands a fighting chance of getting across a designated crossing, unlike in some cities around the world.

Most provincial drivers are understandably intimidated by London traffic. You're going to be surrounded by taxis, minicabs and buses; and there will be bikes and motorcycles coming up on both sides of you at very close quarters. It's close, hand-to-hand fighting for space. There's little room for manoeuvre in London and there's a lot going on. It's fast and furious. You need to press on with confidence and at least pretend you know where you're going. Hesitation will result in angry hoots and abuse. You need nerves of steel to negotiate such dense, unpredictable, movements of vehicles and people.

I'll let you out of a junction if I'm empty, but cab passengers don't like to see you let others delay their journey and bump the fare up. Driving speeds in Central London have reduced to the days of the horse-drawn cart, and they're getting slower – currently seven miles per hour.

The countryside is different. In rural areas I'm always shaking my head at the speed people drive along narrow country roads at; but put the same people on Marble Arch and see if they can judge how much space that cement mixer is going to use, or appreciate the turning requirement of that bus pulling around the Victoria one-way system. The only good thing about London traffic is that things are slower and accidents tend to be less dramatic.

My favourite traffic system has to be the contraflow. Sometimes cycles are coming towards you as part of a very dangerous, but legally sanctioned, contraflow cycle lane. Where cyclists were habitually riding down one-way streets the wrong way, the authorities hit on a neat way of saving themselves the trouble of enforcing the rules: they simply legalised it. Experienced London drivers get used to cycle lanes appearing in the middle of the carriageway. Yes, the actual middle of the road, as on Store Street or busy Shoreditch High Street. Royal College Street in Camden Town is a classic example of an accident waiting to happen. Royal College Street is one way north, and there's a cycle lane on the left side of the carriageway. But beyond the parked cars, and the Camden Council flower pots obscuring your view on the right hand side, there's another cycle lane running south. I've rarely seen a cyclist on the southern contraflow and I can't say I'm surprised; it's lethal.

Another example is in Pimlico. I wonder how many motorists turn straight into Vauxhall Bridge Road from Regency Street without noticing the two cycle lanes? Or from Carmelite Street on to the Queen Victoria Street slip?

My friends in Northamptonshire probably wouldn't believe some of the things I tell them about London's traffic schemes. Then again, it took them a while to believe there were trains running under the ground.

London doesn't have the broad boulevards of the American cities. Park Lane is the nearest we get to it, and on a good day we can actually get up to the legal limit of forty miles per hour. Sadly, your pleasure will be short-lived, as it's only half a mile long. At each end sit two of London's scariest roundabouts. At the northern end there's Marble Arch. While not strictly a roundabout it has all the features of a major London roundabout, including lots of buses, confusing lanes, and maniac driving. Driving on the southbound you are unlikely to break thirty before being confronted by the legendary Hyde Park Corner gyratory.

My only advice on tackling a gyratory is to keep it nice and slow, and make sure you know what exit you want and stick to the appropriate lane like glue. It's knowing what lane to take that's the problem though, and that only comes with experience. What is it about Britain and roundabouts anyway? You rarely see them in the country that sets the gold standard for rational driving systems, the United States.

When things get busy and you are picking up nice passengers, London driving can be exciting. At other times it's a pain in the arse. If you constantly get wound up by the traffic, and other people's selfish behaviour, you won't last long in this job. You learn to try to let it wash over you. I do get wound up, but not excessively. I haven't resorted to road rage for a few years. It was brought home to me how I'd improved when a man I was driving to Euston said two cars had cut me up. He said there would be a fight if that happened in Liverpool. I replied in surprised sincerity that "I didn't even notice."

When I was on the Knowledge, a fellow student asked Derek, the driving instructor at Knowledge Point School, how best to drive a taxi. Derek replied that "you wear it." That sums it up. If I ever become a driving instructor I'm going to purloin that piece of advice and pass it off as my own.

Pricing

The driver isn't responsible for setting fares, and fares throughout the London boroughs are the same, regardless of vehicle. There are different tariffs though, depending on the time of day. The standard rate applies in the daytime; but in the evenings, at weekends, or on public holidays, the meter runs faster. The appropriate tariff is chosen automatically by a computer chip inside the meter. Every year the meter is checked and certified, and a new chip is put in if the fares have gone up that year. Basically, all the driver can do is switch it off and on. Extra charges are rarely added to the meter these days, but when I started, extra charges were allowed for carrying more than one passenger, and 40p could be added for carrying packages over two feet long. Passengers are no longer charged for extra luggage. The old system was a bit complicated and open to misunderstanding, so I'm glad to see it simplified.

Cab fares can appear high, but everything in London is expensive. The city eats money. London's main industry is making money, and you need lots of it to live and play here. If you don't want to take a cab, look what it'd cost to park your own car for a few hours in Westminster. Look at the inflation-busting fare rises on trains every year. Taxi fares are only excessive when you are caught in traffic. This is because the meter runs on a combination of time and motion. If you're moving well, the fare can be less than you expect. No really. On a clear day you can get surprisingly far for a tenner. Conversely, if you are caught in stop/start traffic, a £10 fare can easily go up to £15 or £20. No cab driver likes to be caught in traffic. It's embarrassing asking for a large amount of money for a short, but tortuous, journey sat in traffic. Job satisfaction comes from delivering customers quickly and safely to their destination. We like to satisfy our customers, and we regard it as a personal failure if we fail in that endeavour.

Some drivers enjoy the challenge of working on days when there are widespread road closures. Diversions run the meter up, but they also test your Knowledge as you'll constantly be looking for alternative routes. The Knowledge will always beat a sat nav, but the traffic has become worse with each passing year, and this is something we've had to put up with more and more. I try to remind myself that if driving and parking in London was easy, my job wouldn't exist.

The metered fare applies to the whole cab regardless of how many passengers there are: five or six passengers can be carried depending on the model of the cab. Wise people know that a group of people can move around London by taxi and it can work out cheaper than using tubes and buses. There aren't many cities in which tourists have the confidence to get themselves completely lost, knowing they can be instantly whisked back to their hotel by raising their hand as a yellow light comes in sight.

We're often asked how much it costs to go somewhere. That's what the meter is for. It's difficult to estimate with accuracy. I've learnt to overestimate. If you get there under-cost, your punters are happy. If you underestimate you've put yourself under pressure, and if you come in over the estimate your customer may feel that he's lost out.

In order to compete with private hire, some radio circuits and app-based hailing companies encourage drivers to take fixed-price jobs. Sometimes they are worth doing, sometimes they're not. I often do a £20 job from the City to Paddington. If I have to wait for my passenger and heavy traffic slows our progress I know that the job could normally go about £30. I do it because a £20 job is a decent job, however long it takes. I might otherwise drive around the City for thirty minutes doing nothing but burn diesel. You have to weigh up each job.

Cabs on the street might offer a discount, but don't bank on it. A few lucky customers of mine have enjoyed heavily discounted fares to Luton Airport. One Sunday afternoon I picked up a nice Swiss family on their way to St Pancras to catch the train to Luton Airport Parkway. As we drove the short journey towards St Pancras I thought I'd offer a deal. After confirming the family had yet to buy train tickets I offered to drive them directly to Luton Airport for £60. They agreed. The meter showed £145 (on the slightly higher Sunday rate). It was indeed a big discount, but worth doing for all of us. The family would have paid a similar amount for their train tickets; then they'd have to wait for the train, and then finally the shuttle bus at Luton Airport Parkway Station. I live twelve miles from Luton Airport and would be driving most of this journey in a few hours anyway. It was a quiet day so it made sense to finish early and go home with a guaranteed sixty quid in my pocket (plus £6 tip as it turned out).

On another day, an Indian family approached my cab on the St Paul's Cathedral rank and asked how much it would cost them to get to Luton Airport. I said it would cost about £130, but I was prepared to bargain. I offered a deal to drive them to Luton for £70. My £70 offer was generous. They thanked me for my offer and walked off. It would cost the four of them more than that to get there by train. I was thinking of going home and I would have taken them for £50 had they wanted to negotiate. Maybe they wheeled their bags along to City Thameslink Station and caught the train, or maybe they found a minicab firm prepared to take them for less than £70? After being squeezed into a Prius for a fifty-minute journey they might have regretted their short-sightedness. I thought of chasing them down the road with a better offer, but decided to retain my dignity.

Tipping

It's customary to add on a gratuity to the metered fare: 10% is about right. I only feel I deserve a tip if my service has been faultless. People of some nationalities don't give tips, and I can respect that to a point. A kind word of appreciation on my performance often means more to me than a bit of extra change.

I read somewhere that Australians don't tip because they believe in an egalitarian society, and if they tip you they are displaying power over the poor worker, or something. I can understand that. Still, would they say that when being chased out of New York restaurant for leaving less than 15%? I don't think so.

I suppose tipping cab drivers started when it was a poor man's game. Well, it's becoming a poor man's game again; so if I get you through the traffic quickly and safely, and with a smile on my face, do you think you could spare a pound coin for my trouble?

Talking of nationalities, it's difficult to profile how people behave by their nationality. Some people are suspicious of being taken for a ride, particularly if they come from countries where the local cab drivers are known to be licensed bandits. People that have lived in Britain for a while know that the things that go on in other countries don't go on here.

Station to Station

Like David Bowie, I'm happy to work station to station all day. Driving people to and from train stations is the bread and butter for a day man like me. You'd expect a world class capital like London to have an adequate infrastructure, and its major transport hubs to have a rational system of entry, exit and drop-off facilities. It hasn't, and it's chaos.

Pancras Road runs between King's Cross and St Pancras International stations. The stations sit opposite each other, divided by a stretch of road that resembles Bombay on a bad day. Pedestrians wheel luggage across the road like sacred cows, oblivious to the moving traffic. It's always slow moving, mind; held back by a mess of coaches and double-parked minicabs. Leaving St Pancras on Midland Road could cost you a fiver if you're unfortunate enough to have to queue with the buses to turn left on to Euston Road.

Victoria, Paddington and Liverpool Street, have been building sites for several years. The UKs busiest station, Waterloo, presents a dilemma for the cab driver. The official drop-off will cost your passenger a few quid extra if you're approaching it from Waterloo Bridge, but other options are fraught with problems. Passengers in the know sometimes ask for "The Steps." Setting down on Mepham Street allows the passenger to cross the road and walk up the station steps, but it can be a stressful situation when a bus is behind you waiting for you to move out of the way to let it pass (please don't ask us to process a credit card at The Steps). It would be nice if we could easily drop off on the stretch of Waterloo Road that runs beside the station, but there are over-length bus stops and zigzag approaches all along the road, with just a couple of gaps. There are known to be cameras trained on the bus stops to catch people dropping off illegally.

Access to Liverpool Street Station has not been helped by the closure of Bank Junction and its approaches, and major roadworks have blighted the area for several years.

Euston Station is being redeveloped to accommodate the High Speed Two (HS2) train line. HS2 will shave twenty minutes off the journey from London to Birmingham. Wow. God knows how much it will have cost taxpayers on completion, or how much disruption it's yet to cause. I doubt those on regular Inter City Super-Sizzler tickets will benefit. These things are usually aimed at corporate types willing to pay a premium.

Access to Euston can be difficult. Coming west along Euston Road from King's Cross and St Pancras you can't turn right into the station. Nor can you turn left into Gordon Street and do a U-turn in order to cross Euston Road for the drop-off. You have to navigate slowly through Endsleigh Gardens, a narrow Bloomsbury street.

The whole area has been made worse by the closure of Tavistock Place westbound. Coming from Bloomsbury in the south, you have to queue up in Gordon Street to get across Euston Road. There's a cycle lane on the left on Gordon Street, so it's now effectively a single carriageway. Vehicles ignore the cycle lane and create two lanes.

At present, the drop-off for Euston is down a ramp under the station. The pick-up is even further down into the heart of darkness: a dank, dark, hole; full of noise and diesel fumes from the cabs that shuffle up the underground rank, leaking oil as they go. It resembles a cab garage, and serves as an authentic introduction to the London traffic experience.

It's such a difficult journey from the City to the official set-down at Euston that I sometimes drop-off in Eversholt Street with all the minicabs. It saves the punter a few quid, and it saves me grief.

The Flyers

Station to station work is fine by me, but station to airport is better. It's not always as good as it seems though. If you're a passenger and you've paid sixty quid for a ride to Heathrow you might well get the impression that we're on to a good thing with this taxi caper. You've seen the pick-up rank at Heathrow and you only see a dozen cabs waiting. You reckon we'd only have to wait ten minutes for another job going back to Central London. But what you don't see is the huge feeder park – the queue to join the queue.

Heathrow Airport is a city within a city, and the public only get to see a fraction of it. There are miles of taxi parks and a café dedicated to cab drivers. Hundreds of cabs will be queuing just to be allocated a space on a terminal rank.

The driver has to pay a fee for the privilege, and it can easily take two or three hours before you're allocated a rank. Part of the ranking fee is passed on to the passenger through an extra charge on the meter. The fee covers the computerised system of despatch at Heathrow, and the marshalling needed to stop dodgy practices. At one time, certain Heathrow cab drivers organised themselves into gangs and wouldn't let non-regulars on to the ranks. Cab drivers rarely attempt to rip off customers, but a minority are happy to rip off fellow cab drivers in stealing work. Things at Heathrow were pretty slack until the 1990s before monitoring was made more stringent.

It's a different breed of driver who works Heathrow, and they have their own culture. Some Heathrow drivers flirt with an outlaw image, and established regulars are given nicknames by their colleagues. I've seen former Knowledge Boys undergo a personality change once they start working at Heathrow. Some appear pretty wired to me. I think all that sitting around for hours at a time makes people crazy. Some Heathrow drivers only work the airport and drive straight back if they drop off in Central London. They'd rather sit around for a few hours and socialise with their mates. Drivers like me are known as "town" drivers, and many of us come straight back after dropping at Heathrow.

Most drivers are happy with a ride back to Central London, but what they really want is a left turn on the M4 towards Swindon and Bristol. If a driver gets a job to one of the villages around Heathrow and can get back within thirty minutes, he can join the rank again without charge.

If I wanted to work at Heathrow I'd now been invited to undergo a "Heathrow induction on working practices and procedures". I think I'll leave it, thanks. I've never ranked at Heathrow, and I wasn't prepared to try it as research for this book. Heathrow scares me. All those lanes, signs and service roads: it's scary enough getting off the airport, let alone with someone in the back asking for a town I'd never even heard of.

For the driver, a run to City Airport can be a welcome job, or it can be a nightmare. It depends on the traffic. It's usually a decent enough job if your starting point is from the City, preferably east of Bank Junction; but it can be a tortuous crawl from the West End or from Westminster on the Cycle Superhighway. I accept a lot of fixed-price account jobs to City Airport. The metered fare is always higher than the fixed-price agreement, but it's worth doing if I can get back to Central London quickly. I've never stayed to pick up at City Airport: apart from a long wait, I wouldn't want to be dragged further into unfamiliar territory east of London.

For the passenger, a cab ride to Heathrow can be good value. It's a long slog on the tube, and the Heathrow Express train has its drawbacks. For one, it runs from Paddington, and if you're travelling from the City or West End with luggage it can be a tortuous journey just to get on the train.

Have a look at the price of tickets from Paddington to Heathrow. The fifteen-minute journey isn't cheap, and the fare rises regularly. The Heathrow Express was built with private money and is not subject to the fare regulation that other rail lines have to adhere to. For three or more passengers travelling to Heathrow from Central London, taking a cab all the way will work out cheaper. The same applies to many other journeys.

All-London green badge drivers can pick up passengers at Heathrow and City Airports. Suburban yellow-badge drivers licensed in the Newham sector can pick up at City Airport only. None of us can pick up from the ranks at Luton, Stansted or Gatwick. These airports are outside London and are served by drivers licensed in those areas. We even have to pay to drop off at some airports outside London, such is the greed of the airport authorities whose customers we serve.

You don't have to pay to drop off at Gatwick, but it's a job I often try to talk my way out of. It pays well, but it's a long slog through South London, into Surrey, and finally into West Sussex. The last time I went it took two hours and fifty minutes from the West End. The eighty-mile drive home on three congested motorways took two and a half hours. It's always the last job of the day whenever I go to Gatwick, regardless of time. Driving back to London is just too debilitating. It's about the same distance as Luton Airport, but the motorway going south doesn't even start until you cross the Surrey county line.

Protocols

I shan't bore you too much with taxi drivers' etiquette, but there are unwritten rules concerning stealing other drivers' jobs and such like. Basically, if another empty cab lets you out of a junction the next job belongs to him. If an empty cab overtakes you, he should let you take the next job. A passing cab shouldn't pick up close to a loaded rank. You wouldn't pick up a fare on the other side of the road if there are cabs in sight coming that way. Cabs and buses also give way to each other whenever practical. It's courtesy based on common sense. Sadly, etiquette is being eroded in today's cut-throat society. Many drivers blame the younger drivers, but there are plenty of old boys who should know better than to nick fellow drivers' jobs. It happens to me all the time on the Old Bond Street rank.

Sharp Practices

Outside London, cab drivers have to pay a fee to pick up at train stations and other transport hubs. This can cost the drivers thousands of pounds in annual fees. The fees don't go towards anything as sophisticated as computer-monitoring of ranks; it's just a money-spinner for rapacious transport providers and their shareholders.

If the taxi drivers refuse to pay, the companies will just get minicab firms in. In 2016, Luton Airport sold the rights to service their customers to the London-based minicab company, Addison Lee. Local taxi drivers who had served Luton Airport's passengers for decades were suddenly marginalised. It's not as if they couldn't cope with the work. Airport work kept these drivers going, and they'd been disgracefully sold out.

Minicabs are meant to be pre-booked, but there is the unseemly situation where minicabs are effectively ranking up alongside official Luton taxis. Many visitors arriving at Luton Airport naturally think they are taking a ride in a taxi rather than a minicab. Are they told the difference when they book? Addison Lee's cars are all painted black and blend in with the official taxis. Arguably, a Ford Galaxy looks as much like a taxi as the Mercedes Vito – which is licensed as a taxi in London and other places. Sadly, taxi drivers outside London have little power and often just have to suck it up.

A minority of taxi drivers have arrangements with hotel doormen to supply them with lucrative work. All it takes is a call to a driver's mobile phone to arrange a nice run to Heathrow or beyond; for a commission, of course.

Hotel staff will often mislead their customers into taking a private hire car. They will tell you a taxi will cost more than a private hire car and book you a minicab. Private hire can charge what they like and a minicab may well cost more than taking a taxi from the rank outside the hotel, especially once the hotel wallah has taken his cut. The hotels are sensitive to bad publicity and have purges from time to time where they warn off their staff and reassure the cab trade that they are behaving honestly. I rarely rank at hotels, and on the rare occasion I've been given an airport job, I have neither given, nor been asked to give a commission.

A more subtle practice is to sit outside a hotel or other hotspot with your yellow For Hire light off, hoping someone will approach you and ask you to drive them somewhere nice. If the driver doesn't like the destination stated, he can just say that he's not for hire. The practice is known as "Hanging it Up" and strictly speaking it's touting. Those who do it will say that minicabs do it all the time, and they are only depriving minicab drivers' work. Such people are in denial, as they are also depriving taxi drivers' legitimate work. Some cab drivers are reluctant to report sharp practices but those who break the rules are opting out of the cab drivers' code and should be condemned.

Dress Code

From time to time we hear calls for a dress code. True, your average Uber driver looks resplendent in his black suit, but isn't it a bit of a con? The passenger likes to pretend he's hired a high-end chauffeur, and the driver is dressed as if he's about to attend a business conference. In reality, the customer has chosen the private hire arrangement because it's marginally cheaper than a taxi. Even if the car is a high-spec, highly-polished BMW, it's still a minicab. And the chauffeur is still a minicab driver. I reserve the right to wear shorts in the summer – though I draw the line at flip-flops. I'm driving you to Euston; I'm not trying to sell you a hedge fund investment.

Some taxi drivers could do with some smartening up, but we didn't become our own bosses to be told what to wear. It's impractical to wear a suit for an eight-hour stint in the driving seat. It's in everyone's interests that the driver is comfortable, not hot and sweaty.

Occasionally, oil needs to be checked and fluids need to be topped up. Under many cabs you'll notice a pool of oil or radiator fluid. Sometimes wheels need changing. Even opening the bonnet of a diesel taxi is a dirty business. However much technology has improved motor vehicles, oil still leaks and batteries still go flat – no doubt because of all the electrical devices we have in our cars these days. If I leave my cab for a week without driving it I sometimes take the battery fuse out, as in the past my battery has died after a few days of inactivity. I eventually had a VARTA battery the size of a fridge fitted and it appears to have more power in it than the battery that came with the cab. Punctures are common, and tyre technology never seems to improve. Come on tyre technicians – get your fingers out!

The Annual Cab Inspection

Each year, your cab is presented for its annual licensing inspection. The standards and procedures have changed over the years. It's not quite as traumatic as it used to be, but it would be foolish to treat it lightly. Your cab has to be in first class condition, and all the paperwork must be in order. In my early days, the chassis had to be painted and the engine would be steam cleaned. Every tiny malfunction would have to be put right.

You still have the meter checked and certified, and of course, all your Vehicle Excise Duty and insurance payments must be up to date. These days you can get your cab passed with a few minor dents, but if you blow a bulb on the way to the testing station you'd better have a spare ready to put on (I still don't know how to fit a headlight bulb).

Maybe it depends on the mood of the vehicle examiners: my former Knowledge Examiner colleague, Dave Morgan, had his new tax disc ready when he took his cab along to be inspected, but he hadn't got around to fixing it to the windscreen. He left it on the floor of the cab so it'd be easily seen. Dave is a retired Detective Chief Inspector and he's faced down many horrible scroats. When the examiner failed his cab for not displaying a tax disc Dave just looked at him. When Dave looks at you it's pretty scary.

You need to thoroughly clean your cab, even those greasy little corners that don't see a soapy sponge from one month to the next. It's essential to lift the seats up and clear out any rubbish and dirt. I know someone whose cab failed after the inspector found some syringes under the back seat. I can't tell you whose cab it was as it's my policy not to mess with Russians, especially ones who run Knowledge schools. I've never found any syringes or anything nasty like that, but I once found an unregistered Oyster Card charged with £30. Yowser.

You'll need to show a recent MOT certificate, so your cab would have been checked over, and probably serviced, by a garage. The MOT will have taken care of most of the mechanical and safety aspects of the inspection, but the cab is still put on a ramp and given further tests. The MOT also covers the emissions test. I bought my Euro 4 cab from new and it failed its first two emissions tests. I still don't understand why it belches out black smoke whenever I accelerate.

You can pay the garage to present your cab at the nearest test centre, or you can take it yourself. In recent years I've taken my cab to the Staples Corner test centre. All being well, the inspection should only last twenty minutes. You'll happily screw the new licence plate on and be on your way.

Down at the Doctors

The drivers themselves need MOTs when they reach a certain age. All taxi drivers have to provide evidence of medical fitness at the ages of fifty, fifty-six, sixty-two, sixty-five, and annually thereafter. Even if you're in good health when the letter comes from TfL asking you to book a medical, you're likely to be ill by the time you've joined the virtual queue to arrange an appointment on the phone.

Medical centres are unhealthy places full of sick people coughing and spluttering up germs. I try to avoid such places as much as possible. The form needs to be completed by a GP, and we need to pay a fee for this. My medical in 2018 cost £60, but the fee varies wildly. There are rumours that Uber drivers do it online. I'm not sure how that works. I find it hard to believe some online Doctor Feelgood is issuing medical certificates for the private hire community, but there's evidence suggesting that even the eyesight test is being conducted online.

Safety and Security

Cab drivers are as lax as anyone else about leaving valuable items on view assuming they are safe. Or even if hidden away. In my early days I had a radio stolen from a locked boot, and on another occasion I had my cash dispenser lifted when I left it under the driver's seat and went off for thirty minutes. Cab drivers regularly have valuables stolen from their cabs when they nip in to a toilet in an emergency situation. There are always people watching. I would never leave a phone, sat nav, or money bag in my cab unattended now, but many still do.

Taxi drivers are targeted because criminals see a taxi as a money box on wheels. Hopefully less so now. These days, most people pay by card or on account. All anyone is going to find in my unattended cab is a roll of over-priced printer receipt paper. After I've paid for my diesel I often return home with less cash than I had in my float at the start of the day.

The rules say a cab driver should check there is no property left in the cab after each hiring. Many people are reunited with their property after they believe it's lost and gone forever. When mobile phones didn't exist, instances of passengers leaving items in the cab were relatively rare. The situation is different now. Almost everyone carries a phone, and they're not easy to spot at night on the back seat of a poorly lit taxi; especially when your vision is obscured by a credit card machine, and the myriad of stickers that we're mandated to decorate our cabs with.

Bags and coats are easy to spot, but a small rectangle left on the back seat can catch the most diligent cab driver out. I have a good record of re-uniting people with their phones.

If it's too late and the passenger has fled the scene, it's often a matter of waiting for the person to call. You answer the phone and arrange to deliver it. You'll often be rewarded for your honesty.

One memorable incident took place several years ago when I noticed a phone on my back seat as I drove home at night. The phone rang the following morning and I spoke to my passenger's personal assistant. As I was near the location of his office I was able to deliver the phone promptly.

I met my man and he was very relieved to be reunited with his BlackBerry. I was prepared to charge my passenger the metered fare to his office from where I took the call, which was about £10. He started to take money out of his wallet, lots of it. I said there was no need, as he would have got his phone back eventually through the lost property process. He said that would take too long – obviously a repeat offender who knew the score. There followed a surreal exchange where he was offering me money and I was refusing it. We eventually settled on £25. I sometimes wonder what was stored on that phone.

I once had two lost property incidents in one afternoon. I took a Lord to the House of Lords, then realised he'd left his wallet on the back seat. It was an account job, so he was easy enough to track down. I received a modest cash tip for returning the wallet to the office I'd picked him up from.

All day I'd been hearing a ringing sound in my cab. I turned my ComCab computer off thinking this might be the source of the noise, but it wasn't. When I heard it again I realised it was coming from under my seat. I reached under the seat and pulled out a phone. I thought I'd solved the mystery. I'd just returned from holiday and had left my cab in a hotel car park at Gatwick Airport. I figured someone had moved my cab at the car park and left their phone there. I had a dilemma: spend half a day driving to Gatwick and back, or make contact and offer to post the phone back? The next time it rang I answered it. I discovered that it didn't originate from Gatwick, but had been left there by an Iranian bloke at the Paddington cab wash. He offered me a cup of tea when I returned the phone. I declined his kind offer and went back to work.

If we find lost property we're obliged to hand it in at a Metropolitan Police Station or the TfL Lost Property Office on Baker Street, within twenty-four hours. This isn't as easy as it used to be as the Lost Property Office keeps office hours, and the police also keep funny hours for a twenty-four hour city like London. Many police stations have been permanently closed: four hundred police stations closed in England and Wales within a ten-year period. It's more than likely that should you pop along to your nearest police station you'll find it's been converted into a block of luxury flats; probably with a jokey name like "The Nick" or "The Old Station". The site of Marylebone Police Station on Seymour Street is being developed as I write. Developers promise "boutique apartments in the heart of Marylebone." If any residents of London's fashionable Marylebone need to report a crime they will no longer find any police in the neighbourhood. They'll just have to talk to Russian gangsters about it and hope for the best.

You might eventually get a community policeperson round in a yellow vest and some forms to fill in, but in reality a thick-necked Chechen might make a more thorough job of it or at least point you in the right direction. Just post your application for justice at the dead letter box of your choice and wait for a man in a furry hat to make contact. A poisoned umbrella tip to could warn off noisy neighbours, and an auld babushka could take round a nice samovar of polonium-210 tea in more serious cases.

I can assure passengers there's always a good chance you'll get your property back, even if it's cash. In 2017, Erhan Bodhur, found a bag left on the floor of his cab containing £10,500 in cash. The bag was left there after his passenger went to use a cash machine to withdraw £10. The driver of ten years standing handed the cash in to the police.

Passengers themselves can be lost. Stories abound about the cab driver who traps a nice job out to Heathrow before realising he's running low on diesel. With the passenger's permission he stops en route at a fuel station. The driver fills up and continues the journey. To his horror, as he pulls up at Heathrow he finds the cab full of luggage, but no passenger! The passenger had availed himself of the toilet facilities back in Hammersmith and neglected to tell the driver. I'm prepared to believe this has actually happened, and more than once.

I haven't lost any passengers, but I have gained a few. I once dropped off at Victoria Coach Station. It's a busy stretch of road, so I got moving as quickly as possible afterwards. I then heard a voice behind me, a little old lady asking me for the Hilton Olympia. She'd got in as the last person got out, while I was concentrating on making my escape. Had she not said anything, my next stop would have been the northern suburbs of Northampton.

Our customers' lax attitude to security sometimes astounds me. They'll get you to stop at a cashpoint and leave the door open with coats, phones and bags proudly displayed on the back seat. I have the ability to lock any possessions inside the cab remotely, but a surprising number of people take the risk and leave the door on the latch.

Certain Middle Eastern gentlemen enjoy the showmanship of peeling off a fifty pound note from a huge roll as they pay you off at Harrods. Women never show off their money like that, they wear it. In my experience, it's only men who leave mobile phones in taxis. Women only lose them in their bags, so they're not really lost at all.

Christmas and New Year

I love the season of goodwill, but I can never afford more than a few days off to enjoy it to the full. Christmas is the most fraught period of the year if you are working. The traffic builds up from the beginning of December, and by the middle of the month you can hardly move. Folk drive in to do their Christmas shopping and to admire the Christmas lights, delivery vans park up everywhere oblivious to bus lane cameras, and there are stationary lines of buses caused by all of the above – and the perennial roadworks of course.

Christmas attracts out-of-towners who treat themselves to a cab ride once a year. These passengers are often suspicious of their annual encounter with the Cockney wide-boy trying to fleece his family to subsidise his Christmas box. They sit bolt upright, anxiously counting out twenty pence pieces in their hand as the meter ticks over each painful increment. It's not our fault though. This is the time of year when we fully experience the result of the year's road modelling projects. Passengers pay more for their ride than at this time of the year because they're caught in slowly moving traffic.

I've worked quite a few Decembers in my time, but thankfully haven't suffered too much from passengers who have had a few sherberts and have become difficult. I sometimes get caught out by the odd group of fired-up geezers on their way to annoy Arab families at the Winter Wonderland, but I'm usually OK. My anti-social passenger filter is set at paranoid mode all year round and not many get through the net, even in December. Then again, I don't work at night. On the rare occasion I pick up account customers coming from an office party, they are as straight and as buttoned-up as they are on any other day. They probably worry that we'll get word to their boss if they create.

Trade goes dead on the last couple of days before the big day, but thankfully the traffic levels reduce. Christmas Eve is a jolly day to work, though it doesn't pay well. I've never worked Christmas Day or Boxing Day but I might try it one year in order to satisfy my curiosity.

There used to be a tradition of putting up Christmas decorations in your cab during the festive season, but the practice has faded. I sometimes put tinsel up, but if you do that you need to accept that you'll be picking up slivers of silver foil throughout the year and possibly beyond. It's like when you've had a broken window and you find yourself picking up bits of glass throughout the period of ownership of your cab. Christmas decorations are therefore best suited to rented cabs.

The roads are closed from late afternoon on New Year's Eve for the firework displays, and remain closed the following day. I usually work on New Year's Eve up to about 5 pm. I've worked a couple of New Year's Days in recent years, and it paid well because there were fewer drivers working.

The closures have become more extensive over the years. I worked New Year's Day in 2017. On my first job I was forced to take a circuitous route because of bridge closures and it was embarrassing asking my customers for what should have cost half the amount. I went home after that one job and vowed never to work New Year's Day again.

When all the excitement of Christmas is over, we can use the coming New Year to take stock and look forward. There's the Kipper Season to endure first though. We always hope the work will return early in the New Year. Sometimes it does, sometimes it doesn't. Soon, our working days will bring a bit more daylight, a bit more warmth – and hopefully a bit more income.

Refreshment Breaks

Parking charges in Central London are exorbitant. It'd be nice to have somewhere free and easy in Soho that would allow me to take advantage of an inexpensive meal in Chinatown, but there's nowhere I've found that fits the bill. There are parking opportunities in Belgravia and Knightsbridge, but you're not going to find many lunches under a tenner around there.

Cab drivers find their favourite spots. There used to be a handful of cab driver-only cafes in Central London, but the land they were sited on rocketed in value and the land was sold to developers. They were always popular as they offered parking and toilet facilities. With the price of land in London, the remaining two must be considered permanently under threat.

There's an inclusive, interactive, atmosphere at cafes used by cab drivers. Everyone is encouraged to join in the mad discussions. They can be noisy places. Huge, traditional fry-ups are still popular, but these days you'll often see some kind of salad on people's plates. I'm of the "if it ain't fried, it ain't food" school. I believe the Good Lord painted certain foods green and orange to warn us not to eat them. The milk is semi-skimmed these days. What's that all about? What's the point in supplying supposedly healthier milk when you need to use twice as much of it? Years ago, it was the cranks and freaks who drank semi-skimmed milk. Now I'm considered a freak for wanting the proper stuff.

At the cab cafes you won't necessarily see a Food Hygiene Rating on display, or invitations to look up their reviews on *Trip Advisor*. We take the risk anyway, bearing in mind the maxim that what doesn't kill you makes you stronger. Besides, there's free parking and a toilet. There's probably no paper in the bogs, mind.

In order to service the rise of Uber, TfL were licensing several hundred minicabs every week. Running concurrently to saturation licensing there was a decrease in infrastructure. TfL's policies ensured that we all had less road space in which to work, and fewer facilities in which to freshen up. Councils were closing public toilets, where they should have been opening more places to service the new drivers. Consequently there were reports of taxi and minicab drivers toileting in residential streets, particularly minicab drivers parked up around Heathrow Airport awaiting bookings. Taxi drivers have rest ranks where they can park up for a while, but private hire drivers enjoy no such luxury. Life can be made difficult for any taxi or private hire driver who finds such facilities open. Those using the free public "Iron Lung" toilet in Regency Place discovered fines in the post as

Westminster had cynically trained cameras in the immediate vicinity in order to catch people parking on yellow lines. The Lincoln's Inn Square toilet offers a Rest Rank – short-term parking for taxis: usually for thirty minutes, sometimes for an hour. The toilet facility there keeps erratic hours, and is often closed when it's meant to be open.

There's one public toilet I'd never use, and it's the temporary one that Westminster Council have delivered on projected high-alcohol weekends. It's situated on the corner of Haymarket and Jermyn Street in the heart of the West End. It's one of those open-view stand-up pissoirs that offer relief at music and beer festivals. It's on a very busy corner and it's very public. The toilet is by the taxi rank next to a prestigious office block full of our most esteemed account holders. I'm often sat there waiting there for a customer.

I'm surprised anyone would use the toilet, but they do. In broad daylight, captive in my taxi, I observed a man approach the ugly grey plastic khazi. He proceeded to unzip himself and took a pee, just a few yards from my cab and right in my line of view. Not wishing to witness the full horror of this spectacle I busied myself with checking my ComCab account screen.

I wonder what the good, unsuspecting burghers of St James think as they go about their honest business? Or visitors passing by, hoping to soak up the glamour and sophistication of London's fashionable West End? I wonder what my account customers would think, should they emerge from the office at this moment? What has this country come to? (And what a job it must be for the people unloading these contraptions!) Maybe I shouldn't have been offended? I do tend to be caught out by modern practices that would have been considered disgraceful in my younger days: wearing pyjamas to go to the shops is one recent practice that has me shaking my head.

My first thought concerning the toilet stall was that there was no need for it. Any pedestrian caught short can try a pub, café, or coffee shop. Most of these establishments would be sympathetic enough to let non-customers use their facilities. Confident folk might get past a hotel doorman.

Without adequate facilities, we will continue to hear about taxi drivers dumping bottles full of urine in residential streets, and of Uber drivers using people's gardens around Heathrow as toilets. Disgusting behaviour, but London councils should do more to help people whose work involves driving around all day, scared to stop moving. I'm often tempted to nip into the terminal building at Heathrow to use the toilet, but I know there are cameras watching, and I know I'm liable to a fine, or to see my cab go up in a controlled explosion at the hands of a paranoid police service.

Cab driving doesn't tend to be a young person's game. There are quite a few drivers with bladder and bowel problems, and holding it in can bring on urinary tract problems. Taxi drivers are understandably concerned with their own situation, but the lack of facilities for private hire drivers is even worse, as they have no official rest ranks. It all contributes to an unpleasant and unhealthy environment. People don't generally pee for fun – though I understand some people use toilet cubicles for fun.

As a humorous footnote to the display of public toileting above, five minutes later a man walked his dog up to the toilet and lifted it up to the urinal so it could have a pee. That's really taking the piss.

6

Passengers

There are many reasons why people take taxis. Trains, tubes and buses cover most of London well, but public transport isn't convenient in some situations. Sometimes people have luggage they need to get across London to a rail station or airport. A ride in a cab could be part of a holiday or a Christmas treat. Sometimes a cab is taken in an emergency. It's an uncomfortable feeling knowing we sometimes thrive on the misfortune of others.

In an ideal scenario, smiley happy people get into your cab, and you convey them swiftly to their destination. Kids are always enthralled with a ride in an iconic London taxi because it's nothing like the car their parents drive. A once-a-year family can barely contain their excitement in December when you become Santa Claus himself.

You can gain considerable satisfaction when things are running well, but there are many factors conspiring to ruin our job satisfaction: traffic congestion, road closures, special events, other road users and pedestrians. As for customers, some don't know where they live, or where they want to go to. Some will hold you responsible for the traffic, or for their own time-management deficiencies. Some don't know where to hail a cab and expect us to stop in front of a bus on Oxford Street, or park on red routes while they use a cashpoint. They get hot, they get cold. They're happy, they're miserable. And all customers are in a hurry.

I always try to respect my customers. I don't refer to them as "fares" because I don't like being seen as a "cover" in a restaurant, or a "human resource" by a company that might employ me. I can't abide rudeness, and I'm always insulted when an account customer walks off without a "thank you." There are a few idiots and ingrates, but 95% of my customers are nice people who treat me with respect. Without passengers, my job wouldn't exist: therefore, our customers should be valued and respected.

If in what follows I'm hard on those who pay my wages, I don't mean you, dear reader: you hail a cab in a sensible place; you request your destination clearly; you appreciate the difficult task I have negotiating roadworks and madcap traffic schemes; and you are pleasant and polite throughout. No, I mean the others.

Keeping the Customer Satisfied

The general public are unpredictable, and dealing with strangers can be unsettling. You can't tell by looking at someone if they're going to kick off if things don't go their way.

Starting out for work in cold weather I always put the heater on in the back as I approach Central London. My aim is to provide some warmth to my first passenger of the day. Sometimes my aim to provide comfort is wasted and the passenger opens the windows as soon as he gets in. When my passenger leaves, my cab feels cold. I put the heater on again. Some people are always hot, some are always cold. It's the same side of the coin with the air-conditioning in the summer.

In matters of customer liaison, a firm but fair approach is best: you neither want to scare customers off, nor show any weakness. Some people will exploit any hint of vulnerability. Some folk are big people in the office and have never heard the word "No". In a cab they are just another punter. Stay firm and they might respect you for it. Or they could write a stiff letter to TfL and try to get your licence suspended.

It instils confidence in your customer if you show you are at the top of your game and you know what you are doing. We are victims of our reputation. The moment a passenger sits down we are expected to move off immediately. There is no time to consult maps or sat navs. If you really can't think of a destination and haven't time to look it up, asking in a cheery, matter-of-fact way to confirm the address they have on their phone usually clarifies things. We all forget things from time to time.

It's fair to say there are a fair few grumpy old men driving cabs in London. I'm convinced some passengers like a grumpy driver. It's a popular image of the London cabbie that some people come to expect. It's like going for a Chinese meal in Soho. Restaurant service in Chinatown has its own name: "Soho Brusque". I'm sure some people are disappointed if they get a jovial waiter come to take their order. One who lets you linger over your jasmine tea for a while after your crispy pork. I'm always a bit apprehensive when hailing a cab: will he be chatty or grumpy? I prefer the quiet driver, but I like a smile and some acknowledgement. It's the same with Chinese waiters.

Many cab drivers are sociable, but we respect the fact that most customers prefer a chat-free ride. This is often reinforced by the passenger who's plugged into an electrical device before they even enter the hallowed portal of a London cab. Being sociable, and making small talk, doesn't come naturally to me. When I did personality tests as a Careers Adviser I was always off the scale on introversion. Perhaps I've always been in the wrong job? I don't like teamwork, and I don't enjoy conversing with strangers. I'm in awe of people who can talk to strangers without any self-consciousness. Why do you think I've written a book rather than deliver my thoughts at a public lecture?

A reality TV show in 2016 showed staff at work at the Mandarin Oriental Hotel. I remember thinking at the time how difficult I would find this job. I was amazed at the patience of hotel staff as they pandered to the whims of wealthy guests accustomed to five-star service. The enduring image for me was of an Arab woman having her luggage delivered to the hotel in a removal van, complete with explicit instructions on how her suite should be converted into a children's play pen. We drive these people around all the time, though I don't get too involved. The rich and powerful generally inhabit a world beyond my experience or understanding. I sometimes wonder where I went wrong in life when I've dropped some people off at the Hotel de Posh and I'm about to go off for a botulism burger and a pint of instant coffee.

To speak truth, I prefer animals to people. I'd rather muck out the elephants' enclosure at a zoo, than pander to demanding people in a hotel. As a Knowledge Examiner, one of my valued customers was a doorman at The Ritz. I'd sometimes see him go about his business when I dropped off passengers there. I was impressed with the easy way he had with people: just the right balance of brevity and formality.

Hotel staff must deal with some *very* difficult people. I find it hard to keep a smile on my face dealing with people I can't stand.

The Optimum Route

Customers, we are on your side. We do everything we can to get to your destination as quickly and as safely as possible. In London, there are many ways to run the same route, and the skill of the driver is in deciding which way might be best on any given occasion. Some passengers tell you what way they want to go. This is good because it removes the responsibility from the driver.

We're trained to know the shortest route, and that's not necessarily the fastest. An experienced cab driver learns to set the sat nav in his head to the quickest route to avoid conflict, particularly with corporate account holders.

Many people don't realise that the River Thames doesn't run straight as it flows through London, and that not all of the bridges run in a north–south direction. The shortest route from a point in the Chelsea area to the City is by way of two bridges. I rarely use two bridges because it makes people suspicious. One man knew the score when I picked him up in Holborn bound for Dolphin Square, Pimlico. I'd normally head towards Trafalgar Square, then down past Parliament. My man asked me to use two bridges. He didn't specify which two bridges, so he was possibly testing me. I went over Waterloo Bridge, then back across the river at Lambeth Bridge. It was a quick, though slightly longer, route than the one I would have taken. My customer was pleased, and that pleased me. Sometimes there's real job satisfaction in this game you know.

Many customers take the same journey regularly and expect every taxi driver to choose their preferred route automatically. The customer isn't always right though. Just because they're taken the same way every day, it doesn't mean it's the best way; it might just be the way they are used to. Although customers sometimes teach the driver something, it's more frequently the other way round. Often a driver can show the customer a new way, but taking a new route is always risky. In a city where new road closures happen every day, the fear is that your particular favourite streets will be coned off once you've committed to a particular route.

It's best to talk over the options with your passengers. Usually, they'll leave the final decision to you. This can make you uncomfortable, as you're going to be held responsible if you get to the top of Mabledon Place and there's a giant crane blocking the last few hundred yards to King's Cross. Traffic can be heavy on Sunday evenings. I took a man from St Pancras to Paddington. Basically, you just turn right onto Euston Road and keep going. Down the slip off Bishops Bridge Road, and you're there. Rather than queue to get through Euston Underpass, I bypassed it by turning left into Gower Street, then took the quieter roads through Fitzrovia and Marylebone. I delivered my customer swiftly, but from a different direction. I'd analysed the situation and had used my skill to get my passenger to his destination as quickly as possible, and without extra mileage. And how did he react? He had a pop! It wasn't the route he was used to.

I took a woman from Hermitage Lane, NW2, to Victoria Street, at about 10.30 am. I drive down Finchley Road every day on my drive into Central London and I know it's always slow. I therefore took Heath Street down to Swiss Cottage.

Unfortunately, Heath Street was slow going. "This is the worst road possible," the lady said. She wanted me to use the bus lane on Finchley Road as I'm legally entitled to do. Using the bus lane helps a bit, but you are still swerving around coaches and builders' lorries most of the way down. It isn't a bus lane after 10 am anyway. Confidence is everything in this game, but it's easily dispelled. As self-doubt crept in I wondered if she was right. Maybe I made the wrong call? Maybe I'm incompetent? This sort of thing really shatters your confidence.

The following day I trapped a job from the same area to Abbey Road, St John's Wood. I used Heath Street again, and this time it was clear. On arrival the lady said I was the only person that's driven her the right way. Confidence was restored. The truth is, *you* usually know more than the customer.

An experienced driver will have the skill to chop and change the route, and in many cases it works. Where there is congestion and you take evasive action, it's best to let the passenger *see* the queuing traffic before diverting. After all, if the passenger hasn't seen the congestion with his own eyes he might be wondering why you're taking an unorthodox route. For example, if I know there's a huge demonstration march coming down Regent Street, I'll pick a different route. This route might be a little bit longer, but it gets us out of trouble. The passenger isn't aware of a thousand soap-dodgers about to block our progress and wonders why I'm using Wardour Street and cutting through Soho. If other drivers have the same idea, Wardour Street could be jammed too. Who'll get the blame? Me of course. Let them actually *see* the mayhem caused by the demo taking up the whole of

Park Lane, Regent Street and Piccadilly. If necessary, point out the yellow diversion signs that have suddenly appeared without warning at the entrance to Regent Street. If the passenger doesn't see documentary evidence, he might not believe you.

All I'm doing is employing a method I use when washing up when the wife's gone to work. If I wash everything up and put all the crocks and cutlery away in their proper place, she'll return to a clear sink and draining board. She might not be aware of the hard graft I put in. However, if I wash up, then spread all the clean crocks all over the worktop, it's clear what I've been doing. Same principle: leave the evidence and let them *see* the work you've put in. The pile of washing up can be thus viewed as a clogged up one-way system – let's say The Elephant & Castle.

The Sat Nav Cometh

Cab drivers won't take you the long way round on purpose. Most drivers have too much pride in their job to allow themselves to cheat the public. Besides, many people follow your route on an app and can query it.

I first realised a passenger was following my route on a phone application in 2014. It was a short but fairly complex run from the Mall into Soho. At the end, my Indian man beamed and said "Very Good!" So, our customers are checking up on us, are they?

Satellite navigation has made our job both easier and harder. A sat nav device is woefully inadequate for use in London, but it's useful when you get jobs out of town, or for looking up door numbers. The sat nav has also made it easier for our competition to operate; though as I say, it has limited use in London and other big cities. I've used a sat nav in Sheffield a couple of times. It sent me down roads that were permanently closed off, and around and around a ring road until I got dizzy. My Cabbie's Mate got me to a rural location in deepest Surrey on a package delivery once – I never would have found it without help – and it's invaluable for looking up small hotels on the service roads off Sussex Gardens in Bayswater.

Our private hire competitors no longer need to thumb through the *A–Z* as if they're in the backstreets of Cairo. It's incredible that a person can be recruited from another country to work as a private hire driver without ever seeing a London map. I challenge anyone to try to get around London relying on sat nav: "Turn left Tavistock Place... er, it says Cycles Only. Better carry on until the next junction... That looks blocked off! Next left then... Where are all these people going? Where am I? What now? Sorry madam, I'm not sure how to get out of this..."

You can repeat this all over London. In my experience, even when the sat nav sends you on a route not blighted by closed roads, it's not usually the best way to go. That knowledge comes only with practical experience of driving different routes and at different times of the day and week. Most customers know the score as to London's traffic and appreciate we are doing our best under difficult circumstances. Our strength is that we can often find alternative routes to get out of trouble. Sadly though, with such an aggressive programme of road closures, both driver and passenger are increasingly left frustrated. There is more reason to use our analytical skills when we're really up against it.

Anyway, let's look at a few major consumer groups:

Commuters

Thousands of workers come into London every weekday – and a few at the weekends. Only the bravest souls drive here: those with enough income to be able to pay extortionate parking charges, or the privileged few with access to private parking. The rest swarm out of train stations and continue their journeys by foot, or by tube, bus or taxi. Walking is slow, buses are slow. The tube is OK at off-peak times, but it's a living hell when busy. It's hot, crowded and everyone is getting in everyone else's way. Commuting is a miserable experience. I know what it's like, I've done it. I know the tension as your train is called and hundreds of you rush down the ramp at Euston in order to secure a seat fit only for an arse smaller than that of a supermodel.

When I became a Knowledge Examiner in 2011 my annual season ticket from Northampton cost around £4500 – with no option of booking a reserved seat. Apart from the crippling expense, there's the stress of the actual experience.

Chaos ensued at Waterloo Station in August 2017 when the station closed half its platforms before modernising the station. The train companies advised passengers to avoid travelling at peak times and even suggested taking a holiday in August. The misery was compounded by long-term roadworks on the Westminster Bridge approach which made any road journey to the 'Loo longer and more expensive.

Commuters, I feel your pain. You have to put up with inflation-busting price hikes every year, but with no real improvement in the service: just more people crowding you out and coughing and sneezing germs over you. Even if you can afford to travel first class you're not exempt: when I used to travel back from Euston, the train was so crowded they sometimes opened up the first class carriages to everyone! What's that all about? Surely the whole point in buying a first class ticket is to guarantee a seat in a relatively empty carriage?

I'm still a commuter of course. It's just that when I get to London I drive around the West End for eight hours looking for a parking space. At about 7 pm I give up and drive home.

Tourists

We all love tourists: they're so jolly and easy to deal with. Well would you rather drive a frustrated commuter to Waterloo Station to catch a train that went five minutes ago, or drive some giggly Chinese girls to Selfridges?

Foreign visitors love the Changing of the Guard ceremony, Harrods, Selfridges, Tower Bridge, &c, &c... You need to be careful with Tower Bridge. Apart from the 20 mph speed limit, visitors sometimes confuse it with London Bridge. You get a good view of Tower Bridge and the Shard, but London Bridge is otherwise a rather uninteresting strip of concrete and tarmac. Didn't the Americans buy London Bridge thinking it was Tower Bridge one time? I'm not sure if that's strictly true, but it's a nice story, and one that I used to mention to my colleagues in Louisiana whenever possible.

Bargain-conscious tourists are easily pleased with a trip to Primark, or to watch street entertainers. I often see a gaggle of tourists watching a bloke bang a drum kit on a busy West End street. No other musical instruments, just a drum kit. I don't know about you, but I don't see the attraction.

Tourists are usually in a good mood as they're on holiday. They're not usually so rushed, and they enjoy watching the freaks as we drive through the West End. I'm happy to pose for a photo at the end of the ride too. Tourists are sometimes mocked for being amused by the humdrum things that the locals take for granted. I don't. I can see London through their eyes. I've taken photos of checker cabs in New York myself.

Although there are thousands of tourists around on every day of the week, they aren't getting in taxis like they used to. Maybe they're taking hop-on hop-off tour buses? Maybe they're hiring Boris Bikes, or walking more? We're painfully aware that many visitors are also calling up Uber instead.

Many visitors come to London for sports events, concerts and festivals of every description. Football, international cricket and rugby, and the Wimbledon tennis championships are big events. Many foreign visitors take in a football match. Unfortunately, it's not easy getting hold of tickets for Premier League matches at short notice, so people often have to lower their sights. I've taken several groups of football fans down to Millwall's stadium. On one drive down into the South East London Badlands I had to explain to my Scandinavian passengers why I took my West Ham air freshener down as we approached. Millwall and West Ham are sworn enemies and much blood has been spilt when the two teams have played each other.

Going to Arsenal's stadium is fine, but I generally dislike taking people to football. They've got things the wrong way round in this country. When things get busy, the reaction is to close off roads and underground stations. So instead of keeping the traffic flowing when Chelsea play at home they close the streets entirely.

Boys with Toys

Each summer, drivers bring their flash sports cars over from the Gulf States. Knightsbridge and Mayfair are full of cruising sports cars bearing Qatar, Kuwait and Dubai number plates. I'm not really a petrol-head and I don't know what make of cars they are. They're painted in strange colours though. They park up at the Dorchester Hotel where young male groupies stand and admire the cars and photograph them on their mobile phones (do you think Arab women are as impressed as the teenaged boys?). Each to their own. As a tourist event, it's probably more rewarding than the Changing of the Guard ceremony. I've got to say that Arabs are valued cab customers. They and the Chinese keep the trade going.

Bridge and Tunnel People

Many London residents don't see the need for a car. It's an expensive burden. When living in London, I was well into my twenties before any of my friends bought cars. I had scooters and motorbikes, and I didn't think about driving a car until the idea of being a cab driver came up. Underground trains went anywhere I wanted to visit, as well as to many places that I've still never been to. I've always been fascinated by the tube map, and I still wonder what the difference is between Ruislip, West Ruislip, South Ruislip and Ruislip Manor. If you wonder what goes on in Cockfosters, Totteridge & Whetstone, Fairlop and Theydon Bois, you're in good company. The tube map is comforting, like the shipping forecast. Enjoy it, but don't try to understand it.

The strange-sounding places listed above are all in North London. If you haven't got a tube station at the end of your road, you probably live in South London. Bad luck. At any

London dinner party, the conversation invariably starts with how you got there. Whoever is the biggest martyr draws the most admiration. If your guests are multimillionaires living in central London, a £10 cab ride is not going to impress anybody. If you have spent forty quid on a tortuous trip over bridges, under tunnels, and around dangerous one-way systems, you have a tale to tell.

I've had a few spells living in South London. It wasn't too bad, there are some nice parts. Unfortunately the image is of railway arches, scrapyards, and dodgy geezers. There has always been plenty of gang-related crime south of the river. The East End had Jack the Ripper and the Krays, and there's a lot of misty-eyed nostalgia for East London. And it's fashionable now. There's nothing fashionable about the Elephant & Castle, though they're trying hard to gentrify the area and drive the poor people out.

I can't really say I have much of an idea what goes on south of London Bridge these days. A job going south or east isn't particularly sought after as it's harder to trap a job coming back. And any journey involving bridges and tunnels is likely to involve queuing in traffic. Cab drivers familiar with the lands south of the Thames might try to use a taxi rank, but the good ones are likely to be full. We'll take you to all of these places, and more, and sometimes with a smile on our faces.

Account Customers

Signing up to a hailing app, or a computerised radio circuit adds strings to your bow, and can provide work when it's quiet on the street. The computerised Computer Cab radio circuit I subscribe to services the huge Taxicard account. This scheme is run by the London boroughs to provide discounted taxi travel for those with limited mobility. Taxicard holders typically only pay £2.50 a ride up to a certain limit – usually £10.80 or £11.80. Once that limit is reached, most boroughs allow a second swipe of the card. The customer has to pay another £2.50, but this allows the Taxicard holder to take a longer trip. Anything on top of their allowance means they have to pay the difference themselves. It can be stressful for the passenger who expects to pay a certain amount, and is presented for a demand for more money when his cab is delayed in traffic. I'm sympathetic in such cases and often write off some, or all, of the difference.

Many Londoners find it difficult to access public transport, and rely on the Taxicard system to get out and about. Many also travel by train and need a cab to get to a main line station. Others go to restaurants and the theatre. If we chose to, we could drive customers to African churches all Sunday morning. More commonly, Taxicard customers are going to and from hospital appointments and they need to be there on time.

Taxicard work is a different type of work: it's more personal, and quite humbling. Sometimes the passenger puts you to work. I'm happy to stop to post letters, or to see customers safely into their homes and stroke the cat (that one cost me a parking ticket). One old lady in St John's Wood got me to walk up the road to buy her a newspaper before we set off. I carried out her request without complaint. I drove her to an expensive restaurant at Borough Market. I'd always fancied dining at Roast myself one day. It wasn't until I realised I'd be eating a crummy cheese roll for my own lunch did I feel a slight twinge of resentment.

At the other extreme I ferry around corporate account holders whose employers pay for their taxi rides. These people come from another world. A world of expensive restaurants and luxury hotels, regular international travel, and half-day shopping trips on the meter. There could be £20 or £30 on the meter before they show up. A £50 cab ride is like the price of a cup of tea to some corporate types. In the summer of 2017 I had a nice wait and return ride from the City to Harrods. By the time my lady had been into Harrods, then returned to the City, she'd cost her company £70. I'm not complaining as £70 is a lot of money to me.

One useful function on my radio circuit is the Going Home mode. When I start to think of home I automatically let the circuit know I am looking to go north. A job to Hampstead or Hendon does me nicely at 7 pm. Many well-off account holders live to the north or west of London so a Roader into the country is always possible. My friend Paul, picked up a man heading home south-west along the M3. The customer obviously took this route home regularly. He helpfully advised Paul to turn left when the meter reached £100. A job going above £100 is rare, but gratefully accepted, especially when you're heading in that direction anyway.

One of my most memorable account jobs was from a big house on Regent's Park Outer Circle – about as posh as it gets. My task was to deliver a cold box of food to a private jet at Luton Airport. Luton Airport is a lucrative run, but this one was particularly good because of the waiting time involved. I had to pass security clearance at the private jet terminal, then actually drive on to the runway and park under a plane's wing. Freaky.

Account customers can be demanding, as well as dismissive of the taxi driver. They want to get somewhere quickly, and it's your job, the faceless taxi driver, to deliver Sir to his destination – and right outside the door if you please, I couldn't possibly walk across the road. Sometimes account customers complain when you can't find a parking space outside their door when picking them up. I've had people who haven't bothered to look a few yards along the road, and have decided not to use you. Some don't even bother to contact the circuit to cancel. It's all right, they're not paying what's already on the meter when the job is officially cancelled, their company is.

Most runs to stations and airports are regarded as "urgent" by the account rider, but I have limited sympathy. Look at your time-management and don't try to throw it back to me and make it *my* problem. My sympathy lies with the customer running late for an appointment at the UCH cancer centre, rather than the fat cat banker who might have to wait an extra twenty minutes for his train home.

Bad Attitude

Look at how some people behave on a bus or a train: feet on seats, eating messy food, shouting and swearing at each other. I often wonder if they behave like that at home. I expect some probably do.

I try not to be too precious about it, but I regard my cab as my home, and I don't like people disturbing it. Even when I'm for hire, you still need to ask permission to enter my home. I don't like it when uninvited people fling open the door in stationary traffic and climb in without a word. Maybe I'm over-sensitive but it's almost like walking on to someone's yacht without seeking permission. Some drivers are worse than I am. Passengers can be intimidated by all the signs some drivers put up warning of what's not acceptable: eating, drinking, not slamming the doors, &c., &c. Plus warnings that whatever you are doing is being recorded on CCTV (CCTV is mandatory in some licensing areas outside London). The warning stickers about smoking and vaping are compulsory. We're not the police, but I guess a public school-type might be reminded of his prefects or headmaster, and wonder if he'll be subjected to a humiliating trousers-down six-of-the-best should he open a bottle of fizzy water without asking permission.

The modern term "Man Spread" refers to the way some men sit with their legs wide open on tube trains, owning their own space, and that of the people on either side of them. I don't want your feet on my seats, and I don't want you eating kebabs. I'd rather not hear you shouting either. But you can indulge in Man Spread if you wish. This is one luxury I'm able to condone in my cab. Go ahead, Sir, the cab is built for comfort. Spread out and enjoy yourself.

I don't expect a chat with my passengers, but I do expect to be acknowledged. Brusque behaviour cuts across the social classes. Some people are so dismissive of the driver that their phone call is more important than telling you where they want to be dropped off. When it's half-way convenient they'll shout "Here Please!" expecting you to stop abruptly.

Here's one example of a miserable and insensitive account customer: in March 2017, a Muslim convert drove a hired car into pedestrians on Westminster Bridge. Six people died, including the attacker, and about fifty were injured. On attempting to storm the Houses of Parliament the attacker stabbed a policeman to death, before being shot dead himself. On the following day, when the city was in mourning, I took a job from a well-known American bank in the City to Pimlico. There were many road closures still in place in the Westminster area, and the normally accepted route to Pimlico went right through the heart of Westminster. Having to take a slightly amended route I did really well to avoid the closures and resulting queues of diverted traffic. There were police vehicles speeding around, and as we went past Millbank Circus we saw rows of international TV crews parked up. It was like a war zone. I was sure my passenger would appreciate my sterling efforts in keeping us moving. We were almost there when m'lady commented that it would've been better had I chosen an earlier left turn from Warwick Way, thus saving maybe a hundred yards.

I didn't say anything, as it was a wait and return job and I still had a long ride back with her to the City. All she was doing was picking up some papers, then returning to the office. She cost her bank £53.

Any sensible person would hail a cab on a straight stretch of road; away from a junction, and somewhere where the driver can stop safely. You wouldn't believe how many people stop cabs at busy junctions, traffic lights, or on Fleet Street where it goes down to one lane.

The traffic lights around Piccadilly Circus attract families with pushchairs. You might stop tentatively when you see the man's hand go up as you think he'll only take five seconds to open and shut the door. He'll then call over his wife with the kids and shopping bags. All you can do is wave politely at the patient driver of the bus behind you, while everyone around you is thinking "Bloody cab drivers... Who do they think they are… They think they own the roads…" &c., &c. Of course some cab drivers are complicit in this anti-social behaviour. They're going to have that job, however badly they're having to park, and however long it takes to load up those suitcases. Drivers who indulge in this behaviour can be identified by the dents in the cab boot.

Passengers can be oblivious in this situation. Some don't realise we can't stop on the zigzag approaches to zebra crossings, and that we only get two minutes to load a wheelchair on a red route before we alert the trigger-happy camera operators at TfL who are itching to post us out a fine. Whether it's ignorance or arrogance, their behaviour shouldn't be indulged in.

I don't like stopping outside security-sensitive buildings. I don't like being stared at by armed police outside the Ministry of Defence, and I always fear being shot outside the American Embassy if I get too close. I miss lots of fares by not stopping for people in inconvenient places, but I try to be a responsible cab driver. Some passengers like the excitement of hailing a moving cab at the last moment and having it screech to a halt. They imagine a cloth-capped driver urgently shouting in a fifties cockney accent "Where to, guv?" while pulling a U-turn with tyres screeching. Yes, the occasional joker tells you to "Follow that cab!" like in the films.

You sometimes get real follow-that-cab jobs when two cabs are needed to transport a large group of people. These jobs make me anxious. If you're the first cab in a two-cab convoy you worry that the cab driver behind you will be criticising your route. You feel as if you are in a competition and that you need to put on a show for the following driver. If you're driving the second cab you feel under pressure to stick close to the leader. You don't want to turn up five minutes later when the passengers have been discharged and their cab has disappeared into the distance.

Good Attitude

The traffic in the Christmas period of 2016 was as bad as I'd ever seen it (it was predictably worse in 2017). Still, not every cab customer complained. I picked up a middle-aged visitor from New York. I only took her half a mile from Regent Street around to Selfridges in Oxford Street. We crawled along in near-stationary traffic. She was on the phone and was quite upbeat, telling the person on the line that being stuck in a traffic queue was "entertaining" and that she was "insulated in a cab." Glad to be of assistance, madam. That'll be a tenner please...

In amongst the negativity and big city neurosis, you will see acts of kindness that give you hope for civilisation. Many people are honest enough to hand over items of lost property that the previous occupants have left behind, for example.

One heart-warming incident happened one Sunday as I was stopped by a group of people outside St Clement Danes Church on The Strand. An elderly lady wanted to catch a bus to go a short distance just past Trafalgar Square, but the traffic was held up by a demonstration and there were no buses going past. Two young men were keen to get her into my cab. I took them to be relatives. One gave me a £20 note. The lady noticed this and told him to put his money away. As she got in, the man handed me the note again. I took it, intending to give the lady the change on arrival. She could then get the change to her grandson or nephew at her leisure. There was no traffic and we flew along The Strand and around

Trafalgar Square. The fare was £5-something. I rounded it down and gave her £15 change from the twenty. The lady went into shock when I explained that her grandson had slipped me the twenty, and this was her change. It transpired that the young man wasn't a relative at all. Two young men had come across an elderly lady in distress, waiting for a bus that was never going to come. They were total strangers and they had handed over £20. She gave me a fiver tip.

Code of Practice for Passengers

So, traffic-related issues aside, most of our problems come from our interaction with passengers. It's not always their fault: there's poor communication and misunderstanding on both sides, and either party can be reluctant to make clear their wishes and expectations. To make sure there are no more misunderstandings, I think it'll be useful to compile a quick code of practice for passengers:

- Want to hail a passing cab? Just looking at the oncoming driver isn't enough: you need to thrust your arm out with confident intent. London is no place for limp-wristed hails (an underarm Asian-style hail is acceptable so long as it's clear)

- If you're not hailing a cab, please don't wave your arms around on a London street: we've all stopped for people waving to their friend across the road

- Don't try to get into a passing cab in stationary traffic without asking if I'm free. If my yellow For Hire light isn't on I'm probably not working. Cab drivers are entitled to go for breaks, and to go home when they want to. By all means ask, but don't get upset if I tell you I'm not free. I could have just returned from the supermarket, or be taking the cat to the vet

- Stop a cab somewhere sensible. Don't expect a cab to stop at a busy junction or at traffic lights. Many cab drivers indulge you and stop at such daft places, and they spoil it for everyone. Please don't encourage it

- The same applies to setting down: it takes a couple of minutes to process a credit card, so have your cash ready if you really must get out on double red lines on Euston Road. We also don't like you sitting in the back counting out the contents of your piggy bank with a queue of buses behind us on Oxford Street

- You've done well to get across three lanes of busy traffic to reach my cab on Haymarket rank, but you're not safe yet. There are doors on both sides of a taxi – why not use the one nearest to the kerb?

- Don't stand at the back of the cab at St Pancras expecting the driver to put your bags in the boot. Taxi boots are tiny, and are only big enough to accommodate the equipment we're obliged to carry in order to make us accessible: such as a wheelchair ramp and a harness. There's room for little else

- Please try not to stop a cab on one-way streets if you are going in the opposite direction: particularly on major northbound streets like Tottenham Court Road if you're going south. You're quite within your rights, but it spoils it for the driver who thinks he's on his way home if he stops for you

- State your destination clearly and accurately. I know you've read about a cab driver's enlarged hippocampus, but it doesn't help him read your mind as to what part of Edgware Road you want. It's a very long road. In fact it's the A5 and it goes to Wales

- Don't send your husband out into the street to stop a cab while you're still at the till at the Rainforest Café gift shop. Or before you've got your kids in the pushchair and your shopping bags ready

- Yes, you can bring your dog, cat, rabbit or any other pet with you. It's the humans I'm suspicious of

- Don't put your feet on the seats. Or eat or drink without asking first

- Either inform the driver of your preferred route or leave it to his judgment. Should you get stuck in traffic, respect the driver's decision and don't make a song and dance about it

- Don't ask for Paddington; then add that you want an obscure B&B on Sussex Gardens when we're going down the ramp off Bishops Bridge Road

- It's bad luck say "the roads are clear today" when you are only halfway there. Anything can happen in the next half a mile

- Saying you want to be dropped off "halfway down" is meaningless when the driver can't see how long the road is. Just shout when we're there

- The driver is not responsible for the traffic. Please direct your comments on madcap road schemes to TfL

- The same applies to taxi fares. We have no control over this either

- "I'm in a hurry" doesn't cut any ice. Everyone's in a hurry, and all trips are urgent. I respectfully suggest you look at your own time-management. Don't try to turn *your* problem into *my* problem

- Best not attempt to engage the driver in a discussion on Uber: like the aforementioned madcap traffic schemes, this is another touchy subject best avoided

- I'll stop at a cashpoint if you insist, but it'll be easier for us both if you use a credit card. I am still subject to parking restrictions outside a cashpoint. The meter's still running too. Using a card is always going to be cheaper.

There you have it; those are my top tips for smooth customer relations. I think we now understand each other. Let's now look at a few special categories of passenger.

Celebrities

I never refer to a celebrity as a VIP. Every customer is a Very Important Person. A cab ride is a great leveller. I operate a robust Equal Opportunities policy, and in my cab everyone is treated with respect. Celebrities have always treated me with respect too. I've never felt they were lording it over me. It's the wannabees you need to be wary of.

Most celebrities go about their business quietly without drawing attention to themselves. Some try to disguise themselves with hats, scarves and dark glasses. It's always nice to pick up well-known actors, musicians or footballers. I always respect their privacy and would never try to engage them in conversation if I got the feeling they wanted to be left alone. I don't like to be intrusive, and I don't like to give anyone any reason to show any irritation.

They say you should never meet your heroes. With a celebrity you admire, you don't want them to be anything other than the person you imagine them to be. You want them to remain someone to admire. On two occasions in around 1990, I picked up Manchester United and Northern Ireland footballing legend, George Best, in Curzon Street. He was a well-known figure to drivers working evenings in Mayfair. I found him a quiet, charming, man, happy to exchange a few words. I also picked up Chelsea player, Roberto Di Matteo. A star, for sure; though not quite in the league of George Best.

Also in Mayfair, I picked up veteran actor, Stewart Granger. This guy had presence in spades, a real character. Bound for Fulham, he wouldn't stop talking and referred to Fulham Broadway as a "shit hole" and wondered about the punch-ups that occur at Chelsea Football Club. Irish actor, Richard Harris was another big name from around the same time.

I was particularly excited to pick up a musical hero of mine at the Royal Garden Hotel in Kensington: Robert Plant of Led Zeppelin. He was a really nice, laid-back, guy who wanted to talk about the previous night's television programmes on the way home to Primrose Hill.

Saturday June 2nd 2012. It's the day before the Queen's Diamond Jubilee celebrations and I accepted an account job picking up at a hairdresser's in Knightsbridge. My passenger turned out to be the Duchess of Kent and she was going to Kensington Palace. She came over as posh and confident; but also polite. Rather than order me round to a nearby shop, she asks if I "wouldn't mind." When she returned with an umbrella she said it was "for tomorrow." I'd never been into the grounds of Kensington Palace before so I needed her to direct me from Kensington High Street. There's a turning with signs saying "authorised vehicles only", then further up there's a police checkpoint. The police looked in the back of the cab and waved us through (it's harder getting out as they stop you and take down the cab's details). I'm not sure how one addresses the Queen's cousin, so I kept it neutral and treated her like anyone else. She seemed a character, and I felt she might be up for a chat over a pint sometime. Incidentally, I've never picked the Queen up in my cab, but I've seen her driven around London from time to time. You hear the whistles from the police motorcyclists first; then the traffic parts to allow the royal limousine to glide through. She never gets caught in traffic jams and probably doesn't realise London's traffic has increased since the '50s. I often wonder what she makes of the traffic cones and ugly concrete blocks that have sat outside Buckingham Palace for over a year.

One Saturday in 2013, former boxer, and eccentric celebrity, Chris Eubank chased my cab down Baker Street (Patsy Kensit also chased my cab down Baker Street once). He said he'd left his umbrella in Selfridge's, so he got me to stop there, before going on to Mayfair to collect his car. He then asked me my opinion on the best way to get to Brighton. He seemed a nice guy. Unlike most celebrities, Chris doesn't try to blend in to the background. The next time I saw him he was standing in the middle of Berkeley Square waving his arms around like a Jewish comedian trying to flag a cab down.

It was a busy Saturday, that one. My next job straight after Chris Eubank was an account pick-up at Scott's Restaurant. Bound for Chelsea, I was startled to find we were being chased by the paparazzi on motorbikes. I learned later that my customers were Charles Saatchi and his new girlfriend. Saatchi had been all over the media recently following his messy divorce from celebrity chef, Nigella Lawson. The photo of the pair in my cab made the *Sun on Sunday*.

Songwriter Nicky Chinn knew the way from Sloane Square to St John's Wood and directed the route to the letter. At the time I was playing bass in a rock covers band. I told him we were rehearsing "Blockbuster", one of many hits he co-wrote for The Sweet. He was flattered. Another songwriter, Mike Batt, was on his way from Bayswater to Mayfair. His musical credits include writing the music for the Wombles, and for discovering Katie Melua. He was a polite and pleasant man.

Marc Almond stopped me on a quiet weekend morning at Holborn Circus. He was going to Camden Town. He proved to be a quiet and pleasant chap (for younger readers, Marc was the frontman for 80s techno-pop band, Soft Cell. Get on your smartphone and look it up).

One evening I had a cab ride with a dead man. I stopped on Shaftesbury Avenue in the dark and realised my next customer was to be Les Dennis. It was freaky because his character had died the previous night on *Coronation Street*. He was on the phone talking excitedly about a new play he was about to start. When we exchanged words at the end he proved to be a really nice guy. He told me the person he'd been talking to on the phone was Bobby Davro, a comedy contemporary.

A comedian taught me a new route from St Pancras to Barnes in leafy south-west London. The impressionist, Alistair McGowan, wanted me to use the Westway to Shepherd's Bush, then drop down through Hammersmith and over the bridge into Barnes. It's a longer route than any Knowledge Boy would take, but it was quick. My passenger was as posh and as serious as I expected him to be (I never expect comedians to tell jokes and be funny).

One celebrity customer I admired was the actor, Michael Gambon. He was a very polite fellow. I'd just been watching him on TV after buying the DVD boxed set of *The Singing Detective*, a Dennis Potter work from the 1990s. More recently, he'd also starred in a Harry Potter film. That didn't mean much to me. I should have told him I recognised him as *The Singing Detective*, but I let the moment go. I thought afterwards how I could have said I was "more Dennis Potter than Harry Potter," but my chance had gone. I regretted not speaking to him properly and told myself to seize my chance the next time a celebrity I admired got in my cab.

Turning a corner one afternoon in May 2017, I was aware of a man hailing me. He was out of my line of sight, but on stopping I immediately recognised him as *Monty Python* star, Michael Palin. This one made me nervous. Palin is widely regarded as the world's nicest guy. Would he criticise my route? Would he be furious if I dared speak to him? Would he abuse me in a torrent of four-letter words if I mentioned the Pythons? This man was a comedy genius and no mistake – a pioneer of modern British surreal comedy. I needed him to remain a hero and I wasn't going to do anything to let him spoil my image of him.

Remembering how I'd let the moment pass with Michael Gambon a couple of years earlier I knew that in matters of celebrity encounter, regret weighs more than fear. At the end of the journey I overcame my nerves and we exchanged a few words. Michael was exactly how I imagined: like an old-style university professor, and as approachable and self-effacing as he is on his TV travel programmes. I'm glad to say that my image of Michael remained intact.

Many Lords and Ladies have ridden in my cab. I was intrigued about the Conservative Party Chief Whip I picked up. Imagine going to a party and saying you are the Chief Whip! I bet he's popular with the ladies. Well, a certain kind of lady anyway.

The Truth About Dogs and Cats

Not all our passengers are human, of course. We are obliged to accommodate assistance dogs, and we sometimes get asked to transport pampered pets, and take dogs to and from the park with their owners. Our minicab friends are always in trouble for refusing to carry assistance dogs. Refusing blind people's dogs has been against the law for several years, and the guidelines have been well publicised – there's even a poster up at the testing centre where taxi and minicab drivers take their vehicles for its annual licensing inspection. Never mind the legislation, I go the extra mile to promote equal opportunities for animals. I'm suspicious of people who don't like animals. I've never had a problem with animals in the cab, but I've had plenty of problems with people.

I welcome our furry friends in all areas of life. For me, a comfortable pub is one where you have to step over a sleeping dog to get to the bar, and where the irritable pub cat dares you to try to sit on his chair. I like the way that in France you can take your pet out to dinner as part of the family. I've yet to see a cat or rabbit sat at the dinner table, but I love to see a dog's head emerge from a lady's handbag. Those Frenchies are way ahead.

I always stop to pick up people with dogs, and they're usually grateful as they obviously get refusals. A dog invariably settles straight down to enjoy the ride in quiet contemplation – as our human customers should do. I've never carried a dog that was loud and obnoxious through drink, has changed its mind where it wants to go, has criticised my route, has picked the rubber off the armrest, or has left pistachio shells all over the carpet.

I never had kids because I felt I was never earning enough money. I'm not especially keen on children anyway, and I certainly wouldn't want any in the house. I prefer pets. Dogs are fine, but I prefer cats. Dogs are too conformist. Cats are free-thinking individuals, and I can relate to that. Tell a dog what to do, and it'll do it without thinking. A cat shows a healthy disrespect for authority and will ignore you if it doesn't like what's being suggested, or stare you down in a challenging way. Badly behaved pets are the most entertaining. I like a pet I can have a fight with. It's not all violence though; most cats have an affectionate side. They're just discerning and cautious. They need to get to know you first.

Many people believe dogs are more intelligent than cats, but that's only because cats are uncooperative. They're difficult to test because they get bored and walk off. The cat is the only domestic pet that has total freedom to come and go as it pleases. Other pets must resent that. If you don't feed him right, your faithful house-tiger will simply move next door. Fur Q. You know you are a good person if your pet doesn't run away. The cat thinks of itself as the master and you as the pet. That's fine; let them think they're the boss and they're happy. I have a cat and I have a rabbit. Rabbits are pretty mad too.

Buyer's Guide

If you're thinking of acquiring a secondhand cat, the ones you see sat on cushions on window sills usually make the best entry-level pets. The cats that like the outdoor life too much are the ones you need to be suspicious of. These are the ones who leave rodents on your bed as presents.

Barking

My strangest cab job involving an animal happened in 2014 after responding to an account call in Soho. I waited a fair time until a woman got in with a dog. She sent me to Barking Betty's in Battersea ("Grooming for the Urban Dog"). The lady asked me to wait twenty minutes, then take them back to Soho. Parking wasn't a problem in Battersea, so I was happy to do so. She took the woofer to Betty's, then returned to say it would take an hour. The woman sat in the cab while doggie was pampered, and the clock ticked over 20p every few seconds.

The pampering took even longer than anticipated and the lady decided she needed the loo. She found a café to use, though I thought afterwards that she could have used a litter tray at Barking Betty's.

In the end I waited 2¾ hours, but we got back to Soho quickly and everyone was happy. God knows who the account holder was, but it cost them £164 (plus automatic tip). The dog looked clean and happy, clearly oblivious to the expense involved. I'm not sure who was the most barking that day.

In concluding this section on passengers, it's got to be said that after a dog, my favourite passenger is a package. Occasionally I get offers to deliver a package on my account circuit, and I have been known to travel long distances to pick one up. So long as the delivery address is clear, a package is guaranteed not to give you any trouble. You just switch on the meter and take a leisurely drive to your destination. It's nice feeling that your passenger isn't going to criticise your route or indulge in any anti-social behaviour.

•

7

Know Your Enemy

So who are those making life difficult for us – and our esteemed customers? Let's look at those road users taking work from us, holding us up in traffic, or hampering our progress through the mean streets of London in other ways.

Minicabs

On the surface of it, all a taxi driver does is drive a customer from point A to point B for payment. A deceptively simple business plan, and one that has been exploited for many years by those unwilling to go through the effort of gaining a proper taxi licence.

From the very beginning, London led the way in safety, and stipulated strict licensing rules. As a result, your London cab driver will have had strict background checks, years of testing on his topographical knowledge, and will have passed an enhanced driving test. The cabs are all 100% accessible and are built like tanks. Fares are calculated by a meter that cannot be tampered with.

Taxis and private hire vehicles operate differently. Minicabs are not allowed to solicit or respond to street hails. They have to be pre-booked through a licensed operator. They set their own fares, but cannot use a meter in London.

It's the way of the world that where exists a successful service, someone will come along and undercut you. Our trade was challenged in 1961 when Welbeck Motors emerged to muscle in on taxi work. Welbeck flooded the streets with a fleet of red Renault Dauphines, and exploited technology by using two-way radios. The company secured financial backing, and lobbied for the support of Members of Parliament to run a "mini-taxi" service. They didn't receive explicit approval, but they had sections of the press on their side.

There are clearly parallels with modern day Uber, where lower overheads and lax restrictions allowed minicab operators to undercut taxis and work to lower standards of safety and driver training. Welbeck Motors and Uber both had money behind them which they used to influence politicians and the media. I'd imagine that Welbeck were seen as trendy and as progressive as Uber were when they arrived on our shores.

Although Welbeck Motors went into liquidation in 1965, other interested parties were waiting in the wings to exploit loopholes in stringent Hackney Carriage Laws and create a second tier cab service using two-way radio.

Drivers were recruited to minicab firms, typically operating out of doorways. They weren't officially licensed, but so long as they were pre-booked and their journeys were logged they could operate legally.

Under the cover of darkness, many drivers would also illegally tout for business in the West End and City. Drivers would respond to people approaching their cars parked up outside bars and in other prominent positions. In many cases, someone in a car would pull up and directly solicit for business. They could be minicab drivers working illegally, or just chancers off the street. Blokes with cars still exploit the vulnerable to this day. You can just imagine the crime statistics. Despite warnings to women not to use minicabs without pre-booking, or never to use those touting illegally on the streets, many people still use their services. Taxi drivers complain that touts aren't pursued enough, and they're not. Touts don't just deny taxi drivers and legitimate private hire drivers revenue; they also endanger the public. You are not insured if you accept a ride in a private hire car unless it is pre-booked. The thing is, in the eyes of the authorities they help clear the streets of drunks every night so those in power allow it to continue.

Private hire drivers, vehicles and operators were eventually licensed by the Public Carriage Office in 2000. Some firms got their acts together and ran their businesses professionally, while the weaker ones folded.

In London, there have never been restrictions on the number of private hire licences issued. In the case of taxis, numbers have risen very slowly over the years, kept down naturally by the Knowledge process. Suburban taxi licences were suspended for a while due to over-supply, but private hire licences have continued to be issued in huge numbers – *despite* over-supply! In order to service the Uber organisation, by 2016, several hundred licences a week were being issued (licensing slowed in 2017).

If hundreds of taxi licences were being issued each week, there would be angry talk about congestion and pollution. Many thousands of extra taxis on the streets would be noticed. You barely notice minicabs. London minicabs don't have plates and roof signs as in the rest of the country.

Signage is pretty low key if it exists at all, and the private hire licence sticker on the back window is virtually unreadable. It's often disguised further by the tinted glass that TfL allow private hire vehicles to have, but not taxis.

The private hire industry can always undercut taxis on price because of lower running costs. London taxis are purpose-built in order to conform to stringent safety standards, including the famous twenty-five feet turning circle (I'm unsure if this applied in the days of horse-drawn cabs). Crucially, private hire drivers enjoy a free reign in their choice of vehicle – and they don't need to spend fifty-six grand on a new one.

Most taxi drivers tolerate minicabs and recognise their right to exist. I've read letters in the taxi trade press urging drivers not to let minicabs out at junctions. Think about it: with taxis heavily outnumbered by minicabs we'd only be harming ourselves. Since the rise of Uber, taxi drivers often find themselves fighting alongside drivers working at traditional private hire companies. I can read a private hire magazine and agree with almost every word printed. Traditional private hire drivers are affected by Uber even more than we are. Many private hire drivers and operators also think licensing should be capped, and agree with the tightening up of licensing.

The situation is different outside London, where the lines are blurred between taxis and minicabs. Licensing requirements and regulations between the two services are very similar in many authorities; so similar that the public understandably don't differentiate. The vehicles can be identical: in many licensing authorities, regular saloon cars can be used as taxis (even in London, a Mercedes Vito can be used by both factions). Minicabs licensed outside London can also be fitted with meters.

I unwittingly used two minicabs in May 2018. Following a boozy wedding celebration in rural Oxfordshire, my wife and I needed to get to our guest house in South Oxford. With no cab ranks around, our hosts asked the pub barmaid to call us a taxi. What arrived was a minicab. Never mind, like most boozed-up members of the cab-riding public, we just wanted to get home. I have to say, the experience was faultless.

On leaving the accommodation the following morning Mo asked the chef to help book us a taxi. It was a small guest house, but they had some kind of booking app on their wall. He pressed the button a few times, and told us a blue Toyota would be with us in three minutes. It was a sophisticated-looking booking apparatus; certainly not something I'd expect to find in a £75 guest house on Iffley Road. So, this is what we're up against, eh?

Cycles

Cyclists aren't really the enemy of course, but the proportion of crimes committed by cyclists ensures they are high up the league table for anti-social behaviour. It's a minority who spoil it for the others, but sadly, it's the bad ones we remember.

Year by year, cycling has gained in popularity. It got a boost in 2010 when the then London Mayor, Boris Johnson, launched a bike hire scheme. Ranks of "Boris Bikes" were placed all over London and made available for hire. The benefits of cycling have been heavily promoted, yet the dangers aren't publicised. The onus on driving sensibly is always on the motorist, and too little education given to cyclists (whatever happened to the Cycling Proficiency Test?).

It must be very difficult to ride a bike in London: it would scare me to death if I were forced onto a bike for the day. A cyclist unfamiliar with London would surely find the new road modelling schemes dangerously complex and confusing. You'd also need the right attitude: a sense of your own vulnerability, coupled with respect and understanding of other road users and pedestrians.

I'm sure the first rule I learnt on my Cycling Proficiency course in 1971 was to never overtake on the inside. The problem is that there is so little road space in our cities, and in London cycling on the inside is encouraged. Many roads have a cycle lane – usually, but not always, on the left of the carriageway. Cyclists legitimately use this inside lane and necessarily undertake slow moving motor vehicles. All too often though, they endanger themselves by going straight ahead when vehicles are indicating a turn. Cyclists also ride on the inside where there is no cycle lane. The practice has therefore become tacitly sanctioned on all roads, regardless as there's a cycle lane on the left or not.

Way back in the 1980s I noticed cyclists doing stupid things: running red lights; riding down one-way streets the wrong way; and not using lights at night. Cycle couriers were the worst of the lot, and they had a militant attitude towards motorists. The police rarely got involved, and the situation got out of control. The gendarmerie rarely troubled themselves with enforcing traffic laws abused by cyclists, and rather than nip bad behaviour in the bud, they let it flourish and grow like Japanese bindweed. Cyclists ride straight past a police van going the wrong way down a one-one way street and the police do nothing.

Some cyclists blot the traffic out with headphones, and I'm surprised this is legal. Some have cameras fixed to their helmets to film examples of bad motoring to post on websites. I presume they don't film themselves tearing through red lights and scattering pedestrians trying to cross on zebra crossings. What they don't realise is that many motorists have forward-facing cameras too. I have a camera fitted as part of my cab insurance. Cyclists are often in denial as to their behaviour, and if challenged tend to respond with aggression.

Cab drivers know all the restrictions and they know when you're doing something illegal. Cyclists transgressing the rules probably don't realise they're sometimes being punished by not being given space: when twenty car drivers have watched a cyclist jump a red light they're unlikely to afforded the miscreant any further room on the road to abuse.

Cyclists complain that motorists don't give them enough room, but it's often a case of the carriageway not being wide enough. On the Cycle Superhighways, the cyclist usually moves faster than the motor vehicle on segregated lanes; but segregated lanes reduce the space for motor vehicles, and this in turn adds to pollution. Once they've cycled off the CSH, they are jostling for position with motor vehicles which have taken new roads to avoid the CSH. These roads have probably already been narrowed by modernisation schemes. Cycling is promoted as healthy, yet cyclists are breathing in the same air as everybody else. What they've gained by exercise, they've lost in sucking in London's filth. Like the train commuter, cyclists get strength through suffering and martyrdom. Both groups eventually burn themselves out with the hideousness of it all.

A disproportionate amount of space is given over to cyclists, yet they pay nothing to use the roads. Cyclists are only going to take responsibility when they are licensed and plated. How can they damage a vehicle without being held responsible? They need to be insured and identified, and they should pay a nominal licensing fee in order to fund their licensing. Once they start getting fined for riding through red lights and accrue points on their licences they will surely adopt a more responsible attitude. They will also be taken more seriously as road users, which they will benefit from.

In a collision between a cycle and a motor vehicle, the driver of the motor vehicle is assumed to be at fault. Cyclists have no licence to lose, and if they scrape your car they know you can do nothing about it. As far as our licencing body goes, cyclists are protected from all blame and criticism. Even helpful safety suggestions: a few years ago, a taxi garage placed stickers on its fleet of rented cabs. It was a polite, non-confrontational, sticker found on many other vehicles, warning cyclists not to overtake on the left. Transport for London banned the sticker.

Cyclists could justifiably claim that they were here before the motor vehicle, but things have changed. I wonder what would happen if British motorists went back to the horse-drawn cart? The last horse-drawn London taxi was licensed in 1947, but what if the trade said they were fed up of being blamed for pollution and complained that electric vehicles were too expensive? Would TfL licence horse-drawn taxis and promote them as part of their green agenda? To be honest

I don't know what would happen, though traffic speeds in Central London would probably remain unchanged.

Motorcycles

Most cab drivers learn the Knowledge on a motorcycle, so most of us have a degree of affection for our motorised two-wheeled friends. When I was on the Knowledge there were hundreds of motorbike couriers whizzing around London delivering documents to offices, drawings to architects, and tins of film to production companies. Their work has become largely redundant in the digital age, but you still see the occasional courier bike with top boxes exclaiming "Urgent! Medical Supplies!" "BLOOD!" &c. Right, a white-coated medic calls up a motorbike when he needs a live heart sent across London to an operating theatre? I don't believe for a minute that the NHS are so cash-stretched that they are commissioning motorbike couriers to transport blood and live organs for transport. I've seen courier vans emblazoned with "Medical" spelt backwards like on an ambulance. It's a scam to make other motorists believe they are engaged in life-or-death journeys, and should be afforded the right of way without let or hindrance. Believe me, there's nothing more urgent in that top box than a hot kebab, it's life ebbing away, maybe.

What's this nonsense about writing "Fire" or "Ambulance" backwards anyway? If you can't read Fire backwards you shouldn't be allowed anywhere near a road.

As a former courier myself I still harbour something of a misty-eyed nostalgia for the traditional knight-of-the-road couriers: the ones who wear proper protective clothing, and wait patiently at the stop line at traffic lights. They've largely been replaced by a new breed of rider: aggressive, unthinking; and taking unnecessary risks with their own lives and everyone around them. And your wing mirrors. The worst lot can be identified by the food boxes fixed atop their noisy, but low-powered, machines. They're paid peanuts on a self-employed basis to deliver pizza and other foods, and they're under pressure to get to someone's home or office while the food's still hot. Many take their cue from seeing cyclists flouting the law and riding dangerously. They scrape down the inside between buses and cabs with their huge food boxes, and nobody is going to get in their way. They're on a mission. They don't trouble themselves too much with One Way signs, and they inconvenience cyclists by sitting in their protected area in advance of the motorists' stop line.

We all do the occasional dodgy manoeuvre or illegal turn, but undertaking traffic on the left and going right around Keep Left signs was considered beyond the pale in my day. Sadly, you see car drivers go around the Keep Left bollards now too. I've seen cabs do it, and I even saw a bus do it on Holborn Viaduct.

Cyclists and motorcyclists develop bad habits in different ways. New cyclists often start by obeying the laws and riding carefully, only to pick up bad habits later on. Motorcyclists do the opposite: they start off riding badly, then become sensible later on, if they survive their first few months riding like maniacs.

Motorcyclists often aren't the people you think they are: like cycling, motorcycling in London is largely a middle class game. I always thought the ones riding big serious bikes were greasy rocker-types, but after observing them around

St James's Square I noticed that most of the bikers parking at the motorcycle bays were wearing suits. Not a criticism, just an observation.

One last thing about motorcycles: why do some of them feel the need to make so much of a racket? There's no need for modern motorcycles to make so much noise. I expect it's like the drivers of some of those flashy sports cars: it's pure, unadulterated, attention seeking.

Pedicabs

Otherwise known as cycle rickshaws, these machines started appearing in the 1990s and have continued to multiply. They tempt tourists in with their quirky third world imagery and loud Arabic music. They know their market: Gulf Arabs with more money than sense.

Pedicabs often display an official-looking licence plate on the back. It's a scam, there's no such thing as pedicab licensing. As there are no controls, the drivers charge as much as they can get away with, and they are famous for charging outrageous prices. Rip-offs are well-documented. One memorable incident was the altercation filmed in 2015 after a pedicab rider tried to charge a tourist £206 for a three-minute ride along Oxford Street. Riders exploit foreign visitors' lack of English, then claim the fare was agreed at the start of the journey. Be assured that the fare will be far in excess of what a taxi or minicab will cost. And even more than Uber during surge-pricing periods.

Pedicabs are totally unsuited to British cities. They are dangerously unstable, and totally unregulated. They get in everyone's way and slow the traffic down – look how they park in the bus lane outside Hamleys and force buses to drive around them. Why they're not booked for obstruction, I don't know.

I've taken cycle rickshaws myself in Vietnam, as well as motorised ones in other Asian countries. Well, on holiday, health and safety kind of goes out the window. If a dark fella tells me to stroke a crocodile in Gambia, I'll act the tourist. I suppose that's why people use pedicabs: they're on holiday and it looks like fun. Arguably, it's as foolhardy as patting a crocodile on the head, and it's certainly a very expensive sightseeing tour.

Boris made noises about banning pedicabs when he was mayor, but did nothing. Mayor Khan said little on the matter since taking office, and the result was the launch of a fleet of *motorised* pedicabs in 2018.

I don't know why they just don't send in the taxman and immigration: that'll get some of them off the roads. The Benefits Agency could check if they're claiming unemployment benefit, and the Performing Rights people can charge them royalties for playing music in a public place. Pedicabs don't make much of a dent in our revenue, but they are ripping people off and creating a bad impression. We shouldn't really care if they fleece tourists, but nobody wants visitors coming to Britain leaving with a bad impression. We run a tight ship here on matters of public transportation.

We shouldn't put pedicabs in the same category as pedal buses. These are those huge pedal-powered contraptions you see crawling around the St Paul's Cathedral area with eight boozed-up hen party women on board, swigging from bottles and singing along with "It's Raining Men." They get in the way, but I can't help smile when I see one sail past St Paul's Cathedral when I'm sat on the rank.

Buses

Buses top the hierarchy of London road users and you mess with them at your peril. It doesn't matter much to a bus driver if you lose a wing mirror while they go straight ahead in the left turn lane at Piccadilly Circus. They won't have to pay for any damage out of their own pocket like you or I. Like our pedal-powered friends, they sometimes get in the way, but it would be wrong to think upon them as the enemy.

I might be remembering things through rose-tinted spectacles, but in my youth a bus operated out of a garage. An old Routemaster would pull up and everyone would pile on the open platform on the corner of the bus. The bus would barely come to a stop before roaring off, leaving the conductor to amble along the aisle dispensing unintelligible tickets from a huge Gibson ticket machine. Now, all the passengers have to queue to scan their Oyster Cards before the bus can shut its doors and move off. Their on-street termini now sprawl all over the West End blocking off Henrietta Place and Cavendish Place, and causing a nuisance around Piccadilly Circus. I'm sure buses never used to use double yellow lines or cycle lanes as a terminus.

You can no longer board a bus with cash; you need to swipe a pre-charged travel card or contactless credit card. Many bus passengers are tourists and people are still free to make queries as they board. While the driver points out St Paul's Cathedral on their map, the hapless car driver is sat behind the bus on Praed Street in Paddington unable to get around the bus that's taking up half the carriageway; and there's usually another bus coming towards you. On roads like Shoreditch High Street you can't see when they've stopped, so you don't know whether you can go around them or not. Buses should not be allowed to stop unless there are cut-outs in the carriageway to allow other vehicles to pass.

I'm not sure if buses still have an Inspector Blake-type figure telling drivers to "Get that bus out!" but bus operators clearly have their work cut out keeping to timetables. Timings are affected because of road remodelling projects, and by allowing multiple road and building works to close important roads at the same time. The bus companies are controlled by TfL, who have allowed the chaos in the first place. TfL licence cabs as well as buses, but we get few concessions: buses and cycles top TfL's priority list.

Buses are often allowed to use roads too narrow for their purposes, although to be fair it's the parking of others rather than the driving of the bus that cause the problems. Beware buses with letters accompanying numbers on their destination signs. I'm not sure what the letters mean, but I think it's code for "this bus uses ridiculously narrow roads."

Timings are important to the bus companies because they are losing customers. Half-empty buses crawl along Regent Street, then queue to clear the junction at Oxford Circus, or to block everyone else at Piccadilly Circus. Many of the roads buses use have been narrowed, making it impossible to get past them. It's not their fault, it's the system. I shudder when I see a bus bound for Streatham or Crystal Palace. We often grumble about going into the Deep South, but imagine what it must be like dragging a bus through Camberwell and Brixton? Or sitting on one as a passenger.

We don't need so many buses. Regent Street is a slowly moving convoy of lumbering red giants, many of which are half empty (or is it half full?). Their acceleration is slow, except when accelerating through red lights, which is quite often. At least you can see them coming.

On my way home I used to wonder how buses and coaches would get in front of me when driving north up Finchley Road. Taxis are allowed to use the bus lane, but I usually prefer not to as there are always obstructions and it's more trouble than it's worth. I eventually worked out how it was done: the buses and coaches simply swerve in and out of the bus lane, intimidating other drivers into letting them cut in. They use the same tactics on the Fleet Street cycle lane when they cut in just before Ludgate Circus. Most cab drivers will back down when challenged with behaviour that could put them and their vehicle out of service.

Cab and bus drivers have an agreement to let each other out whenever possible. We have a lot of respect for bus drivers, and we all appreciate that it's one of the hardest jobs in London. Their drivers, in the main, show a lot of patience, as *everyone* is trying to get past them.

Tour buses are the dirtiest and noisiest buses on the roads, and they're particularly annoying as they drive five miles an hour slower than normal buses. When the streets in the financial district are quieter at the weekends, Ludgate Hill still resembles a bus terminal with all the tour buses parked up on the cycle lane.

Thankfully, Boris Johnson got rid of those confounded bendy buses when he was London Mayor. They were simply too long for London, and would routinely block junctions. The last one in London plied its business in December 2011. They are not missed. There are many new shiny red "Boris Buses" on London's roads. This smart-looking bus is an update on the much-loved Routemaster; the one with the open door at the corner. The door is no longer open while in motion, and the bus was dubbed the "Roastmaster" when the air-conditioning failed on early models. It's a nice-looking bus, but not as characterful as the old Routemaster, of which there are still a few running.

Buses operate differently outside London. You can buy tickets with cash, and in most towns you can receive change. The bus drivers in Leighton Buzzard wave at passers-by in the street, and are happy to hold long conversations with housewives while driving – often by shouting to someone at the back. You learn a lot about your neighbours kids' illnesses and holidays in Tenerife on a bus in a small town. When things are quiet they'll ignore the bus stops and operate a door-to-door service. Pollution isn't considered an issue in Bedfordshire. I've enjoyed many a lunchtime pint in the Black Lion listening to ancient buses idling for ten minutes at the bus stops outside.

Post Office Vans

In the 1990s I used to be terrorised by Post Office vans. Either their drivers have improved, or everyone else's driving has become worse. Then again, you don't often see them in motion, as they are usually parked up and in the way. How long does it take to bring down a bag of mail from an office, or empty a post box? The answer seems to be an incredibly long time.

The Post Office are a private company so I don't see how they are afforded so much waiting time. It's the same with those armoured security vans. We rarely see them on the move. They always seem to be parked up for ages at a busy junction.

Emergency Vehicles

Whether we should move out of the way of emergency vehicles is sometimes discussed on radio phone-ins. The matter has yet to be definitively settled. As far as I understand, you can be ordered to move out of the way by the police. Things are more problematic with the fire and ambulance services. Obviously, if you refuse to move to let such vehicles pass you will have a guilty conscience eating away at you for days. You will also have the drivers of all the vehicles surrounding you thinking what a cold, heartless person you are. However, cameras are watching you at many junctions, and people have been fined for crossing the stop line at red traffic lights. It's going to cost you about £70 to be a good citizen – if you pay on time – and that's a lot of money to me. I don't think the NHS are going to pay your fine for you, and I wouldn't bank on getting any joy out of the police either should you put a claim in.

Agricultural Vehicles

I often find myself following agricultural machinery during the harvesting season as I live in the country. If you live in London and are caught behind a tractor during working hours you know you've taken a wrong turn on the way to Stansted or Gatwick. The countryside is a mysterious place to many cab drivers, and we are well aware there are films on the Horror Channel about people who've made wrong turns in rural areas.

Joggers

There was a well-publicised incidence of pavement rage in 2017, when a male jogger knocked a woman into the path of a moving bus on Putney Bridge. A tragedy was averted by the quick reactions of the bus driver.

The right of way means nothing when you're wearing Lycra. Some joggers think they have the moral high ground with their green credentials. Why they don't stay in parks where the air is cleaner I don't know. Probably to show off. They jog angrily on the spot if you spoil their timings and force them to wait on the pavement until you pass. They're particularly good at running across zebra crossings from the blind spot behind you. It's often too late to take evasive action, but like pigeons, they are impossible to run over.

Pedestrians

Pedestrians sit right of the bottom of the London road user food chain. Most of us are pedestrians at times, and it's hard work: certainly harder than driving a cab. Just a short walk through the West End is a frustrating experience, having to overtake slow people and dodge people coming the other way. It's much nicer to be insulated in the air-conditioned luxury in a taxi listening to a soothing radio programme.

Walkers get hassle from everybody, though they also like to give it out. However much cab drivers might complain about bus drivers, van drivers, minicab drivers and cyclists; the thrill-seeking pedestrian presents more problems than any other group. I like the one-way working they have on the pedestrian ramp at Birmingham New Street Station. They need to roll that out in London.

As London councils put more and more paved strips down the middle of major roads, they encourage people to cross the road away from a proper crossing. It's not safe to cross Oxford Street, yet it's encouraged by the paving.

I'd like to see jaywalking become a crime, but I accept it's not practical. Every day we have to brake sharply as some brain-dead zombie walks straight into the road listening to earphones or making a phone call. Often they do it while pushing their offspring in a pushchair. They know the driver will always get the blame should they injure themselves by their own stupidity.

Quick Code of Practice for Pedestrians

- Yes, you can take a photo of me and my taxi, but be polite and ask first

- Don't stand at a zebra crossing if you have no intention of crossing. At the "Beatles Crossing" at Abbey Road, please wait for a gap in the traffic before taking your photos

- Don't stop us to ask for directions. That's rude. I don't stop you in your nurse's uniform and ask you to look at my stiff back

- There are plenty of proper crossing places on Oxford Street – please use them.

Other Road Users

That's the serious road users dealt with, but there are other folk on the streets that exploit the grey area of uncertainty between pedestrian and road user status. For instance: people on roller skates, skateboards, Segways and those stupid kids' scooters that certain middle-aged men seem to favour. I think adults riding scooters should be detained under the Male Menopause Act and kept in a dark room until they are better.

Are they legally classed as road users? Do they have any rights? Or is it totally illegal to ride down a busy thoroughfare on plastic wheels and a plank of wood? Who knows? Nobody's going to do anything about it anyway.

8

When Things Go Wrong

Occupational hazards come thick and fast in this game, and they take many different forms. Apart from drivers of other vehicles, there are many other factors conspiring against us: every day we encounter badly designed road systems, traffic congestion and kamikaze pedestrians. We're forced to drive all day in killer pollution – while at the same time being blamed for causing it. And there's always someone around to tell us off if we do something wrong.

Pollution

There's a killer on the road. Around 40,000 people die prematurely because of air pollution, much of it caused by diesel. Up to 9000 people die in London alone. When things reach critical levels, warning signs are put on roadside matrix signs, and you are urged to stay out of London unless your journey is necessary. That always makes me smile wryly: how many people do you know you drive around London for fun? Apart from suburban boy racers and Gulf Arabs in Knightsbridge, I mean. There are around 24,000 taxi drivers and 113,000 minicab drivers licensed to operate in Greater London. Add to that God-knows how many delivery drivers. None of us have any choice. It's our job.

In April 2015, a Public Health Emergency was declared. In June 2017, the new mayor, Sadiq Khan, triggered an emergency air quality alert on roadside signs, on the underground, and at bus stops (the roadside matrix signs are more frequently used to warn of road closures that the authorities have inflicted on us). Pedestrians are affected, but undoubtedly less than those of us forced to drive, or cycle, around all day. Maybe I'm used to it, but I haven't knowingly been affected by London's poor air quality. Perhaps it's knocked a couple of years off my life, but all I can really say is that you can sometimes smell and taste the filth in the air. It has body.

Boris Johnson, the previous London mayor, decreed that no new diesel taxis would be licensed in London from 2018. It's going to take many years to make the changeover from diesel to electricity, so pollution is going to be a fact of life for some time to come. Minicabs heavily outnumber taxis but they have no such obligation to go electric.

Up until 2018 we had to drive diesel cabs as there were no electric ones available for use in London. When the new electric taxi was unveiled there were few charging points available, so there was a bit of a hollow ring to all this anti-diesel stuff. Fine particle pollution from brake linings and tyres also contribute, so electric vehicles won't completely eradicate the filth anyway.

Pollution isn't just about air quality, it's about noise too. London's a noisy place. Nearly every road is being dug up, or has building work being carried out. There's the banging and drilling from building sites; plus all the noisy vehicles such as buses, lorries, skips, cement mixers, motorcycles – yes, and taxis. If you hang around outside Hamleys or around

Covent Garden there's that confounded Arab music blaring out from pedal rickshaws. Even worse there's the bloke on the bagpipes on Westminster Bridge.

Road Closures & Remodelling

Road and building works are essential, but some seem to go on for ever. What might last for a few months on your local high street can go on for several years in London, and many result in permanent closures. It affects historic buildings too: tourists are disappointed that their view of Elizabeth Tower housing Big Ben is blighted by scaffolding. This is a city that takes four years to clean a bell.

There can be few Knowledge Boys around who can remember Allington Street. This was an important road leading you out to safety from opposite Victoria Station. The Victoria area has been an unholy mess of closed lanes and tipper trucks since at least 2010 when I returned to cab driving. The northern end of Dean Street is another long term closure, and one that severely restricts access to Soho from Oxford Street and the Marylebone area. These roads, and many like them, have been completely closed by building works for several years, possibly to never reopen.

Piccadilly Underpass is regularly closed for maintenance. This crucial east-west through route was closed during most of the summer in 2016. As the days of misery continued I wondered what improvements we might enjoy on its reopening. When the underpass reopened it had the same grimy walls, the same inadequate lighting, and the same puddle of water in the dip. I then saw the improvements: the outside walls had been rebuilt and there was a huge illuminated advertising screen.

Many construction workers' job role appears to consist solely of managing the traffic around building sites. Builders' lorries no longer need to wait for a gap in the traffic before pulling off a site, as a bloke in a fluorescent vest wielding a road-crossing lollypop will walk into the road to stop all the traffic. When was it that builders were given control of the roads?

An individual holding up the traffic for a few minutes is one thing, but other roads have been permanently blocked off by new buildings. How are big corporations allowed to close whole streets off permanently? When the BBC rebuilt Broadcasting House on Langham Place they completely blocked off the through route from Langham Street into Foley Street. This used to be a useful route through Fitzrovia avoiding Mortimer Street.

During temporary closures you sometimes you get yellow diversion signs, but if a sign exists it's usually pretty vague. Those who rely on sat navs are left scratching their heads wondering what to do next. Even those of us with a good grasp of geography sometimes end up going around in circles directed by those confounded yellow signs with arrows on them. Some closures are mentioned on TfL websites, but we shouldn't need to consult websites before every journey. Full details of any closure or diversion should be legally notified by clear signage. The reason for, and the duration of, the closure should also be notified. I love the way they leave the warning signs up long after the event as a warning to other drivers thinking of coming into the area on another day. I suppose it's the modern equivalent of putting heads on spikes at the Tower of London.

Exhibition Road in South Kensington was closed for a year or so. It reopened as a shared-space thoroughfare, with stylishly patterned paving, no kerbs, and lots of street furniture. It looks very nice, but it's confusing; which is not something you want on a street housing three of London's largest museums and with hundreds of tourists wandering around. You don't know whether you're in the middle of the road or on a footpath. Driving south to the junction with Cromwell Place, the layout and lack of road markings, gives the impression you're on a one-way street. Many vehicles move over to the right hand lane to be confronted by oncoming vehicles. I did it myself once. Perhaps this is what caused a security panic in October 2017 when an Uber driver with dodgy insurance crashed into cars and injured eleven pedestrians?

There's circular paving at the junction of Prince Consort Road, but no other indications that it might be a roundabout. There are no signs. People treat it like a roundabout, but nobody knows if it is one or not. If we're not clear what is and isn't a roundabout, how do we know who has the right of way? Maybe that's something the insurance companies will need to sort out.

Driving north from Exhibition Road you come into a road that cuts through parkland – Kensington Gardens to the left, Hyde Park to the right. It used to be a nice drive shaving time off journeys using busy Kensington Church Street or Park Lane. It's now down to one lane in each direction, with over-sized cycle lanes. For the driver, it's become yet another one to avoid. The pedestrian is confronted by two-way vehicle traffic, plus a separate two-way cycle lane. The pedestrian crossings are not marked as zebras and look like speed bumps. Brave pedestrians who use these crossings also find people cycling across them as well.

November 9th 2015 was a black day for London's professional drivers. On this day, Camden Council closed an essential East to West route through the centre of Bloomsbury. Driving west from the City aiming for Bayswater you could make for Oxford Street and continue west, usually through Fitzrovia if there's any traffic; or you could make for Euston and Marylebone Roads. Just getting into Oxford Street is a major undertaking, likely to involve queuing behind buses from the end of High Holborn. The Euston Road option is longer and is no less busy. Being allowed to use the bus lane on Marylebone Road helps taxis heading to Paddington, but you have to clear Euston Underpass first, and that can be a nightmare. The less-congested middle way was through Tavistock Place, until they made it cycles only.

May 22nd 2017 was another dark day. On this particular Monday, the City of London closed off Bank Junction, allowing only buses and cycles into the heart of the financial district. The authorities tried to sell the closure as a safety measure, but could never back it up with figures. Taxis were definitely not major players in the accident statistics in the area, so should have been exempt. It's nothing but a cynical move to keep TfL's buses on time, while making a bit of money on the side through filming drivers confused by the complexities of the restrictions.

Over a two-year period, twenty-five people were killed, and 12,000 injured, in bus-related incidents, most of them pedestrians. The London Assembly cited driver stress, tiredness, and frequent distractions as being partly to blame. Deputy Chair of the Transport Committee, Caroline

Pidgeon, noted that: "The Mayor of London incentivises bus operators to meet punctuality targets, but not to reduce collisions and injuries. It's an outrage."

If cabs are to serve the financial district, Bank Junction is absolutely crucial. Many important buildings, including the Ned Hotel have now been rendered inaccessible: not good if you're in a wheelchair or have lots of luggage with you. Motorists are once again being forced to burn up more fuel and time working their way around ill-thought out closures. I find it hard to believe that the City consider it safer to have cars, taxis and vans tearing around the hazardous slalom of Gresham Street, Lothbury and Bartholomew Lane, rather than queue nicely at the lights at Bank Junction. The closures don't apply after 7 pm or at the weekends, but we don't get a lot of work in the City at weekends as the financial district generally keeps office hours.

Many drivers were fined in the early days of the closure. The map publicising the closures was colour-coded, and gave the impression you could drive into Cornhill from Leadenhall Street, then exit at Finch Lane before Bank Junction. The actual signs at the entrance to Cornhill contradict this, implying you can't drive into Cornhill at all. Fining motorists has proved a real cash from cameras money-spinner. Soon after the closure it was estimated they were raking in £16K an hour!

If you make your way through the junction during the times when the restriction doesn't apply you are still not guaranteed safe passage. Driving up Threadneedle Street towards New Broad Street you run the risk of being caught behind a bus. The bus stop is situated right by a Keep Left sign, so you are stuck. There's a similar situation in the narrow bit of Fleet Street. I suspect this is another cynical traffic-calming strategy.

Away from the City in the West End, access to the Lyceum Theatre has been barricaded off. It's not very convenient if you're going to the theatre in a wheelchair, as a surprising number of people do. Great strides have been made making access easier for people with limited mobility, but it seems to be regressing. What's the point in forcing taxis to be wheelchair accessible if we can't access the roads we need?

Following a terrorist attack on the Christmas markets in Berlin in 2016, in which twelve people died, security was stepped up for London's Changing of the Guard ceremony. During this pageant, vehicles are denied access to the sensitive area around Buckingham Palace for a couple of hours while the guards do their thing. It makes a misery of any journey going towards Victoria. They also erected huge, ugly, metal barriers to form chicanes at the start of Buckingham Palace Road and at the Admiralty Arch end of the Mall. It doesn't look like they're going to be removed anytime soon.

They have also reduced the road space on some Central London bridges as a response to terrorist attacks. Metal barriers have been put in place to stop vehicles from driving into pedestrians. I'm unconvinced the bridge barriers, or the security arrangements around Buckingham Palace, are seriously intended to deter terrorists. Terrorists will simply find other locations – or perhaps take advantage of the artificially-manufactured queue of traffic on the bridges. The authorities wanted to be seen to be doing something, but I suspect it's just as much an exercise in traffic calming as anything else.

Road remodelling is meant to be about safety, but the congestion is causing pollution, which is killing people. The emergency services have complained that they can't get past on emergency calls. This is also killing people. The Bank Junction closure is not *for* safety, it's *against* the smooth movement of traffic. It's generating money for nothing, and we're paying for it.

With road space fast disappearing, shame is heaped upon motorists who use their initiative to seek out alternative routes (as the official signs sometimes advise). The media sometimes refer to a short cut as a "Rat Run". I object to the implication that those of us with the foresight to seek alternative routes should be regarded as rodents. I hope those journalists who use such lazy terms end up sat in the back of a cab on the Cycle Superhighway the next time they're late for a meeting.

Congestion

The result of all of the above is traffic congestion. Congestion isn't necessarily caused by too much traffic, it's more often caused by ill thought-out traffic systems. Traffic has declined in recent years, but congestion has increased. Most cities have a rush hour when the roads are busier than usual, but the London rush hour lasts all day: I'd say from about 7 am until 7 pm and beyond. Some roads can be busy until midnight. You'll find the occasional quiet area during the day, and you learn to enjoy it while you can. Generally though, large sections of London are congested much of the time, and whenever other factors are added in to the mix, whole areas can grind to a halt. Vehicle breakdowns can gridlock London, but are only temporary (drivers who run out of fuel and bring the Blackwall Tunnel to a halt are now fined). Demonstrations and marches can close off an area for a few hours, and special events can last a day or two.

We keep getting told that the economy is improving, though few ordinary people seem to find more money in their pay packets. Some think the building of smart office and residential blocks prove that London is thriving. Those apartment blocks are only for the rich. Ordinary people won't be spending a million pounds or more on a flat in Central London. They might however, be able to shop at the many small supermarkets that have appeared on almost every corner in recent years. This might also be an indicator of an affluent society, but I'm sceptical. Is an affluent society one where you're no more than a five minute walk from a Tesco? Is it worth it? If you welcome the convenience of a mini-supermarket on every corner you must accept articulated lorries blocking up Covent Garden and Hampstead Village as a consequence.

Special Events

The cab trade used to look forward to the events that brought visitors into London. No so much now. Any event that closes roads is disruptive and makes our job harder. I sigh with relief when royal events are held at Windsor or Balmoral rather than London.

Marches and demonstrations happen pretty much every week. Some are so extensive that a day off is the only sensible course of action. When I first started in this game, the main events causing traffic disruption were the London Marathon and the Gay Pride march. You accepted you'd find it difficult to work on these days and you could plan your days off accordingly. Now, every minority group has a day in which they close the roads for an event. Running and cycling races are held so frequently that they've become a real nuisance. There are food festivals, car rallies and bus rallies. Regent Street gets closed for a few days every year for American football celebrations (no, I don't know what's that to do with London either). Major shopping streets have their own Christmas lighting arrangements and each Christmas light switch-on can take a whole day. Certain shops such as Harrods and Hamleys hold Christmas parades. They take up the best part of a day – and happen in early November. How can a shop be allowed to disrupt London's traffic?

I only get sent to the arse end of Hackney about once a year. On April 23rd 2017 I was asked to go to Homerton Park. It was the worst possible day on which to make my annual visit there as I got caught in a half-marathon. This was exactly one week after the London Marathon which closed many roads and made working the cab impossible.

In January 2018, many Central London streets were closed for the Lumiere light show extravaganza. I'm sure it was a very nice event, but I don't know, I was working. Or trying to. We are used to weekend closures, but you can't shut off the West End on a weekday and not expect chaos. TfL are the masters of understatement. They thought "Delays Expected" signs would be adequate. There was no warning as to the true extent of the disruption, just helpful advice to "Plan Your Journey". How can you plan your journey when they don't tell you what roads are affected? Those of us who found the unaffected roads couldn't get off them as at every turn we were confronted by closed off roads that we weren't told about. When you can't move around you can't work effectively as a taxi driver, so I wrote the last day of the event off and stayed at home. I don't know how much the light show cost in wasted time, fuel, and resulting pollution levels.

Regent Street is closed on every Sunday in July: not just Regent Street, but many surrounding roads. This is to allow shoppers a day where they don't have to worry about getting run over. It's all very nice, but London is a working city, not Disneyland.

Accompanying the Regent Street closures on most Saturdays and Sundays in July 2017, were cycling and running events. Such events are sponsored by commercial organisations and largely only benefit the participants and the shareholders of the organisers who get to advertise themselves on barricaded streets.

I know cycling and running are the quickest way to get through London, but it's a nuisance to professional drivers who want to work. It's a depressing sight watching the metal barriers being erected on a Friday evening, and passing piles of traffic cones and No Entry signs ready to be put in place the following day. If they can turn London into a cycle track, why not give over the West End to cab and bus racing one day a year?

It's incredibly disruptive to have all the bus routes changed and essential routes blocked for events – most of which are essentially commercial promotions. I wonder what it all costs in erecting metal barriers, supplying extra police; and in pollution caused by road closures. I'm convinced it's all part of the anti-motorist agenda.

The Police

Cab drivers who've been in the game longer than I reminisce about regular skirmishes with the boys in blue, and I think we can confidently accept that in the old days the police systematically hassled cab drivers. This is no longer the case. The police even have honorary membership of the cab caff I frequent on Camley Street for God's sake.

I think we've already established that cab drivers don't respond well to being told what to do, but a non-confrontational word in your ear can make you think about your actions should you transgress the laws of the road.

In the mid-80s I was a motorbike courier. One morning I was zooming up Albany Street when a motorbike cop drew alongside me at the lights. It was a clear road, but I'd been speeding. Rather than read the riot act, the cop asked if he thought one of our speedometers might be out, as his suggested we'd both been speeding. Just a friendly word made me think. Policing at its best.

I'd been told off a few times for stopping in places I shouldn't in the following years, but I've never been nicked, and I've yet to be shot by the American police for setting down next to their embassy.

In 2015 I was pulled up for driving my cab in a cycle lane. I was proceeding west along Grosvenor Road towards Chelsea Bridge. There was a long line of traffic, but the cycle lane was empty. I looked at the signs: it was a Monday to Saturday cycle lane. Today was Sunday. I got into the empty lane painted blue and overtook all the mugs on the main carriageway. Just after overtaking a police car I heard the siren behind me. I didn't stop at first because I knew I'd done nothing wrong, but I eventually realised I was being pursued. I was invited to get out of the cab and have a word. The policeman wasn't rude, but I was still annoyed at having been wrongly accused. He said he had camera footage of me driving in a cycle lane, and added that he could also do me for failing to stop. I said I was sure the cycle lane wasn't in operation on Sundays, but I thought it best not to argue. It ended amicably. We both got back in our cars and carried on.

My passenger and I studied the Monday to Saturday signs. I was definitely in the right. My man had the air of a left-wing lawyer and might be familiar with stories of police harassment. I briefly considered putting on a show: perhaps shout at the police car as we drove past and wave wildly at the signs. Maybe get out in the middle of the road and rant and rave? Do the police still fit you up if they don't like the look of you? I'm not sure, but I decided I wasn't going to risk it.

Also in 2015, my wife had the police coming to our house looking for me. At the earliest opportunity I phoned them to find out what it was all about. I was told that I'd filled up with diesel and driven off without paying. What?! At first I was in denial, but as the details came out I had to own up to my crime. The policeman said they had camera footage, and described me coolly wiping down the excess fuel from around the cap before leaving the scene. The policeman said it happens all the time: even the police do it.

I started to piece together the events leading up to the crime. We'd just returned from a weekend away in Yorkshire and I was tired. I'd filled up at an unfamiliar fuel station attached to Morrison's supermarket. I had my shopping list and was excited about the bargains I was going to snap up. There was nothing I could do but plead guilty to being Middle Aged & Absent Minded. I returned to the fuel station to pay my bill that evening.

I am a bit nervous around the police though. On the rare occasion I drop off at Heathrow, I often stop for a coffee or a Whopper Meal at Heston Services on my way back into Central London. A policeman started to make conversation as I waited for my over-priced cappuccino – a daylight robbery if I ever saw it. I just couldn't speak normally and felt he was building up to an enquiry into where I was on a particular day in 2010 when I made an illegal turn off Oxford Street. I couldn't have made myself appear shiftier. From that day on I worked on my attitude towards the police. I'm all right with detectives; it's the uniform that makes me nervous: all that authoritarian dark clothing and all that scary equipment hanging from their belts. By the time I involved the police in a non-payment of cab fare in 2016, I had got over my phobia. You'll read about that later. Anyway, I'd take my chance with the police in this country over other places. I just wish they'd nick more cyclists.

Cash from Cameras

Wherever you are in London, there's someone watching you on camera. We all want safe road systems and we all condemn other road users when they cut up, cheat or inconvenience us with their selfish actions. We like road systems where lanes and signage are laid out clearly. We see the need for speed restrictions, banned turns, and for traffic lights and box junctions. All these measures have their place in making driving safer and easier when used intelligently. Sometimes though, it seems that councils are just out to catch us out as a money-making exercise. More than in any other city, London's traffic cameras are poised ready to make a killing.

Many boroughs are increasing their 20 mph zones. Islington Borough is the capital of speed bumps and 20 mph speed limits, with many of the borough's roads employing both traffic calming methods simultaneously. Of course, driving above 20 mph is often a luxury in inner-London, so it's annoying to get filmed and fined should you find a clear stretch of road affording you that opportunity.

Some traffic calming systems are plain daft, particularly in Islington. On Theberton Street regular motor vehicles have to squeeze through a seven-foot gap to the left of the carriageway. The centre of the road is a designated bus lane, though it's not on a bus route and no buses use this particular road!

In 2017, the tide finally seemed to be turning against speed bumps when it was announced that some would be removed. The authorities finally conceded that vehicles slowing and accelerating at speed bumps added to pollution. Speed bumps also damage people's cars, and the braking and accelerating used in negotiating these artificial hills add to noise and pollution.

I've yet to notice any removal of speed bumps. They've spent all that Council Tax on putting useless speed bumps in, and it's going to cost more to take them out. Many cash-strapped boroughs are facing cuts, so if you live in Islington and wonder why your swimming pools close down and your libraries only open half a day a week, you'll know why. Console yourself with the thought that you still have some top class traffic calming systems.

Local authorities enjoy a lot of sport at box junctions, and London's road systems make it extremely difficult to avoid putting yourself on offer. If you pull forward driving normally you could be caught in the box junction when the lights change. If you hold back, another driver is likely to zoom in to the space in front of you. All too often, that car will just continue to crawl through the junction in time, but you, the responsible driver, will be caught on camera.

One particularly busy camera hot-spot is the corner of Berkeley Street and Piccadilly. Many drivers have been filmed and fined there, me included. As the two lanes end in Berkeley Street you're forced either left or right into Piccadilly. Lane markings would help motorists decide what lane to get in before they attempt their turn, but that would be too simple. Why not just let people get caught with their wheels touching the sacred yellow grid and zap them with the camera?

You get about five seconds to complete the turn. Piccadilly is a busy road, with another set of lights waiting for you immediately after the turn. Only a few vehicles get around the corner before the lights change. Sometimes only one vehicle will get to make the turn, particularly if there are buses involved. At each cycle there are usually a few unlucky vehicles that get caught in the box junction, and they are at the mercy of whoever is watching the camera footage. I got done when I wanted to turn left into Piccadilly, then make the next right into St James Street. I made my turn from the left lane as common sense dictates, but got caught behind vehicles that came around from the right lane and forced me to stop in the box junction.

Sometimes they use camera vans to catch people out. Berkeley Street/Piccadilly needs some kind of control, but I see no good reason to ban the left turn from Phoenix Street into Calthorpe Street. Knowledge Boys reading this are going to love this... For a week or so I thought I'd invented a new and exciting cut-through from Clerkenwell to King's Cross. From Clerkenwell Road I'd use a few little-used roads, then make a left into Calthorpe Street and a right into Gray's Inn Road. As I didn't expect to see a No Left Turn sign at Calthorpe Street I missed it. Unfortunately a camera car saw it and I received a fine in the post. You're not getting in anyone's way turning left into Calthorpe Street: it's not busy or dangerous. Right turns are always more hazardous, but strangely, you are allowed to turn right there. I notice that Camden Council still park their stupid little camera cars in Calthorpe Street, ready to catch out an ex- Knowledge Examiner who perhaps should've known better.

For all the good work I do at St Pancras, that Christmas I thought I might receive a card from Camden Council and a note of appreciation for all the help I have given the good people of that borough over the past year: perhaps a card depicting a wintry scene and a Victorian hansom driver muffled from the bleak mid-winter. All I got was a grainy photograph of my cab and a demand for money.

However much enforcement may appear overzealous, some roads are relatively free from enforcement. I'd advise any driver coming into the West End looking for free parking to try the busier roads like Haymarket or Bond Street. Nobody seems to get ticketed here. You'll be in good company: from Oxford Street to Piccadilly you'll see minicabs, vans and builders' lorries, parked on both sides of

Bond Street. In the Haymarket area, it's best to keep off the side streets as you get parking wardens patrolling there. You can park up in the loading bay outside Planet Hollywood, or on the double yellows opposite Tiger Tiger all day. Keep your hazard lights on to give the impression you will be returning in a couple of minutes. Serious free parking enthusiasts might like to consider surrounding their vehicle with orange fencing to give the impression they are doing essential road maintenance. Or drive a Spanish coach.

The Speed Awareness Course

Every professional driver gets done for doing something illegal eventually. Should you be lucky enough to get up to a decent speed you may well find yourself invited to take a speed awareness course. I've never been caught speeding in London, but I've been done a few times in more rural areas.

In 2017 I was filmed driving at 48 miles per hour in a 40 mph limit. This was on the A5 approaching Dunstable as I drove home from London one evening. I had the choice of a £100 fine and points on my licence, or to attend a speed awareness course at my own expense. I'd attended such a course seven years previously when I lived in Northampton. I was filmed rushing back with a KFC Bargain Bucket a mile from my home. Since then, they'd turned off all the speed cameras in Northamptonshire to save money. I assumed they did the same in Bedfordshire. I'd lived there for over two years and I'd never seen any camera flashes go off.

Sunday 30th July was an ideal day to take a day off to attend the course: Regent Street was closed for summer shopping, and there were cycle races all over London too. Checking the TfL website it appeared that nearly every useful road would be closed.

I was interested to learn that you can book a course in any location you want to. At first I thought I might like to make a day of it and book a course in a seaside town; maybe even work a weekend in Devon around it. Thinking more seriously, it wouldn't really be fair on my wife to leave her to amuse herself for several hours while I attend a lecture on road signs.

I decided to go somewhere on my own, nearer to home. So, I found myself in an office block in Newport Pagnell on that Sunday morning. Newport Pagnell is only thirty-five minutes away – if I put my foot down. The courses also vary in cost: mine was one of the cheaper ones at £80.

I've got to say, it was quite an enjoyable experience. There was a case in the news at the time concerning an MP who got his wife to say she was driving his car when it was caught speeding. After checking there were no wives of politicians present, proceedings commenced dead on 8 am. Talk about speeding: the male trainer clearly wanted this event over with as quickly as possible, and spoke so fast it was hard to keep up. He set a challenge: if any of us could correctly identify the speed limits on various classes of roads, we could go home at coffee break. None of us managed it. It took me the full four hours to get into my head the difference between a single and a dual carriageway (what looks like a dual carriageway is actually a single carriageway if there's no central reservation. The speed limit on a dual carriageway is 70 mph unless otherwise indicated, so you don't want to get it wrong).

Our two-wheeled friends weren't discussed very favourably, but when one man claimed that "all motorcyclists break the speed limits," the trainer reminded us that out of the twenty-four of us, there were no bikers present.

I learned that we concentrate for about fifteen minutes in every driving hour, and that we tend to drive faster if the music we are playing is faster than our heartbeat. The trainer assured us that we should be OK with Coldplay (I suspect I was blasting out Motorhead on that fateful day in June).

Do you get irritated by the constant changes in speed limits on smart motorways? The red-circled speed limit signs aren't triggered by a person, but are set automatically by radar in the cats' eyes. Rather than having everyone come to a halt on a congested motorway, the system merely slows you down. The idea being that you progress smoothly through.

I don't want to give the impression I'm a serial speeder. I rarely go above 65 on the motorway, and I'm always scratching my head at the speeds some people drive at on country roads – the deadliest roads of all. The course did its job: I try to drive more carefully, and I'm thinking of switching to Classic FM. I don't intend to get done again. Though if I do, I have a few weekends free next July when they close Regent Street for its Shopping Sundays.

Mistakes

These are inevitable, but as the driver gains experience, mistakes become only occasional. Many mistakes are caused by poor communication. The passenger's English might not be good, or if they're English they might be slurring after a few light ales. In any case, it's hard to hear anything over the noisy rumble of a taxi's diesel engine. Remember, there's a Perspex partition with a tiny gap. Modern taxis have intercom systems, but they're not very effective.

Early in my career I took a lady to Mornington Crescent rather than Warrington Crescent, a couple of miles away. Another time, a bloke asked for New Kent Road, then fell asleep soon after getting in. At Elephant & Castle I asked him where he wanted to be dropped off. I was horrified when he said he wanted dropping off at New *King's* Road, several miles in the opposite direction. I completed the journey at no extra charge. He was fine about it, and so he might. That was over twenty-five years ago, and I'm still convinced he asked for New Kent Road.

When I returned to the cab trade in 2010 I invested in a Cabbie's Mate device. This works as a regular sat nav, but you can switch in to A–Z mode and draw a line on the map. The device also pinpoints thousands of Points of Interest. This is very useful if you can't remember all those hotel chains that change their names every month. It's got me out of many an embarrassing situation.

I could've done with satellite technology in about 1990 when an Arab gentleman asked me for a hotel near Heathrow Airport. Airport hotels can be difficult to find and difficult to remember, particularly if you rarely go out to the flyers. I suppose I should have asked my passenger for the precise address, but I thought I'd ask another cab driver when I drew alongside one on the drive out to Heathrow. I was told that the hotel I wanted was the one facing you as you exit the roundabout off the M4. I relaxed knowing that it would be easy enough to find. As I drove along the M4 and on to the exit slip off the roundabout I saw it was a different hotel completely. I drove past the entrance and was now back on the M4 heading west. I eventually found out that the hotel was on the edge of Slough, a town that I've still never been to in all my years of cab driving.

I made a similar mistake when I missed a turning near Heathrow and headed into rural Buckinghamshire. It's a novel experience for a London cab driver to drive past sheep grazing on green pastures. It usually means you're on your way to Gatwick Airport, or you've have trapped a lucrative roader deep into Twattinghamshire. It's a sickening feeling when you have an irate passenger in the back that's going to arrive home late, and you're burning time and diesel. Your humiliation gauge is glowing red on the dashboard and you want the M25 to swallow up you and your cab before things get even worse. All you can do is apologise and knock a generous amount of money off the fare. This usually calms things down. People like a discount, and this was a Black Friday deal twenty-five years before it'd been invented.

I find airports confusing with all those fast-moving lanes going in all directions, over-complicated direction signs, and all those car parks. I was therefore a bit on edge after trapping a nice ride to Heathrow. My passengers wanted Terminal 2, then Terminal 5. I dropped at T2, then followed the signs for T5. Terminal 5 is some miles past the three main terminals, so I followed the signs on the airport service roads. I was just congratulating myself on following the complicated route around roundabouts and dead end car park lanes when I saw one last sign, reading "Taxis Only". I'm driving a taxi, I thought, so I took that lane, I then found myself on the back of the cab rank. Thankfully, I managed to get out of trouble by driving over the kerbing. Embarrassing though.

The Westfield shopping centre at Shepherd's Bush has caused me anxiety ever since it opened. It's a convoluted route to the official taxi drop off, and it's a bit like an airport, with lots of confusing lanes and car parks. On my first visit there I panicked and dropped a Caribbean family off inside the customer car park. I pretended this was where cabs normally set down. My passengers were none the wiser, and would even have saved themselves a couple of quid on the shorter route. I, on the other hand, paid a pound to get out of the car park. I did the same thing again a few years later when they changed the road system.

It's best to confirm the destination before you set off. French people have a particular way of asking for "Saint Pancras" or the "Saint Giles Hotel", and it takes a while for you to attune yourself to the way an Arab visitor will pronounce "Edgware Road".

When someone asks you to taken them to "to… to… to… Regent Street" they don't necessarily have a stutter; they might want 222 Regent Street (those Russian cab drivers again).

A young Chinese couple asked for Old Street one Sunday afternoon. I was glad to get out of the busy West End and headed up though the quieter streets of Holborn and Clerkenwell. It transpired they'd asked for Oxford Street in the opposite direction. Argh! When they initially asked for Old/Oxford Street I repeated Old Street back to them, but it clearly got lost in translation.

When an American couple got into my cab on the Haymarket rank and asked for "Reubens" I repeated back the destination to confirm. I ran a nice quick route up to Marylebone and stopped outside Reubens; London's celebrated kosher restaurant. "Where's the hotel?" asked the man. I realised my mistake immediately. They wanted Rubens Hotel opposite Buckingham Palace. There was a fair bit of traffic on the way back, and of course the extra fare was down to me. The couple were fine about it; in fact he implied it was his wife's fault. The fact was, we couldn't hear each other over the noise of the traffic when we set off from one of London's busiest roads.

Anyway, that was a selection of my own mistakes, and I feel relieved to have got them off my chest.

Big mistakes often pass into folklore. There's the story of the driver who took a passenger twelve miles out to the town of Croydon. He then realised that the passenger wanted John Bell & Croyden, a well-known chemist's emporium on Wigmore Street in Central London.

Another story I like concerns the passenger who was taken a fair way into the deep south of Tooting Common. He'd asked for Tutankhamun in an American accent and wondered where the exhibition was. It was at the British Museum, six miles away in the direction he'd just come from.

The most horrific story I've heard needs to be taken with a pinch of salt, and has almost certainly become embellished the more it's been told. It involves an American couple staying in a Central London hotel. They were booked on a luxury cruise and hired a cab from the hotel rank to take them to meet their cruise ship at the port. The hotel linkman asked the driver to make for Harwich. In his excitement, the driver neglected to confirm the destination with his passengers and set off for the east coast of Essex, no doubt with pound signs spinning in his eyes like a one-armed bandit machine. At Harwich he asked the couple which quay they wanted. The number of the quay didn't exist at Harwich. It existed at Southampton on the south coast. Thanks to Jonathan Harvey for that one. It's at least third hand, but I like to think it's a true story.

Bilking

Most cab rides pass off smoothly: the customer gets to his destination, the driver gets paid, and both parties are happy. In a mercifully small minority of instances, the customer opts out of the contract and fails to make payment. Occasionally, someone genuinely realises they have no money on them until it's too late. In more sinister cases, the customer has no intention of paying. This is known as bilking. Cab drivers are experienced drivers, not experienced criminals. We trust people. We don't understand the criminal mind, and we find it hard to understand how someone could cold-bloodedly defraud a working individual of payment for a service rendered in good faith.

Sometimes, the police try to fob a bilked driver off by claiming it's a civil matter. It's not. Making off without making payment is an arrestable offence, and one that any cab driver should press charges on. After all, if a store detective catches a shoplifter, the culprit will most likely be detained and handed over to the rozzers to deal with. It's the same principle with a cab fare. In the case of a cab fare, the lost fare may represent the difference between a financial loss or profit on that particular day, and it's not something the driver would be able to insure against.

On two occasions I've trusted passengers to post me a cheque after they claimed they had no money to pay their fare. In the early days I drove a distressed young woman home after she told me she'd had her purse stolen. She offered to send me a cheque. That was the last I heard from her.

Many years later I drove a posh old lady from Mayfair to Harrods. This time I received a cheque in the post in excess of the fare and a nice handwritten note. This incident restored my faith in the honesty of the public, but I'd only accept a cheque in desperate circumstances.

I've been bilked a few times by runners, and even by two or three walkers. You have to weigh up whether you run after them or not. I never have. I'm careful to the point of paranoia as to where I pick up, and the appearance of a person hailing me; but bilkers don't have notices around their necks advertising their speciality. Most appear perfectly respectable.

One Saturday in 2016 I was thinking of home when I stopped for one last job in Shaftesbury Avenue. A stroke of luck, he was going north to Hampstead, only ten minutes from the M1. It was about 6 pm and still light, but I felt a bit uneasy about him. He was a young bloke with a posh accent, but he appeared nervous. When we arrived at an upmarket address off Frognal he indicated for me to wait two minutes while he went inside to get some money. Tension mounted.

After about ten minutes he came out and stood by the door, fiddling with his headphones. After another five minutes, he walked past me at a brisk pace and disappeared. I suspected he wasn't coming back any time soon.

There appeared to be nobody at home when I knocked on the door and peered through the letterbox. I gave it about ten minutes before phoning 101. I told the police what had happened and that there was £41 on the meter. I was told to leave it with them.

I didn't think of taking a photo on my phone until afterwards. Had I photographed the person on his doorstep when I first felt suspicious, it could have sped things up with the police enquiry. I also neglected to print out a receipt as evidence of costs and timings.

I knew it wasn't the crime of the century. Even in leafy Hampstead there must be enough crime to keep the gendarmerie busy: burglary, dodgy antique dealing, dog fouling, &c. I was therefore prepared for a brick wall of silence, perhaps to be treated as an irritation. Not so. I received texts, phone messages, and emails to reassure me they were still on the case. I asked if I should make contact myself; after all, I knew the address. I was advised to leave it to them.

I eventually got to speak to a policeman on the phone. He was chatty, and was interested in the cab trade. He'd visited the address but found no signs of occupancy. He told me houses in the area are often rented out – at £2000 per week – so have periods of being unoccupied. We agreed that it looked a very posh house: it looked like a setting for *the Antiques Roadshow* when I looked through the letterbox. There was no CCTV in the road, and as you know, I neglected to take a photo of the miscreant. Unless something new came up, there was no more they could do. I asked if one of us should post a letter at the address. The PC said he'd do that.

A week or two later I had an email to say the case was still live, but I was realistic enough to know I'd probably have to write off my £41. I tried to forget about it and move on.

Several days further on, I received a voicemail message from my PC. He said he'd "identified the culprit." He went on to say that he'd "facilitate payment." My PC had turned into a bank manager, but I didn't care, I was going to get my money!

My knowledge of police procedural is informed by TV programmes. I imagined a couple of detectives celebrating the solving of this heinous crime over a pint at a pub on

Hampstead Heath, like Inspector Morse and Lewis would've done in Oxford. I wondered if the offender had come quietly, or if there had been a struggle. I imagined a crack team of cops in checked baseball caps kicking the door in, and a hardened criminal shouting "You won't take me alive, Copper!" The response would surely be a splintering of the wooden door, and the miscreant dragged out with a few licks of a truncheon, and perhaps a Taser for good measure. I'd have the opportunity to put on a show in court by pointing out the thieving scroat: "It's him wot done it!"

Fantasy over. There would be no day in court as I didn't want to waste any time on all that. I told my PC I just wanted my money back and no fuss. The PC said he would get the money and I could pop into the station to collect it. I asked what it was all about. It was pretty much how I imagined: a first year student was horribly drunk and took a cab home (the drunkenness was cunningly disguised by dark glasses). He knew he had no money but took a gamble on his parents being in. They were out, and he panicked.

It's a bit silly doing a runner from your own home though – he must've known he wouldn't get away with it. All he had to do was ask me at the time if he could send a cheque (remember, I've done this twice before, with a 50% success rate). The PC had had a lot of contact with the young lad and his parents. Apparently they'd dragged him down to the cop shop by his ear and he was embarrassed about the whole thing.

At my suggestion, the PC contacted the family again and asked they send a cheque to me directly. The young man's mother sent a cheque for £45 and a note apologising for her son's behaviour, crudely-written in blue felt-tipped pen.

It was a pretty pathetic apology, particularly as she hadn't ensured the lad apologised himself. I could have ended his career before it'd even started had I been cruel enough to take the matter to court. Some parents, honestly.

Funny Money

I keep meaning to invest in one of those pens that identifies fake banknotes. I could have done with one early in my Butter Boy days. A youngster gave me a £50 note. I foolishly took it. Later on at the Royal Oak cab café I used the note to pay for my lamb chops and chips. The man behind the till refused to accept it. Under fluorescent lighting we could all see it was a fake.

The following day it was reported on the radio that some people had been arrested for producing fake banknotes. As I entered Tottenham Court Road Police Station to hand over my dodgy note I was quite excited. Maybe this note had come from the team recently arrested for counterfeiting? Would I get an award? Well, I'd get a "Thanks, son" at the very least. Not really. It was depressingly mundane. The copper put my £50 note into a plastic bag and that was about it. To think, I'd lost a £50 note, plus about forty quid that I gave the bloke as change. And I had to pay for my own lamb chops.

Turned Out Nice Again?

This country rarely experiences extreme weather, though it is unpredictable. When the first snowflake drops, the roads and rails grind to a halt, and all the schools close, just in case they face legal action for forcing children out into the cold. As much as I like to pretend I'm driving my rig across Alaska like on *Ice Road Truckers*, anything more than a dusting of the white stuff and I'm on my way home. We rarely experience snow in London, but if it snows, I don't work. The only time I enjoy snow is at Christmas when I have a few days off. When the first rays of sun hit our shores, British people head to a pub with an outdoor seating area and order a pint of lager with a wasp in it. Others strip off and lie around drunk in our parks. Or try to get into cabs in Soho. We need to be wary. Driving in hot weather is very debilitating, even in a cab with air-conditioning. Driving in rain is depressing. I don't like the dark either.

At the end of February and the beginning of March 2018, I lost four days work because of snow. Little over a month later we had three boiling hot days. April 19th was the hottest April day since 1949. It was a great day to find my air-conditioning had packed up. We then had over a week of cold, rain and hail. I forgot about the air-conditioning and put the heater on.

9

Examiner

One day I picked up my usual copy of *Taxi* magazine. Among the advertisements there was one detailing Knowledge of London Examiner vacancies. In a fever of excitement I sat in the cab café and planned my application. Many cab drivers fantasise about becoming Knowledge Examiners, but it's not something you can plan for. There's no career structure allowing you to apply for promotion from driver to examiner after serving a certain period of time. Examiners were known to be ex-police officers fortunate enough to have secured a cushy retirement posting. They didn't give up their jobs easily. But things had progressed a little since my days of visiting the Public Carriage Office at Penton Street. Transport for London had taken over the PCO, and its examiners were longer police civilians.

I knew I stood a reasonable chance of success as I had been a Careers Adviser, and had relevant experience of working in the public sector and of conducting interviews. Sure enough, I was invited to take an assessment at their West Kensington outpost at Ashfield House.

TfL's personnel department advised on how best to approach their system of competence-based interviews, and I duly tried to anticipate likely questions and bone up on some possible answers. I would be tested on my English, maths, and Knowledge of London skills. The English bit would be fine, but the maths bit worried me. I scraped through a GCSE C-grade equivalent at my adult education college in Birmingham, and that was fifteen years ago. The Knowledge section wouldn't exactly be a walk in the park either.

I needn't have worried about the maths, as this turned out to involve very basic arithmetic. The Knowledge was more challenging. My general sense of geography was good, but I struggled with writing out the sort of Runs that a Knowledge Boy would be asked for on an Appearance. I left the room knowing I could have done better. I can only think that my flowery use of English earned me an interview a few weeks later.

The Public Carriage Office was now known as London Taxi and Private Hire. They had recently moved out of the grim grey office in North London to the flash glass Palestra building south of Blackfriars Bridge.

I was greeted in reception by the Knowledge of London Manager, Nicola Danvers, and a man whose name I instantly forgot in the excitement of the moment. I found him quite austere, and I never did find out what job he did. This wasn't anything unusual for TfL. I was later to find out that people's jobs within the organisations were vague, and changed frequently. You'd wonder why you stopped seeing a particular person in the kitchen, then find out they'd been seconded to another department months ago.

I was left to wait on a comfy chair until they were ready to interview me. I felt anything but comfortable, and seriously considered getting in the lift and leaving the situation. I have a good record in securing job interviews because I'm skilled at writing CVs and personal statements, but I am well out of my comfort zone in face to face interrogations. The job interviews I attended from 1978 onwards were informal chats about who I was and what I was about. By 2001, the Careers Adviser job interviews I attended featured scenario-questions, such as, "What project might you set up if I gave you a free afternoon a week?" The questions were usually posed by a panel of interviewers, rather than a bloke sitting on the edge of a desk, as in my school-leaver interviews. The Transport for London interview process felt even more formal and intimidating, and the whole set-up at Palestra was pretty oppressive, as I was to find out later. I was called in, and we were away. Nicola and the other chap asked long questions where I'd have to give an example of how I'd handled a variety of situations: for example, how I'd collaborated with other agencies; how I'd overcome something; how I'd made a quick decision, &c. I answered some questions well, while others I wasn't happy with.

On the Firm

When I heard I'd got the job I considered it one of my life's biggest achievements. I was only offered an eight-month contract, but I'd fulfilled my dream of becoming a Knowledge Examiner. I celebrated with champagne at home a few hours later.

Subscribers to a Knowledge web forum discussed the appointment of six newly appointed examiners. A buzz had been created in the close-knit Knowledge world and I was excited to be a part of it. The appointments would please Knowledge candidates as the current shortage of examiners had resulted in longer waiting times between exam appearances: the fifty-six day interval between testing could now run to nearly double that.

The Knowledge Boys would all be wondering what the new examiners would be like. Would they be hard or soft? Would they be austere or approachable? I could now fantasise about what kind of examiner I'd like to be.

I was invited to an induction day back in West Kensington. This didn't fall on an ideal day, as the wife and I had tickets to see Iron Maiden in Sheffield the night before (Mo really wanted to see Peter Kay, but he wasn't gigging). We made the fairly long drive up from Northampton aiming to take it easy and try to get home at a reasonable hour. Maiden put on a great show, and I was disappointed to miss "Run for the Hills", as we left early to catch a tram back to the park and ride.

I could have done with more sleep, and I didn't relish the thought of a gruelling journey to West London for a 9 am start. I had to get up ridiculously early, but I made it in good time. The induction was set up for a variety of new starters across TfL's directorates. I met Mark Gunning and Kathy Gerrard, who had also been appointed examiners. We got on well and stayed friends. The induction was quite jolly, and full of interesting facts and figures. One fact stands out: tube trains now run throughout the night at weekends, but it's unlikely they'll run all night every night because unlike the New York system, there's only one track in each direction, and this doesn't allow trains to be run when maintenance is being carried out.

In the section about our responsibilities as employees, Kath articulated the question that some of us had been thinking, but were too afraid to ask: "Are we allowed to drink at lunchtimes?" The answer was an emphatic "No." Lunchtime drinking was strictly verboten. I found out later that we'd be getting a measly forty-five minute afternoon break, so had inadequate time for either a drink or a proper lunch anyway. This was a shock to a person who regularly enjoyed a leisurely beer and burger at Wetherspoons as a Careers Adviser. Tube workers couldn't even have a beer after work if they were wearing their uniforms. Welcome to the strange world of TfL.

Many things are on a need to know basis at TfL. The induction finished in the early afternoon, and we were unsure if we were expected to show ourselves at our new workplace before going home. Mark phoned the Knowledge Department, who told us we were expected to put in an appearance. Mark, Kath and I, made the tube journey across London to meet our new manager and work colleagues at the Palestra building. Mark became known to be very particular about cleanliness and hygiene. He's a man who wears a three-piece suit every working day and he's not used to rubbing shoulders with the great unwashed on the underground. He just doesn't do public transport. It wasn't especially busy on the tube, but it was enough to freak him out. I thought Kath might have had to bring some smelling salts out of her bag. He was barely conscious as the train pulled into Southwark Station.

I thought the other examiners might have resented new people coming in to disrupt their tight-knit regime, but they were all very kind to us. We were now part of a close band of brothers and sisters. This was a unique job and we were one of the few to be admitted into this privileged position. There was no work for us to do today, so we were all allowed home at 4 pm. Before I left, Nicola marked my card, and told me my mismatched jacket and trouser combination was unacceptable. It was to be a proper suit from now on.

It would've been useful had my new employers informed me of my hours of work. Yesterday's induction started at 9 am, so I assumed my normal working day would start at the same time. Only now did I find out I'd be starting at 8 am. Blimey, how long would it take me to travel seventy miles from the northern suburbs of Northampton? And what time would I have to get up in the morning?

Thankfully, I didn't have any appointments with any heavy metal bands up north the night before my first proper day. I settled on a 4.15 am alarm call. This would allow me forty-five minutes in which to get dressed, watch a bit of BBC News, and fix myself and the cat a quick breakfast (from that day on Rocky insisted he was fed at the same outrageous time). I'd drive the cab a couple of miles and park near the train station. At Euston I'd catch a tube to Waterloo and walk the rest. I felt like a brain-dead zombie making this journey, but as a morning person figured my body would get used to it. It never did.

Over the next few weeks, the other three new examiners joined us: Jonathan Harvey, John Shaw, and Dave Morgan. We spent a lot of the early days observing the established examiners in action. We'd pull a chair into the cramped offices and watch Knowledge candidates being interrogated. All examiners have their own philosophies and styles of delivery. I learnt something from them all.

After a couple of weeks of observation we took our first Appearances, observed by Nicola. I don't know who was more nervous, me or the candidate. I gave my first candidate a C and I was happy with my performance. Nicola was satisfied that I could fly solo from now on.

I brought in a length of string and some Blu Tack so I could check my Runs in the traditional fashion. I also brought in my own one-way A-Z map. The Knowledge department was woefully under-resourced, and if you wanted a map showing new-fangled areas such as Canary Wharf, or one-way systems in the present century, it was best to bring your own. I set out my desk with my Who, Clash, Pink Floyd and West Ham United coffee mugs, and looked forward to starting my examining work for real. I also managed to source a red *Keep Calm and Carry On* mug. I placed this in a prominent position on my desk, as I felt it gave sound advice to my candidates. Several people appreciated this, though one Millwall supporter complained on a web forum that my West Ham mug distracted him.

Finals and Map Test

After a candidate has learnt a certain number of Runs, he is invited to take a written exam. This is known as a "Map Test". Only after passing the Map Test would the candidate be invited to start the Appearance process. Candidates are asked to identify Points of Interest on a map under exam conditions. The task is harder than it sounds, even if you don't have the pressure of sitting opposite an examiner. It's not a very clear map, and no roads are marked. After observing our colleagues in action we'd conduct our own map tests and we'd mark the papers afterwards.

If I wasn't sure what mark to give, I'd ask another examiner what they thought. Opinions differed widely: one examiner would suggest I give a lower mark, while another would recommend a higher mark. I'd usually err on the side of the latter. The examiner who suggested leniency reminded me that candidates spend a lot of money to take these tests, and unless they have clearly made little effort to prepare, borderline candidates should be given the benefit of the doubt. I agree. If they are making inadequate effort they will be weeded out at a later stage, and no mistake.

The Finals Talk is a jolly little ceremony where candidates who have completed all formalities are awarded their badges and licences. The head of Taxi and Private Hire Licensing usually says a few words, and the examiner conducting things gives a talk about the responsibilities of running your own taxi business. The new cab drivers and their families are all booted and suited as they pose for photos with their favourite examiners after the ceremony. The candidate has worked extremely hard for around three years, and his family would have suffered too. It's a huge achievement. I've attended two of my own degree graduation ceremonies, but I'd say this modest gathering was as meaningful and emotionally charged as my MA ceremony at Birmingham Symphony Hall was.

Dress Code

Official advice to candidates states that "in order to become licensed you are, therefore, asked to prevent a clean and smart appearance when attending the Public Carriage Office." Despite TfL's official policy, Knowledge Boys were still being sent home for being inappropriately dressed. Knowledge Examiners often had discussions about whether to send someone home for not wearing a tie. Suits and ties weren't mentioned in policy, but some examiners were determined to penalise anyone who didn't stick to tradition. Candidates weren't expected to remove their jackets until they were invited to once in the interview room, and only then on a hot day. Muslims wearing gowns was a contentious issue. I felt it best not to go there on this one.

Candidates were allowed to use the coffee machine in the kitchen attached to the waiting area, but this wasn't generally publicised. I never saw anyone returning from the kitchen with a steaming cup of coffee, but it was certainly allowed – Nicola said so. Nicola also told me something interesting about the examiners' dress code. Envying other staff members walking around in Led Zeppelin T-shirts on Dress Down Friday, I asked Nicola why the examiners couldn't dress down on Fridays too. I was surprised when I was told that we could. The examiners were just too conservative to do anything else.

Getting to Know my Colleagues

Mark and Kath quickly became known as hard examiners. Not because they wanted to make names for themselves, but because pushing candidates to the very boundaries of insanity was part of their philosophy. An examiner's philosophy is understandably shaped by the way he or she was treated by their examiners when they were on the Knowledge.

Dave Hall was known as the "Smiling Assassin" and was feared by the candidates. On occasions a Knowledge Boy would suddenly feel ill and leave the building rather than face Mr Hall. He'd had it hard as a Knowledge student in the 1980s and wasn't going to give anyone an easy ride. I saw him in action several times. It's all calm and pleasant on the surface, but Dave is like a kindly doctor about to impart grave news. At the end of the consultation, Dr Hall's diagnosis was often grim.

I was a Knowledge student at around the same time as Dave, but my philosophy was at the other end of the scale; probably because my experience of being examined wasn't as traumatic. Jonathan Harvey talked about an examiner throwing his appointment card across the room at him in frustration when he was on the Knowledge. Jonathan himself would never do anything as demeaning, but he asked a lot from his candidates and was unpredictable. If my colleagues were sometimes harsh, it's only because they were treated harshly as students. Ultimately we were all working to maintain standards.

Later, in April 2017, *The Knowledge: the World's Toughest Taxi Test* was aired on television. Current examiner, Paul Whitehead, gave his opinion on the Knowledge: "If it's not taking over your life, you're not doing it properly." Paul is a moderate examiner, so this gives an idea of what is expected of the candidates.

The examiners discussed between themselves the legalities of certain manoeuvres. Opinion was divided whether you could enter Melcolmbe Place from the east in order to set down at Marylebone Station. All the other examiners said you couldn't, I said you could. Mark Gunning was adamant that you had to do a U-turn, which is illegal. I said that you don't do a U-turn; you turn right into Harewood Avenue, then right into Melcolmbe Place north side. These are the sort of manoeuvres that are routinely discussed by those in the cab trade.

When I started the Knowledge the second time I expected it to take me two years. Had I not been invited to a retest I would have been having Appearances with Mr Hall and Mr Gunning. I think it would've taken me longer than my estimated two years. I'd probably still be there now. It makes my blood run cold thinking about it.

All the examiners had an intellect shaped by life experience, and a razor sharp wit. Tony Swire chatted amiably to his candidates and worked his questions into the conversation. I watched him examine a fireman. After chatting about which fire station he worked at, he asked him a Run from the Chinese takeaway opposite. Many people left Tony's room hardly realising they'd had an Appearance.

John Wilkin conducted his Appearances with humour. Knowledge Boys learned to laugh at his jokes. He was nobody's fool though. John always kept an enigmatic smile on his face and tried not to let the crazy bureaucracy get to him. He saw the absurdity of the situation we were all in: we were cab drivers, but also employees of the authority that was making life increasingly difficult for us. John had been a motorcycle cop for twenty-five years, but TfL managers wanted to put him on a motorcycle awareness course before they'd give him permission to bring his motorbike in. I think they wanted to put stabilisers on his bike. There were no light switches at Palestra. It was John who told me that if you sit still long enough the lights go out. John was good at sitting still. He'd often be sat in his room waiting for the lights to go out.

I used to call Hugh McDowell "London's Grumpiest Examiner", but he was actually a really sharp, funny, guy. He had the comic timing of Les Dawson; and as with all the great comedians, his deadpan delivery added to the performance.

Dave Morgan had clearly left the Murder Squad too early. He complained that he used to lead complex investigations, and the examining routine was sapping his motivation. At a health and safety training session he told us he "never compromises." He has a bright future at TfL, I thought. He used to take his shoes and socks off and put his feet on his desk after the last candidate had gone. I don't think Nicola was best pleased, and I predicted an eventual showdown.

Dave wasn't just a former Detective Chief Inspector; he was also something of an authority on the punk rock scene of the late 70s. A right Captain Sensible he was on the quiet. That might explain the attitude.

A few examiners liked to provide history lessons as they examined candidates. Jonathan Harvey started as an examiner a few weeks after myself, and from the outset entertained and informed his candidates. He was fascinated by the origin of the term "On the Wagon" and built a Run around it. The Run asked was a simple one from the site of Newgate Gaol to Tyburn Tree, where the condemned felon was to be hanged by the neck until he be dead. The condemned Knowledge Boy would escape a D if he could name all the pubs the hanging party might have stopped at.

It was quite common for examiners to ask Runs embellished with their own virtual road closures (usually the same examiners, they know who they are). I only did this a few times, asking for a Run that would normally utilise Oxford Street, but on the day Westminster Council closed the road to put up the Christmas lights. Examiners might also ask Runs where the candidate is asked to avoid traffic lights or speed bumps. I didn't resort to such gimmicks. For one thing, I found them flaming hard to devise. Examiners used their discretion whether they allowed candidates to be similarly flamboyant in their answers. Old Street Roundabout was colloquially known as Silicon Roundabout because there are some technology companies based in the area. Examiners aren't always in the mood for clever dick candidates, and some would object to colloquialisms or slang.

One of my role models was an examiner I remembered from my Knowledge days, "the gentleman" Mr Lippit. A more current role model was my colleague, Steve Thomas. Steve was a decorated ex-detective. He was probably the hardest working man I know, and one of the funniest. He'd work his cab before and after his examining work, and at the weekends too. He'd fly back in the early hours from a Chelsea match in Spain or Russia and still drive his cab for a couple of hours before starting his working day with us. Urbane and particular, Steve was highly organised and obsessive over detail. He was passionate about the cab trade, and meticulous in his work. His coloured pens were arranged in rows on his desk, and all his questions were written out weeks in advance. Like myself, I suspect Steve used antiseptic wipes to clean down his desk on changeover day. His working area was as spotless as his cab. Steve didn't feel the need to show off. I looked up to Steve because I wasn't going to showboat my cleverness either. My ego would also stay at home.

Some examiners had nicknames: I've already mentioned Dave Hall, the Smiling Assassin. Hugh MacDowell asked a lot of Runs in the West End, and was known as "Mayfair Hugh". I'd drive down from the M1 every working day, so North London was my area of expertise. I'd often vary my route and check out junctions in Golders Green and Hampstead. I wanted a nickname too, but of course, it's down to others to give you a nickname; you can't pick your own. I fancied something like "Hampstead Chris", but it was DCI Dave Morgan who got in first. I was known as a moderate examiner who would pass most people each day. When I said I'd failed three people before tea break Dave came up with "Killer." Thankfully the name didn't stick.

I briefly tried to cultivate a fearsome, yet eccentric, image of myself by fondling a length of string as I went to call my candidates from the waiting area. I felt self-conscious, as being fearsome is not really me. I dropped the idea and got sensible. Almost. Some examiners write down their favourite Runs in a notebook. My notebook bore the legend *Mr Ackrill's Dead Hard Runs & Killer Points*. I sometimes left it on my desk for the candidates to see, but it was really an ironic joke to amuse my colleagues.

Appearances

Candidates sit in the waiting area, doing what nervous people do. Some sit in silence, and a few whisper to their colleagues. If you prefer, you are welcome to take a TfL magazine from the rack and read about bus suspensions.

We'd get our Appearance lists from a cabinet and plan what questions to ask. It wasn't good form to see the same candidate three times running, so we'd dart around each other's rooms arranging swaps. The idea was that candidates would experience the full range of hard and soft examiners.

Most examiners planned their questions in advance, while a few did it from the top of their heads when the candidate had sat down. I planned my questions a day in advance. In 2011, candidates' files were paper-based. We would read the questions they'd been asked before, to see if they had previously "dropped" any Points. If the candidate couldn't previously identify the Points of Interest being asked we'd often ask the same Run again to see if the candidate had taken the trouble to learn them. Examiners might also write comments in the file on the candidate's performance or attitude. In the past, personal comments on candidates' background, and opinions on their likely progress were normal, but examiners were now under instruction to only record relevant information. Eventually, only a list of questions asked and their scores were recorded. All protocols were discussed at brief, but lively, weekly team meetings.

We could pretty much ask anything we wanted so long as both Points of Interest were within the six-mile limit. Incredibly, it was only in 2011 that TfL had the knowhow to actually put an accurate six-mile circle on a map. We attempted to manually draw circles on the maps in the examination rooms with felt-tipped pens. I was tasked with drawing the first one as I was the one with a degree. I made a right pig's ear of it. I would have felt more comfortable in a supervisory role.

They started to crack down on examiners asking Points proved to be outside the exclusion zone. The All England Tennis Club is an important Point of Interest to cab drivers during Wimbledon fortnight and examiners had been asking candidates for it for many years. One day, we were told it was off limits as it was proved to be over six miles from Charing Cross. Thereafter, if any Point outside the six-mile limit came up and the candidate told their Knowledge school, the Knowledge department would receive a complaint and the examiner would have to account for his actions.

At 8.20, we'd walk around the corner and see a sea of nervous faces looking up in anticipation, wondering whether it was their turn to be called. We'd call our victim, and he or she would respond with "Yes, Sir." The candidate would follow us around to our small office, and wait to be asked to sit down. The routine is formal and intimidating. It's a minefield of protocol. Examiners don't take kindly to candidates who sit down before being invited to, and it would get our backs up if a candidate moved the chair towards the examiner. In *The Knowledge*, the examiner asks the hapless candidate who moves the chair, whether he works for Pickfords as a furniture remover.

There would be a few pleasantries before the first question if time permitted. It was always "Sir" or "Ma'am." Knowledge Boys trying it on with a "Mate" were virtually asking for a D. Unbelievably, female examiners were occasionally addressed as "Darling." In a magazine article I later wrote about the Knowledge process, I reminded candidates that "Darling" starts with a D.

Most examiners have a map secured to a desk lectern, and they trace routes with a piece of string, or similar. My map was too large to fit on my lectern, so the bottom part was missing. This is one reason why I didn't ask a lot of Runs involving South London.

An Appearance isn't quite as formal as it was when I was appearing in the chair, but it's still more formal than most job interviews. I was happy to chat a bit to break the ice, but there wasn't always the time. If an Appearance runs over time you are under pressure to keep the next one to the allotted twenty minutes or less. If you have a run of over-long Appearances, that's your coffee break gone. If, after the break, you continue to let things slip, you could lose some of your measly forty-five minute lunch break too.

You want a confident candidate who has worked hard and calls Runs fluently. If he doesn't know, or can't remember, the first Point of Interest, he'll be asked another. This is repeated until he identifies the starting Point correctly. He'll then be asked the finishing Point. For each "dropped" Point he'll be deducted marks. Only when both Points are identified can the Run be called. The examiner will mark him on his accuracy. If the examiner feels he has taken a longer route than necessary, or has been hesitant in calling the Run, he will be deducted marks. Four questions are asked. If the candidate scores twenty-four points out of a possible forty, he will gain a C-grade pass. Higher scores are available to candidates who excel, but not all examiners mark across the full range. An A is a rarity. An AA is awarded to candidates who get the maximum forty points – that's every Point and route run perfectly. This is almost unheard of.

Standardisation of marking isn't something you can easily apply to the Knowledge, so much of it is subjective. Candidates are expected to know the shortest driving route from one Point of Interest to another. This is still open to interpretation in a large, complex, city like London. What one examiner sees as a good line, another sees as too wide. If you take a minute before calling a Run, a reasonable examiner would view that as using reasonable thinking time. Another examiner would see it as a lack of confidence and deduct points for hesitation.

You can tell which school a candidate attends by the patterns of roads he uses. The schools sell books of Runs with their suggested routes, but they use different roads for reasons of copyright. I was surprised to learn that Knowledge Runs can be copyrighted, but if music can be copyrighted with only seven basic musical notes, why not Knowledge Runs? There are thousands of roads that can be used. I'm still not sure there's an actual formal copyright on road patterns, but the schools certainly avoid listing their suggested routes the same as their rivals.

The Blue Book had recently been rewritten to cover modern London more effectively, and the 468 runs had been reduced to 320. We'd often examine "New Starts" – those on their first Appearance. New Starts were asked questions based on one of the 320 prescribed Runs from the Blue Book; the routes that all candidates were expected to have learnt by this point. New Starts had passed the Map Test, but otherwise had no history as far as we were concerned. Some New Starts really impressed and came away with a nice B or C to start off their Knowledge career; others clammed up and could barely speak. Sometimes it was nerves; sometimes they hadn't put the work in and were found out.

We'd see up to sixteen candidates a day. We'd have a fifteen minute coffee break, and forty-five minutes for lunch. It was quite a tough day. It was fun and emotional in turns, depending on how the candidates performed. The same questions could be put to all candidates on the same stage. Seeing ninety candidates a week eats up a lot of material, so the same questions would come up regularly. Examiners have their favourite Runs and these are known as "Bankers". When a candidate has finished his Appearance, he takes his card to the administration desk and makes his next appointment.

In order to succeed in an Appearance and gain a C, the candidate must gain six marks out of a possible ten on each of the four Runs. If a candidate connected the two Points in a coherent way, but without using the shortest possible route, I would probably still judge his efforts worthy of a six. Any candidate on any stage should be able to get in and out of Waterloo Station and find any of the major hotels. If they don't, they deserve to be caned. Many examiners make it more challenging by asking obscure Points. My philosophy is that the Run is always more important than the Point of Interest. Most candidates would "score" with me if they connected the two Points up in a reasonable way, and this is what I would tell New Starts in my introductory spiel. If a candidate used bus routes, or did it by the "Oranges and Lemons" – the roads coloured orange and yellow on the A–Z – they'd usually leave my room happy.

I don't recall being asked for silly Points as a Knowledge Boy, so I didn't tend to ask many as an examiner. If a candidate can find his way around London with confidence, that is good enough for me. If you can handle a complex cross-London Run, but can't identify an obscure statue of some bloke on a horse, I'm not going to hold you back. I'd sometimes ask for the Joe Strummer Subway or Billy Fury Way. I wouldn't penalise candidates for not knowing these quirky little corners of London. Like the pubs and breweries I would ask on a Friday, they were asked largely for my own amusement.

Examiners who ask a lot of difficult Points say that it forces the candidate to get out on his bike and look for them. Fair enough. All too often these days, Points are "found" on the internet, or on Knowledge school lists.

An examiner might start the Appearance by asking for Drake House. Should the candidate not know that, he'd be asked Raleigh House. Should he drop that Point, he'd be asked other apartment blocks in Dolphin Square until he ran out of Points. If you drop nine Points you can't complete a Run. You score zero for that Run and 25% of your Appearance has ended with nothing. You'd be very lucky to pull things back at that stage.

As you progress to the satisfaction of the examiners, you move through stages: from being seen every fifty-six days, to every twenty-eight days, and finally every twenty-one days (in the 1980s there were also eighty-four and fourteen day stages). You would normally stay on each stage for four, five, or more Appearances, depending on how well you progress. Even if you study full time, and are good at it, you are still likely to spend two years on Appearances.

The job could be emotionally draining. I always looked to pass people rather than fail them, but when candidates performed badly you'd have to give them a D. This means they were no further on than they were when they walked in twenty minutes ago. Four Ds on one particular stage and they get "Red Lined". This sends them back to repeat that stage. That's months of wasted work. I don't approve of this system, and I don't think candidates should be put under such intense pressure. However tough things were in my day, you weren't knowingly put back a stage.

Knowledge candidates have respect for the system and take success and failure with good grace. Some examiners are known to be easy-going and ask straightforward questions, while some are known to be hard. If they want to make life difficult for you, they can. A series of obscure Points, or a particularly difficult Run and you are sent no further on than you were when you arrived. You studied for months and woken up in the early hours fretting about a mere twenty minutes of your life. You'd experience elation if you answered well, but a living nightmare if you performed badly. It would be totally demoralising to leave the examination room having made zero progress. Most candidates accept defeat with dignity, but it hits people hard. Candidates have worked intensely hard to ensure they put in a winning performance and leave with a score. Some people get themselves so worked up that they make themselves ill. Candidates have soiled themselves in the chair, and candidates have collapsed, needing medical attention. Putting in a bad performance affects families too. After I passed one Arab chap, he told me that after he failed to score last time his wife cried for two days.

Knowledge Boys and examiners alike have their weak spots. We tended to ask Runs in the geographical areas we were most familiar with. If an examiner made a mistake we wouldn't hear the last of it. In my day, you wouldn't dare question your examiner, but TfL promises transparency for its valued customers. If the candidate was too nervous about questioning anything at the time, Knowledge school tutors were happy to make enquiries on their behalf. I made a few mistakes, as did all of us. In my early days, I was mortified when I asked a candidate to take me to the Mirabelle restaurant in Mayfair, without realising it had closed down. I drove past the blue neon Mirabelle sign every day and it looked like a going concern. It was an easy mistake to make.

Certainly easier than penalising someone for making an illegal turn at a junction I'd driven through that very morning. I realised my mistake when he left the building, so all I could do was leave a message of apology on his pho~ Embarrassing, but rather that than have him tell ev~

on a web forum that I didn't know what I was doing – which he probably did anyway. It was doubly embarrassing as I should have given him enough marks to move him up a stage. Everything was rectified within the hour, but my carelessness had caused us both distress. I made sure he was down to see me next time so I could apologise in person.

I always advised candidates to bring up any queries at the time, so the examiner can consider the situation. It's two people in a room so it's always your word against theirs. The examiners have pride in their work. If he or she has made a mistake, they will usually admit it and amend any marks immediately. It's no good coming back a week or more after the event and trying to argue the toss. I couldn't remember the Appearances I'd taken the previous day, let alone a fortnight ago.

I learnt early on not to give too much away. In an Appearance I admitted I wasn't sure where a certain hotel was. The candidate told his Knowledge school, who mentioned it to another examiner. The other examiner reminded me that we are Gods to the candidates, and we should never show weakness.

There's nothing the keen examiner enjoys more than searching out Knowledge Porn on his days off. Dave Hall in particular, would spend hours on a Sunday researching junctions and drawing up detailed plans indicating restricted turns. Photocopies were handed out to examiners on Monday morning prior to meeting our first candidates. On a Monday Appearance you might be asked Runs based on journeys that the examiner completed in his cab at the end. Best hope he didn't go anywhere complicated.

Out of fear and respect you won't read anything nasty about the examiners on social media sites. As I said to Nicola soon after I joined: "I'm not used to being respected." Only we vain ones would bother to read what the Knowledge Boys were saying about us, but it could be fun trying to identify who was writing about us. I identified a candidate who told everyone on a Knowledge forum that he mistakenly came up for his Appearance a day early. He was listed to see me the following day. As he sat down I asked if he was sure he'd got the right date. He probably wondered how I knew. We probably weren't meant to, but towards the end of my placement I replied to a few web postings. The Knowledge candidates made some nice comments when I left. That meant a lot to me. I continued to comment on a Knowledge forum when I went back on the cab full time.

Learning the Knowledge wasn't all one-way traffic. Sometimes a candidate would teach you things: maybe they'd use a pattern of roads you'd never thought of before, or tell you that a Point of Interest had moved or closed down. Points that had closed down were known as "Ghost Points". When police and fire stations started to be closed down, the Knowledge world was subject to regular hauntings of Ghost Points. A candidate questioned why I asked for St John's Wood Police Station, reminding me it had closed down. I asked him if he knew the Nag's Head on Holloway Road. He said he did. I replied that the pub closed down years ago. The trick is to say you know it's a Ghost Point, but the building is still a valid Point of Interest. It's all a bit of fun.

The examiners know more than the candidates, but they can sometimes turn you over. Things can be checked quickly on a computer now, but if a candidate calls a turn that sounds illegal, you have to be pretty sure of yourself before docking marks. It's human nature that if you're told something with conviction, it can sow doubt. One candidate made a right turn from Marylebone Road into Cosway Street. It jarred when he called it, but I had to be sure. Just because I'd never made that turn myself, it didn't mean it was illegal. But rather than spend ten minutes fiddling with the computer – that probably wasn't switched on anyway – it was easier to let it go.

I had to laugh taking a New Start Appearance. I used to ask my favourite real ale pubs as Points, and I asked for the Seven Stars, in Carey Street. Many experienced Knowledge Boys had dropped it, so I was impressed that this young bloke nailed it in his first Appearance. When I told him I was impressed he revealed that he was a student at the London School of Economics and it was his local pub. Nice one, son! Years later I wondered why an LSE student would be on the Knowledge.

Some people think you have to be a genius to be an examiner, but I have the memory span of a goldfish and I'm not exceptionally gifted at the Knowledge. I examined many people who were undoubtedly better at the Knowledge than I ever was, particularly on Points.

I don't think I'm being controversial in saying that female candidates were more likely to be held back by excessive nervousness. The whole environment was very male and macho and it must have been particularly intimidating for those who found the sharp end of the Knowledge uncomfortable.

One of the best candidates I examined was Vera. We all looked forward to her arrival when her name came up on our Appearance list. She was exceptionally good at the Knowledge and had a first class delivery. Steve Thomas and I commented on how her words were as calming and reassuring as the shipping forecast. I'd seen her once and gave her a high mark, a B I think. The next time with me she ran four Runs perfectly and only dropped one Point. She earned an A and only needed a basic C pass next time to complete the Knowledge and gain her Req. Unfortunately she came up against an examiner who gave her a D and failed her. She therefore had to try again three weeks later. Steve and I were horrified when we heard. I see her on the road occasionally, but not to talk to. She drives too fast and I can never catch her up. She didn't strike me as the type you'd find in a cab caff munching on a bacon roll. I'm sure she's a first class cab driver. I like to think Vera is the type to help old ladies with their shopping and see them safely across the road.

Nervous Req

The most satisfying part of the job is awarding a candidate their Requisition, indicating they have passed the Knowledge. A candidate who is three points away from his Req has already proved himself as most people would have dropped out long before this stage. Examiners expect great things from someone up for his Req, but it's up to the candidate to keep focussed right to the end. Examiners are not usually disappointed, but some candidates turn up expecting an easy ride having taken their foot off the pedal. I'd give quite complex Runs to a Req candidate, and if they were scoring well on the first three Runs, I'd often end with a gift: Run number one: Manor House Station to Gibson Square. I'd ask it straight like that, or I'd sometimes tease them a bit, while letting them know that they are home and dry:

"Take me from Manor House Station to… Where do you want to go to?"

"… Gibson Square, sir?"

"Righto, away you go…"

Virtually every Knowledge Boy on any stage will bang out this simple Run perfectly (try asking your driver the next time you get in a cab). If the candidate lived within the six-mile limit, I might ask him to take me to Gibson Square from the road he lived in. I would only be half-listening as I'd be underlining his appointment card with a red pen, and writing "Req." on it. After the candidate had set down safely in Gibson Square, I'd congratulate him and reach over to shake his hand. It isn't uncommon for candidates to shed tears when they gain their Req. I would feel quite moved myself.

I'd outline what happens next by way of his suburbs, as he'd need at least one more Appearance on his knowledge of the main routes outside the six-mile area. There wasn't much point in trying to impart detailed information as the candidate wouldn't be taking anything in, but I'd advise him to make sure he physically drove around Heathrow and City Airports before he gained his badge. A candidate won't be examined in detail on his knowledge of every little service road at Heathrow, but it's best to learn how to get in and out of the five terminals before you're driving passengers around for real. I only go to Heathrow about once a month and I still sweat with anxiety as I approach the airport, worrying that I'll panic with a coach behind me and miss the turn. I still congratulate myself every time I exit Terminal Four correctly and find my way back on the road to London.

The Suburbs

Not all candidates study for the green All-London badge. There's a yellow badge available for those who choose to study a suburban sector; for example Enfield, Croydon, or Barking and Dagenham boroughs. It doesn't take as long to study a suburban sector as it's a smaller area and the streets aren't so densely packed. We didn't all like examining suburban candidates as it took us out of our comfort zones. When we collected our files in the morning and there were yellow ones mixed in with the green, we knew we would be examining Suburban candidates. We'd often swap the yellow files with an examiner who was stronger on that particular sector than we were.

In an attempt to strengthen our grasp of the suburbs we were sent on "Out Days" every few weeks. An examiner would borrow a car from TfL and run a handful of suburban routes, just as we would if we were studying the Knowledge. We'd make the short, but fraught, tube journey from Southwark in the morning rush hour, and book a Toyota Prius out from underneath Victoria Coach Station. Top management said we weren't allowed to learn routes in our own cabs, probably because they thought we'd take a few fares when we're meant to be working. In the past, examiners had taken liberties on Out Days. We had to put down our mileage and timings, and not clock off until our normal home time of 4 pm. We'd write out the Runs and Points and put our findings in files for future reference.

We were allotted our own areas to learn. I was happy to take on Enfield and Hounslow boroughs. I like my food, and had visions of enjoying weapons grade curries in the Indian area of Southall, and taking regular luncheons on the golden mile of kebabs on Green Lanes in Haringey. As a day driver, I didn't often go into the outer suburbs. I thought Gordon Hill was a footballer from the 1970s, rather than an area in Enfield. Enfield Highway, Enfield Wash, and Freezywater, were mysterious places to me. Places, I'd fancy, where one might get chased by Tottenham fans should they not like the look of you.

Parking in curry-friendly urban areas was always tricky. I thought driving a car with TfL branding all over it would exempt us from parking violations – after all, we were Transport for London, we own the freaking place! But no, we were subject to the same rules as anyone else.

I never got my curry in Southall, nor did I did pick up many Points in Enfield. I do, however, know where to find a decent Yogurtlu Adana on Green Lanes. The suburban Out Days eventually ground to a halt: possibly because no one would take responsibility for washing the car and putting petrol in it. Well it did look like a minicab.

The Weird and Frightening World of TfL

Folk at TfL aren't encouraged to personalise their working area with comforting knick-knacks, and the rule was that examiners had to change rooms every week so we didn't get too comfortable and mess the rooms up with our hoarding of personal belongings. Consequently, the last twenty minutes on a Friday was spent wheeling cabinets on wheels – known as "dogs" – around, and arranging our maps the way we wanted them for the next working week.

I was fifty in 2012. There were plenty of examiners older than me, though I sometimes felt the more mature. It's possible that Nicola saw me as part of a new, modern breed of examiner. When our cohort of new examiners arrived we heard snippets about things that had happened in the past; events that had resulted in the six new vacancies that we had filled. We heard about rows, sackings, disciplinary hearings, and examiners walking out on their first day. Nicola was strict, but she had to be. She was responsible for a group of very strong characters: mature men and women who'd been around a bit. They weren't first-jobbers who could be moulded into a corporate way of thinking. They had life experience, and their own ideas about doing things.

Someone said I was Nicola's favourite. I don't know whether that's true – Jonathan Harvey reckoned he was her favourite too (that's right, grown men bragging over who is teacher's pet – very mature). She was said to have been a dental nurse before becoming a cab driver, but I never got to ask her about it. Knowledge Boys probably imagined us all chatting in our breaks, and between Appearances, but the workload was too heavy to allow us much time for socialising.

All examiners were required to hold an All-London cab licence. Cab drivers tend to be fiercely independent and resistant to authority. They don't like being told what to do, and aren't slow in showing it. As a cab driver, Nicola knew this, but she still had to pass down orders from those above. Nicola was in a difficult position, and had to adopt the role of headmistress. It makes me smile remembering the way she'd look pointedly at her watch if we were five minutes late calling our first candidates after lunch.

At team meetings Nicola would tell us how things had to be done in the future. The examiners resented her when she insisted changes were needed to practices that had been done the same way for donkeys' years, and they'd ignore her if any directives went against their own views. Disobedience was rife, and it could result in disciplinary measures. Before my time, Nicola had objected to an examiner who put the candidate's chair in an unorthodox position. The issue went all the way to a disciplinary hearing. This and other issues, caused resentment among some of the established examiners.

Nicola wanted to modernise. She wanted to reform the old conservatism and over-formal reverence. Nicola didn't see why candidates had to wear ties, and she wanted to make things less scary. She objected to me referring to the fourth floor as "the floor of fear." I joked that she'd like to bring in teddy bears and warm milk for the Knowledge Boys, but I later came around to her way of thinking and started to question the formality of it all. I got on all right with Nicola, and I felt sorry when I learned that she wasn't invited to the occasional after-work pub visits. She rarely examined candidates herself, but when I observed her, I noted she was a moderate examiner.

There are a lot of people at TfL who earn a lot of money. Many TfL managers earn more than the Prime Minister. Remember, Transport for London are nothing more than a publicly-funded transport provider. I never got to see the top people, and they wouldn't have known who I was. They never ventured down to the shop floor. I only knew who the main players were through seeing their pictures in *Taxi* magazine. They had a mystique around them. As with all corporate types, their aim was to maintain their position until it was time to move on to the next gig. The top managers would leave when things got too hot for them, as we saw later when their mistakes over Uber's licensing became exposed.

There was little scope for examiners to change things for the better. There were few opportunities for consultation with members of senior management, who weren't necessarily experts in anything transport-related. Their expertise was in general management. They had little idea of how the cab trade worked, or how to best run the Knowledge department. They were professional bureaucrats. Everything was dictated by the latest client-focussed trends imported from the USA and disseminated through Nicola at team meetings. Those above Nicola knew how they wanted things done. I was used to being programmed to accept new jargon and the latest trends in political correctness from my days as a Careers Adviser, but it was on a bigger scale here. My previous managers at Connexions would listen, and good ideas might be implemented. At TfL – forget it. Don't come to work at TfL if you have ideas and want to change things. Your creativity will be sapped and your individuality sucked out of you.

When the examiners had a good idea they'd take it to the manager. Nicola would send it upstairs and we'd wait for a response. Invariably we'd be told that they said "No." The people making the decisions would rarely come and speak face to face about anything, it was always through a middle-man, and it was typically a response with no explanation. Most TfL staff members got on with their work quietly, and didn't make waves. There were plenty more people who could be brought in to do your job if you didn't toe the line.

There was a cloying atmosphere of oppression about Palestra. When I'd previously worked in an office, people would go and sit on a colleague's desk with a coffee, or chat in the kitchen. There was too much formality and too little joy here. I was always nervous about talking to people from other departments, especially women. I was quite sure I'd find myself on a harassment charge should I say the wrong thing in the kitchen. When I had any contact with others I found them to be nice people, but they were forced to adhere to a strict regime. Socialising in such a work-focussed environment wasn't encouraged. The examiners occasionally arranged evenings in a pub, and staff from other departments sometimes came. TfL were too tight to arrange a Christmas party or drink-up. It was down to individual staff members to fund anything that might possibly result in fun.

One reason the examiners were so bolshie was that if they were rubbed up the wrong way they could go straight to work as a cab driver the same afternoon. The examiners enjoyed more autonomy than staff from other departments, and could make their own entertainment. The atmosphere between the examiners was in contrast to elsewhere in Palestra. The examiners tended to be older and louder than staff from other departments. They weren't on such a tight leash, and weren't afraid to put an ice cream down the cleavage of political correctness. I sometimes felt like I was on the set of the 70s TV comedy *On the Buses*. In the serious, right-on, world of TfL, the examination floor was an oasis of free speech, irreverence, and... fun. Practical jokes and comments were made all the time. It was most refreshing. Humorous notices were put on each other's doors. Someone would always be humming the theme tune from *The Sweeney* when ex-Flying Squad detective, Steve Thomas, went by.

Some examiners work part-time, and the part-timers often left personal belongings in their office after changeover day. Sometimes Jane Ayres's high heels would be visible in an open cupboard. One Knowledge candidate mentioned seeing the shoes in my cupboard on a Knowledge internet noticeboard. I found this observation most amusing, and for a few days had a notice up blaming the high heels on John Wilkin, suggesting he wore them on his Soho night outs.

We had freedom within the job, but we were aware that we were part of a larger machine. We couldn't criticise the regime. Resistance was futile.

As an organisation, TfL have no sense of humour, and I found it a strange place in which to work. There were no clocks to be seen: a disorientating tactic used by casinos to keep people on task. There were no calendars, but make no mistake, it was forever 1954 on the Knowledge floor. There were no phones on desks either. There were dedicated rooms with free phone lines. I wondered what would happen if you tried to make a call to an international sex line. I didn't try it though. You can be sure there's some TfL law against it.

End of Contract

For much of the year I was leaving and returning home when it was still dark. I was operating on autopilot, an unthinking zombie. I was permanently tired. One morning I closed the front door behind me without picking up my door and cab keys first. I therefore couldn't drive to the train station. I walked the four miles, and actually found it quite invigorating.

On another morning I dressed for work and hurriedly picked up a pair of shoes in the porch and put them on. When I got to London my feet didn't feel right. I looked down and discovered to my horror that I'd put on one black slip-on and one brown Dr Marten. I did the lace up on the

Dr Marten, but it looked ridiculous. I was the madman on the underground that day.

In the office I hoped none of my candidates looked at my feet when I called them into my room. If anybody noticed they never showed it, and I saw no comments on the Knowledge websites about the incident. At tea break, Dave Morgan, was the first to notice. Mind you, he used to be a Detective Chief Inspector and he's trained to notice stuff like that. Nicola seemed amused by it. I thought she might put me on a charge for bringing TfL into disrepute and send me out to buy a new pair of shoes.

The physicality of the morning commute was all right as it was completed before London had properly woken up. Leaving for home at 4 pm was more stressed. At Euston, hundreds of us would peer up at the departure board, ready to strike. As soon as the Northampton train flashed up, a big group of us would rush to the platform aiming to secure a seat when the train arrived. I'd usually get a seat, but occasionally I'd have to stand until a seat became available at Leighton Buzzard, half an hour away. I remember thinking that I couldn't carry on doing this for too many years.

I started to give myself an extra fifteen minutes in bed, but I was still struggling with tiredness. I'd now get up at 4.30 and would be out of the door in thirty minutes. My body never got used to the early starts though. I dreamt of the Knowledge and cab driving every night. In my anxiety dreams I'd always be in an embarrassing situation. I'd often get lost or break down. In one dream I couldn't find my way out of Victoria one-way system. Occasionally my cab would turn into a different vehicle such as a bus or a bike. One time I had to ride my passengers over a puddle on my taxi-cycle.

The dreams were less frequent once I left, but they remain common. In a recent dream I was driving a skateboard. I also couldn't find Belsize Square (there's a touch of reality in that one).

Driving the cab at the weekend didn't help my tiredness. Five months before starting work as an examiner I had bought a new cab on finance. I had to find around £1000 every month to keep it on the road. I therefore worked at least one day in the cab over the weekend in addition to my examining duties. After a few months I would often drive the cab into London, then work a couple of hours when TfL had finished with me at 4 pm.

I was on an eight-month contract, so as far as I was concerned, I would be back driving a cab full time before long. In the end I decided to leave a month early. It wasn't until after I put my notice in that I was told that my contract could have been extended. Had I known that I might have taken a long-term view and looked at other options, such as renting my cab out or moving further south.

I had vague ideas about becoming a writer, but I neither had the focus, nor the confidence to make a go of it. In my final weeks I wrote an article for a private hire magazine, in response to their claim that taxi drivers had a monopoly. That was my first published article. With a bit of pride and confidence behind me, I wrote another piece for a new Knowledge magazine called "Call Over". My piece went in their second ever edition and I wrote for them every month until I could no longer spare the time. Nicola had a word with her manager about my writing. I was told I might have to use a pseudonym, as TfL didn't want anyone criticising them in print, particularly their own employees. This added to my reasons for my leaving my eight-month contract a month early.

I had an attitude problem in my job as a Careers Adviser. I'm fiercely independent and I have problems with authority. But in my time at TfL, I found I could do my job well without giving problems. Let's just hope my next spell as a full-time cab driver would be trouble-free as well.

The other examiners were very kind to me when I left, and we had a drink-up at Doggett's by Blackfriars Bridge. It was nice that a few people from outside the examining clique came.

I was sad leaving the job I enjoyed. Stopped at the lights by Southwark Station I used to gaze up wistfully to the fourth floor at Palestra whenever I was passing. I settled back in full-time cab driving, but I missed my former colleagues and my examining work. I had to keep reminding myself of how tired and miserable I felt after all those early starts and the 140-mile round trip. I wouldn't rule out returning if my circumstances changed though. Nicola said I would probably be able to by-pass the recruitment malarkey should I ask to return while she was still manager. I wondered if I'd get to put that to the test one day in order to stage a dramatic return. She refused to name a bridge after me though.

10

Back on the Cab (Again)

One of the first jobs I needed to do when I left TfL was to return my badge and my piece. I was no longer a sheriff. This isn't as easy as you'd think as you have to get past the security staff at Palestra. Palestra's front-line are nice enough people when you take the trouble to see beyond the black-suited intimidation, but I had no luck with the Men in Black on Saturday morning, when I went to hand in a pack containing my laminated identity card and my staff Oyster Card. Although I'd been a staff member only a few days previously, my security man had to be strongly persuaded to take the pack to give to Nicola on Monday. TfL don't like strangers visiting their offices, and they're suspicious of folk handing in packages. They have a strict policy for everything. Complaining to TfL is not like taking a jumper back to Marks & Spencer's.

The Olympics

Of course, we had the Olympics to look forward to… I expect you thought the meter was running faster than Mo Farrar as we sprinted backwards and forwards to the Olympic Stadium? No, 2012 was one of the worst years for tourism many of us could remember. Opportunistic hoteliers hiked up their rates in anticipation of a bumper summer, but nobody came. Restaurants stayed empty. Generally, people kept out of London. As for the cab trade, we got royally shafted by those administering the traffic arrangements during the Olympics. I came home early on the opening day as there was so little work around. I caught the wonderful opening ceremony on TV featuring the Spice Girls cavorting on top of London taxis. It's a disgrace that taxis were exploited to provide iconic images of London while the real working taxis had been marginalised. We knew that VIPs connected to the Olympics would be chauffeured around in black BMWs. We had been warned to expect widespread road closures. Many cab drivers talked about going away on holiday. When we realised the extent of the disruption, some drivers got jobs as Olympic chauffeurs, which was probably the sensible thing to do. With few ordinary spectators going all the way to Stratford in a cab, we struggled to find work. Those customers we managed to scrape together found roads narrowed or closed, and many journeys were beset with problems. On at least one occasion I went home distraught half way through my normal eight-hour shift, as road closures had made it impossible to get around.

I saw little on TV after the opening day, and every time I caught a bit at a cab café there seemed to be an arse-kicking contest going on between two women in white towels. But it was the cab trade that got its arse kicked at Stratford. We saw few Olympic vehicles on the roads, but many empty lanes dedicated to them. As we sat and stewed in stationary traffic overlooking an empty VIP lane we didn't realise that in five years time, many of these lanes would be permanently closed and given over to cycles.

As an event, the Olympic Games were hailed as a great success. Putting aside the travel arrangements it was organised brilliantly, and the British athletes excelled.

Back to School

One day I discovered an email inviting me to have a chat about tutoring at the Eleanor Cross Knowledge School. I was interested and went along to see what they had in mind. I agreed to run a one-hour session a week.

At my first session I outlined my career to date, and my role as an examiner. I then took questions from the floor. The session was largely about dispelling myths on how candidates are examined and scored. I treated all questions seriously, though some questions were quite off the wall. They wanted to know if examiners discriminated against minority groups or women. I took satisfaction in telling my charges that everyone is treated equally. There's another question that's always asked. It sounds daft, but enough Knowledge Boys believe this old chestnut to make it worth clarifying. I was happy to put the idea to bed and say that examiners do not put a date in your file indicating when you'll get your badge.

In subsequent sessions we'd look at Runs on a theme: such as London squares, or bridges. I'd also offer mock Appearances. I would take those interested into a room and ask four Knowledge Runs as an examiner would. Invariably, the students would do well. This was sometimes contrary to their real Appearances at Palestra. Either they were being asked for ridiculous Points of Interest up at the Towers, or they were hampered by nerves once in the chair.

In the formal environment at Palestra there's little discussion. What the examiner says goes. There's a lot of emotion, and most of it is on the candidate's side. It could be a devastating day for the candidate, but a run-of-the-mill day for the examiner. The examiner puts it from his mind and calls the next punter. You just step over the chalk outline where the sorry cadaver of a Knowledge Boy had lain, and ignore the flashing blue lights and the crackle of DCI Morgan's police radio. Nothing to see here, sir. Move on. At the Knowledge school however, the examiner-turned-tutor is the focus of raw emotion. On this rare occasion, school subscribers were free to pick the brains of an ex-examiner, someone in the know. People were looking to me for the definitive answer. Students would sidle up to me at the end of a session and expect me to know why they didn't perform at their last Appearance. I had no answers to this. They seemed competent enough handling mock Appearances in a school setting, but would be full of self-doubt after they scored a couple of Ds up at the Towers. They were hard-working people who were good enough to pass the Knowledge. My only answer was that it's all about confidence, and as an individual you have to find your own individual way to handle your nerves and show the examiner what you know.

How to handle your nerves is a difficult one to answer. Emotions run high in the Knowledge world. Candidates put too much pressure on themselves, and this makes them nervous. Candidates feel anxious if they don't know every Point on the school's lists. Knowledge Boys look for patterns in the examiners' questions and try to build up a profile of the examiners. Sometimes it works, but candidates often waste time and effort chasing old questions instead of learning something new. Many Knowledge students compare themselves with others too much. Knowledge Boys and cab drivers can tell some whopping fisherman's tales, including exaggerations on how hard they work. Their stories are best taken with a pinch of salt.

Many candidates over-complicate things. Excessive use of online Knowledge forums can give you a sense of inferiority, and get you wound up over trivial matters. Knowledge Boys and cab drivers can spend hours discussing the best route, often arguing over things that don't matter. The Knowledge internet noticeboards are full of Knowledge Boys obsessing over shaving a few yards off a Run.

Many Runs asked for in an Appearance are based on the Blue Book of 320 prescribed Runs, and these are sometimes neglected in favour of chasing obscure Points. You need to concentrate on learning the bread and butter Runs, then focus on areas you're not confident on. Confidence comes from knowing you're working as hard as your individual circumstances allow. You need to accept that a person working a full-time job can't devote as much time to the Knowledge as someone who's given up work to study full time. As for feeling nervous, I'd remind people that it's just a bloke in a room asking you to show him what you know. I'd remind them that the examiners are fellow cab drivers, and they want you to succeed.

Tutoring at the school was very humbling. You feel the fear and pressure as an examiner, but I found being a tutor the most challenging episode in my cab-related career. The experience reminded me how seriously everyone takes it, and how it affects people. As cab drivers we always need to remember this.

You don't have to be Jewish to Work Here...

Friday wasn't a good day to run school sessions as many subscribers take time off to visit the mosque. The ethnic make-up of the cab trade has changed over the years. When I joined the trade it had a Jewish flavour to it, but that's fading. Although I'm Church of England, driving a cab kind of made you Jewish in those days.

Salt beef sandwiches are still available in the cab caffs, but I don't think the current drivers are very devout judging by the amount of bacon consumed.

These days, your driver is more likely to be Muslim than Jewish. Knowledge students include many men and women from Africa, Asia, and various other regions; including some countries I'm not allowed to visit due to the Israeli stamp in my passport. In the democratic world of the Knowledge, anyone can excel. At the school, there was a quiet, personable chap from Mongolia (I didn't ask whether he was from the Inner or the Outer part – not that I'd know the difference). I later examined him in an Appearance and he could find his way around London really well. Aziz from Afghanistan was one of several students I met who were better at answering Knowledge questions than I ever was.

Recognition

Knowledge Boys thrive on conspiracy theories and rumour. Whenever I met one of my old customers on the road, they'd often tell me the latest gossip they'd heard from their Knowledge school: what TfL were doing; which examiners were leaving; and the reputations of those who were joining. They try to find out as much about their examiners as they can, work their brains out, and try to second guess what questions they're likely to ask. Sometimes they knew more about the workings up at the Towers than I did, but often they were way off. One chap proudly told me he knew where all the examiners lived. He provided a few examples. I don't know where he got his information from, but it was nonsense.

It was always good to see my old Knowledge examinees on the road. They'd wave from their cabs, and say "Hello Sir!" at cab cafes. I met lots of my old customers on the day my cab broke down at Charing Cross Station. Hardly a day goes by without a smiling Arab or Somali beaming a "Hello Sir!" from his cab and touching his heart in respect. I was never really comfortable with the "Sir" bit, but had I met my old examiners on the street I would probably address them similarly. I was always a bit in awe working alongside John Wilkin, as he'd examined me for my re-licensing in 2010.

I could've done without the "Hello Sir" I received on one quiet August bank holiday. There was little traffic around as I swung into the top of New Bond Street from Oxford Street. Suddenly, the silence was shattered by a police car blaring out blues and twos close behind me. I pulled over to let it pass, then realised it was after me! At times like this, every dodgy thing you've ever done flashes through your mind: did he not like the way I scattered the tourists like pigeons who ignored the *Don't Walk* indicator at the junction? Was it the right turns I'd routinely been doing from Poland Street into Oxford Street? Or my occasional right turn from Spring Gardens into Praed Street?

As he indicated for me to pull up I knew that this was going to cause me some embarrassment. Any incident, however minor, could cause untold anxiety when I had passengers sitting inches away observing everything. Were my Middle Eastern gentlemen anticipating some authentic police brutality to film for Al Jazeera on their smartphones?

As the police officer started his "Hello Sir…" routine, familiar from TV reality shows, I thought he looked a bit familiar. Indeed, once my brain stopped whirring I felt sure we'd sat opposite each other before in an interview situation. Yes, another of my old customers from Palestra! I'd been spooked by a Knowledge Boy! Knowledge Boy or not, my policy is not to mess with London's finest, so I tamely said that it was nice to see him again. I'm not sure my passengers heard the exchange, but I laughed all the way to Harrods, hoping to give the impression that we Brits are so eccentric we even find it funny being stopped by the police.

Dog Section indeed – I'll set the cat on the pair of them.

Country Life

Towards the end of 2014, my wife and I decided to move. I'd been driving seventy miles into London from Northampton for over four years and it was becoming a pain. From time to time I'd think about moving back to London. I never did, and I probably never will. In my youth I would have loved to have lived somewhere fast and exciting like Soho. As a young adult I'd chose somewhere like Islington. I lived in Highbury for a while and that was nice; but any of those North London areas I had lived in were now out of my price range: Highbury, Stoke Newington, Stamford Hill, Haringey and Wood Green. I'd probably find Islington too raucous now I'm older. The wife and the cat wouldn't like it either. I'd now aspire to suburbs like Finchley, Golders Green or Hendon (if you're familiar with London, you might wonder if driving a cab really has made me Jewish in my tastes, already).

I'm ambivalent towards London. I recognise it as one of the great cities of the world, but I wouldn't choose to live there. It's overcrowded, and it's a bit full of itself. It's all about the latest trends and fads, and you are constantly push, push, pushing, towards the totems of success that always seem out of reach – particularly if you're spending two grand a month to rent a flat. It costs twice as much to live in London than in most other cities, and for what? You can't even get a seat in a pub any more – even on a Sunday. People don't move to London to relax or retire, and young professionals can no longer afford to buy their first homes here. London's great to visit, but you need a million to insulate yourself from all the crap. London is very hard work.

Many fashionable areas of London would be regarded as concrete shit-holes if they were in other cities. When I wore a younger man's clothes I much preferred bourgeois Islington over tatty old Camden Town. I don't see what's great about Dalston or Bethnal Green. There might be a nest of hipsters up every lamp post nowadays, but in my youth you'd only go to these mean inner-London districts if you wanted to get kicked into a canal by skinheads. I've never really understood the appeal of Shoreditch either, but then I'm no longer twenty-one. In modern parlance, I "don't get it".

Young people like the edginess of London, and middle class people can't see how dangerous some parts of London are. However many trendy wine bars mushroom up, I wouldn't walk around Ladbroke Grove Station at night. Plenty of people do though.

I share Mr Trump's disappointment at the American Embassy moving from Mayfair to Nine Elms Lane. Is it Battersea or Vauxhall? Wherever it is, it's yet another soulless area of development that's going to be an ugly mess of concrete and cranes for many years to come. Eventually it'll settle into being a soulless enclave of rich people, but without the cranes; rather like Imperial Wharf.

I always enjoy a day off in London, and although the wife says she doesn't like the place, she always enjoys our visits there. Unless we've just seen West Ham go down at home, and there's a replacement bus service on the Euston line. Or if Mo has experienced any worrying paranormal activity. Mo is very sensitive to the supernatural and often sees apparitions in the atmospheric old pubs we visit around the country. She brought a ghost home from the Coal Hole on The Strand. A man in black haunted the garden shed and would communicate through vivid dreams. When we left Northampton the ghost wished her luck and assured he'd be there for her if she needed him in the future (Ye Olde Cheshire Cheese on Fleet Street is simply creepy, no ghosts).

I'd enjoyed fifteen years in Northampton, but if I stayed in the cab game I'd want to be a bit further south. Feeling the chill wind of middle age I knew I would be happy in a rural location, or in a smaller town on the edge of the countryside. I stopped thinking about a move to London and started to research smaller towns. My tastes had changed over the years. I no longer strived to be an urban rebel, but a pillar of the community. I saw myself a bit like the village vicar, though with purple Dr. Martens on. I loved the idea of the rural idyll. The happiest part of my working day is when I cross the Hertfordshire county line on my drive home. As

I look across the sweet yellow rape fields I imagine a be-smocked farmer leaning on a pitchfork and chewing hay. Cows, sheep and bunny rabbits are gambolling; and ruddy-faced milkmaids are coming o'er the lea. Oh yes, my future was going to be one of sheepdogs, county fairs and scarecrow festivals. I got excited imagining clubbing together with the villagers to buy a cider press, or to run our own pub. I could confuse townies with crop circles and help to build the wicker man for May Day. You twisted Firestarter.

We couldn't afford to live in a village, so we decided on the Bedfordshire market town of Leighton Buzzard. I would save driving time and fuel costs by being thirty or so miles nearer to London. I shan't bore you with the details of the move, but the whole process of moving home has become increasingly traumatic each time. I found out why people say moving home is one of the most stressful things you can do. As an independent adult I used to enjoy moving around different areas of North London. When all your belongings fit into a small van there's no problem. By the time I moved house in Northampton it was like touring with Pink Floyd.

A Return to Examining

I'd felt a bit sad conducting mock Appearances at the Knowledge school over the summer. I missed the real thing. Now I was moving closer to London, the time could be right to stage a dramatic return to examining. It's not that easy though. Examiners don't give up their jobs lightly, and examiners who have left and later regretted their decision have found it virtually impossible to make a return.

Just before Christmas 2014, I phoned Nicola and asked if there was any way back for me. I was surprised to be told that there was likely to be a vacancy in six months time. She promised to contact me.In the New Year Nicola surprised me with a phone call. She said they were looking for temporary cover and could I cover six weeks? Of course I could! I dusted down my coffee mugs and my *Dead Hard Runs* book and made arrangements to re-join my old colleagues on the Floor of Fear.

11

Examiner 2

I was invited back as a temporary worker to cover staff shortages for six weeks. It took a few weeks to navigate the complexities of my contract with Hays Recruitment, who were brokering my placement. There was more paperwork and there were more questions than when I started as a permanent employee in 2011. My case was being handled from Leicester for some reason. I had to take documents into my local Hays office in Northampton, and in an endeavour to speed things up I also signed some papers at their Leicester office when I happened to be in that city on a day trip. I finally reported for work at Palestra at the start of March 2015.

Metal bollards had been placed around the hallowed Palestra building. They were erected after the riots of summer 2011. Transport for London leave nothing to chance. Walking around on different floors I noticed there were certain rooms into which access was forbidden. Some examiners said that all of London's traffic lights were controlled from these mystical rooms, and the integrity of the computers within had to be protected at all costs. If you've seen *The Italian Job* you'll understand that reasoning.

Living thirty-five miles nearer to London I allowed myself a bit more time in bed, but it was still an early start. I misjudged the traffic levels on my first day and I embarrassed myself by turning up forty-five minutes late. I was never late again, but I was getting up uncomfortably early every day. Had the job started at 9 am rather than 8 am I could have enjoyed an extra hour's sleep, but thinking about it later I realised that commuting an hour later in the morning peak would have been unbearable, whether I drove in or caught trains.

The traffic would be starting to build as I drove through Central London at 7.15, and I'd sometimes have to queue to get over Blackfriars Bridge. I was introduced to a car park under some railway arches off Southwark Street. A few of the other examiners parked their cabs there and it cost us £10 a day. At first I resented having to pay to park, but I later realised that it saved me time parking within walking distance of the office.

At 4 pm we'd all walk down to collect our cabs. We'd usually do a few hours work before going home. Mark Gunning and Kathy Gerrard tended to push it out until quite late, but a couple of hours graft was enough for me – just enough to get my diesel money to get home really. I liked to be home by about 8 pm, then relax for a couple of hours before bed. The next thing heard would be the dreaded alarm clock at 5.10.

Lunchtime

I started to bring in sandwiches for my lunch, but found it boring. I preferred to walk around a bit outside and get some air. The other examiners were less keen on visiting Capital Kebabs than I, though I persuaded a few of them along there for an occasional Friday blow-out. On Friday, we'd often go out and eat locally. We'd sometimes go to the pop-up eateries under the railway arches off Great Suffolk Street. It was a grim environment, but the food was invariably good.

I pondered on how London lunch culture had changed over the years. When I first started work in 1978 it was normal to go to the pub for an hour. I tried to continue in this vein as a Careers Adviser, but by 2010 going to the pub was frowned upon. These days, the few that ventured out of the office queued anxiously at the fashionable takeaways of the day, and fretted over how long it would take to make a Lebanese shawarma. The food was bolted before their meagre lunch breaks were up. It seemed joyless and unsatisfying to me. Time seemed less precious in earlier days, and I'd have time to sit down to a meal on a plate with proper metal cutlery. I was now reduced to eating out of a cardboard box with a plastic fork under a railway arch. This was the way that lunchbreaks were going in modern London. I found it most disturbing.

These days most people sit at their desks with salads, especially women. As if eating a salad in a stuffy office is healthier than getting some exercise outside. These salads and diet drinks aren't particularly healthy anyway. I also note that the diet-freak's daily cake and biscuit intake is never included in the calorie count.

Good to be Back

Starting as an examiner again felt good. In some ways it felt as I had never been away, but in other respects it felt different. The paper-based candidate files that we used to refer to had been phased out and transferred to computer files. It freed up storage space but it made looking up candidates more difficult, especially as the system went down so frequently.

One of my first tasks was to get authorisation to use the photocopiers. A department at Palestra can issue you with your identity card, but you have to make a phone call to activate it. I think the people activating the ID cards are based in Sheffield, though one examiner said they were in Croatia. I'd say the accent was more Yorkshire than Yugoslav. This took four weeks to sort out. Until my card was activated I had to ask another examiner to help me photocopy my examinees feedback sheets every afternoon. I did find TfL bureaucracy strange: I thought it absurd to receive a letter from TfL in Sheffield, signed by a person who sat yards away on the same floor.

Before I was allowed to examine candidates I had to sit in and observe other examiners. This was fair enough as I was rusty. The examiners who were recruited at the same time as me in 2011 were now old hands. One or two had blossomed into the popular stereotype of the grumpy examiner.

A few people had left in the period I was away. I wasn't surprised to hear that DCI Dave Morgan had left. I like to think he stormed off following a punk rock-style outburst, though he probably just got bored.

I'd been looking forward to seeing Nicola, but she was off sick. I wanted to thank her for facilitating my return to the examining fold, but she never returned. Dave Hall had been appointed temporary manager. This was good news for the candidates, as The Smiling Assassin now had little time for examining and was safely ensconced in a room on his own juggling paperwork.

A Moderate Philosophy

As we had to move rooms every week, we got to sit opposite different examiners. Paul Whitehead had joined the team in the three years I was away. He was a calming influence and I liked the cut of his jib. Before we saw our first candidates he always started the morning by saying how he wanted a nice peaceful day, with good candidates and no problems. I also started the day with optimism, hoping for a smooth run of candidates who had all worked hard and would all earn positive scores. I still try to carry Paul's optimistic approach with me in the cab.

Some of the other examiners expected the worst, and usually got it. Where Paul and I expected people to pass, other examiners presumed guilt, and sat poised with a red pen at the ready. I never liked to be grumpy or negative in any way. The people we were examining saw us as role models. We were all cab drivers and the candidates were working hard to do the job we were doing, and to be like us. I can identify with that. At my adult education college in Birmingham I was in awe of the university students drinking in the Varsity Tavern up the road. Before that I had of course looked up to cab drivers in a similar reverential way. I expect many Knowledge Boys also wanted to be examiners too, just like I did when I was sat on the other side of the table in the 1980s.

I remained a moderate examiner, but I had toughened up a bit. In the time I'd been away, I believed standards had slipped. Examiners noted we saw fewer Knowledge Boys on the road learning Runs. Many attended Knowledge schools, but too much learning was going on in the classroom, and not enough on the streets. Students relied too much on sharing intelligence on Knowledge forums. If they weren't sure whether a particular manoeuvre was legal, they would ask someone else rather than go and look for themselves.

It's true that you don't see Knowledge Boys out on their bikes like you used to. It's clear much of the studying is being done at home in front of a computer. The examiners made it their vocation to discover who the sit-at-home students were, and to penalise them accordingly. To score zero you need to fail to complete any of the four Runs given. In my second period as an examiner, several students scored zero with me, whereas only one or two people had performed so poorly three years previously.

If candidates answered my questions well, they would earn a good grade. Not all the examiners marked across the range. Some had never given out an A or a B in their lives. Giving difficult Points of Interest helped to prevent having to award a high grade, but I didn't believe in holding people back with unnecessary Points.

I started to turn against the overly formal and reverential Floor of Fear concept. Austerity and formality was what I'd experienced as a Knowledge Boy in the 1980s, but that didn't mean it had to remain so. Nicola had always favoured informality and I was coming around to her way of thinking. Others examiners might still refuse to see candidates inappropriately dressed – i.e. not wearing a tie – but I no longer considered it important. I discussed Dress Down Friday with Jonathan Harvey and suggested we dress more informally ourselves. He advised against any such involvement with dressing down, and added that other examiners probably wouldn't speak to us if we broke ranks and tried to modernise. I left my tie off for one Friday afternoon Appearance, but that marked the extent of my rebellion.

Office Move

There was a bit of excitement in May when the Taxi and Private Hire Department moved out of Palestra into a new office a few hundred yards up the road towards Blackfriars Bridge. It wasn't such a prestigious building, but it provided a more intimate environment. Feedback from the candidates was positive.

In the first few weeks of the move I enjoyed asking candidates to locate the Prince William Henry pub. I'd then point out the building just about visible through the window behind me. Having a window to look out of was a welcome luxury after Palestra, even if overlooking a pub made me want to go off for a pint.

Technology wasn't a big part of the job, but by 2015, virtually all of the candidates' files only existed on computer. Most examiners still conducted examinations in the traditional way, and followed the candidates' Runs with a length of string on a map. The tool of our trade was a box full of maps and A–Z atlases. The maps hadn't been updated for several years and some were now ridiculously out of date. The ones that existed were often falling apart and there weren't enough to go around. Another examiner suggested I buy my own. I didn't feel this was good enough. I'd been brought in as a temp for six weeks, and I was on less money than everyone else. Should I really be buying my own maps?

Pay Dispute

I started to realise how tight and how awkward TfL were. We didn't know it at the time, but the examiners who joined on short contracts in 2011 were paid less than those already established. Some of those underpaid examiners were now involved in a long-running pay dispute. They were continually fobbed off as TfL obstructed talks. As far as I know the dispute is continuing.

I was being paid even less as a temporary worker, and I enjoyed none of the perks the employees had. The permanent staff were entitled to free train season tickets from their home, a TfL Oyster travelcard for themselves and one other designated person, membership of a pension scheme; and they could buy into private health care if they wanted to. Of course, all employees also received paid holiday and sick pay.

Hays agency's policy was to review my pay after six months to ensure I was being paid the equivalent to everyone else. When my placement was extended I went through the temporary manager, Dave Hall, in order to request my pay be adjusted forthwith. In true TfL style I received a curt "No" from those upstairs.

When my review came up, Hays informed me that TfL had assured the agency that I was on the same money as the other examiners. This was nonsense as I was being paid less than the examiners I joined with in 2011 (as mentioned above, they in turn were being paid less than those who joined earlier). I should have pursued the matter, but I wanted to be taken on permanently and I didn't want to come over as an agitator. I didn't want to rock the boat, I wanted a job on it.

When I got my next pay slip I saw that my hourly rate had been raised by one pence an hour.

Towards the end of my tenure we all attended a conference for the whole Surface Transport Department. Listening to all the pompous rhetoric on how TfL value their staff I sat there with my coffee and biscuits brooding over my one pence per hour pay rise. Soon I would suffer the ignominy of applying for my own job.

Complaints Department

Few cab drivers think TfL are treating them fairly. All the examiners hold taxi licences and I think I speak for them all when I say that their loyalties lie with the cab trade rather than TfL. We all want to improve the cab trade, but the examiners are powerless to change anything. Our views count for nothing and decisions are taken regardless of what we think. We are all opposed to much of what our licensing body has done to the trade and to the roads of London. TfL's anti-car offensive has made life a misery for many who live or work in London. These decisions are made by people with scant knowledge of the cab trade, or the London driving experience.

A couple of examiners made it their business to take photographs of suspicious activity on the roads. Photos of out of town minicabs working illegally in London were sent upstairs with full details, in the expectation they'd be investigated. Invariably, the eagle-eyed examiners never heard anything more. We knew that if we did anything wrong in our cabs, they'd be down on us like a ton of bricks, but the department couldn't be bothered to investigate dubious activities presented to them on plate, or on mobile phone footage at least.

Part of the examiners role was to advise on customer complaints against cab drivers. Letters of complaint were shared out between us and we were tasked with assessing if the driver had taken a longer route than necessary or had attempted to rip-off the customer in any other way. In some cases the cab driver was clearly an idiot who should have been suspended, but in others, the customer was being unreasonable and didn't know what he was talking about. We'd write down what we'd expect the fare to be for the journey under discussion and state if we thought the driver was in the wrong or not. We were all striving for a better cab trade and we'd all say so if we thought the driver was at fault. In the majority of cases I'd say the customer had got it wrong.

In order to feel fully part of the machine it's necessary to see how all the cogs worked. Sadly, this wasn't TfL's philosophy. After sending the paperwork back upstairs I would've expected to hear back on how the complaints were resolved, but we never heard back.

The Times They Are a-Changin'

The examiners all had their idiosyncratic systems for following a Run during Appearances. I used a simple Blu Tack and string arrangement, featuring a large map, and a smaller *Knowledge A–Z* for close-up work. Mark Gunning favoured a huge map spread out over two lecterns. The double-lectern method allowed him to cover the extremities of North, South, East and West London. Anyone who'd been examined by Mr Gunning knows he likes to cover every corner of London, sometimes in the same Run.

Jonathan Harvey defied convention and laid his map flat on the desk. On days he was feeling rebellious he wouldn't use a map at all. Highly irregular.

Steve Thomas's working methods were only understood by himself. They featured coloured pens, strange coding, and bits of paper cut and pasted (not cut and pasted as on a computer programme, I mean actually cut and pasted).

Paul Whitehead used a complicated Heath Robinson-type arrangement of elastic bands, magnets, pins, bulldog clips and other plastic bits and bobs.

In my final days I went to have a word with Kate Chennels in her room. I was shocked with what I saw. Rather than cluttering up her desk with a huge map spread over a lectern, Kate was following candidates' lines on a... on a.. on a LAPTOP COMPUTER. This was the Knowledge equivalent of Dylan going electric. This would shock Planet Knowledge to its very core, and no mistake.

Unsurprisingly, Kate was appointed Knowledge of London Manager soon after her pioneering work. I hoped to be around to be part of the brave new world that brought the Knowledge into the twenty-first century at last. Sadly, I was never to see Kate plug her red Strat into a Marshall stack and carve out a searing opening to "Like a Rolling Stone". By this time my days were numbered, and it was me who was the rolling stone.

Thoughts on my Career

The job became easier. I didn't feel quite as tired as I did when I was commuting from Northampton, and this time around my sleep wasn't interrupted by dreams every night about the Knowledge, cabs, or one-way systems: I still dreamt of these things most nights, but not every night as before.

Early into my placement I broached the subject of my writing with Dave Hall. I'd been writing regular articles for two trade magazines and I wanted it to continue. Dave took the matter higher up. The message came back that while I was working at TfL I wasn't allowed to write anything for publication, whether cab-related or not. I found this ruling rather extreme.

With my fledgling writing career on hold, I considered examining to be a more secure career option. My placement had been extended beyond six months and was looking open-ended. Kathy Gerrard had asked if I missed my freedom. No, I could leave whenever I wanted to, particularly as a temp. I felt I would be exercising my freedom by staying as long as possible. I decided that I would like to make my career as an examiner, and hoped I'd be asked to stay on permanently the next time a vacancy came up.

The Beginning of the End

At a team meeting, Dave announced that an examiner vacancy was about to be advertised. I'd been doing the job for several months and was disappointed not to have been offered the permanent position outright. Disappointed but not surprised, as I suspected the managers would want to advertise the job externally.

Making an online job application is a complex business at TfL, and it has to be completed to strict specifications. They even tell you what font type to use on the application form. I emailed my completed application off and was eventually asked to sit a written assessment.

It seemed absurd to me. I finished my examining work early, then joined a room full of be-suited cab drivers ready to be assessed for a job I was already doing. Dave Hall advised me to put my suit jacket on so I looked the part. I found the assessment a bit easier than I did when I applied to join TfL some years earlier. The assessment's focus was on Knowledge skills, and I was considerably more accomplished this time around. It wasn't a pushover though by any means.

I was offered an interview a few weeks later and I worked hard on my preparation. I needed to prepare a presentation related to the Knowledge. I was satisfied with my presentation. I'm not a natural presenter, but I was happy with the content and delivery. The interviewers, Dave Hall and another chap, seemed satisfied.

In the actual interview there were a few general questions to break the ice before things got serious. Interviews at TfL aren't individually tailored and there are few opportunities for the interviewers to go off-piste and explore what people are all about. There is little emphasis on exploring whether the candidate can actually do the job or not. Questions are pre-set from above and give little opportunity for the candidate to shine. The questions are probably the same if you apply to be a bus driver or an executive. I had experience of actually doing the job, but the practicalities of the post weren't discussed. It was disappointing that I wasn't given the chance to outline my philosophy of examining.

The questions were longer and more abstract than the ones I answered at my first interview. They were so long that I'd sometimes forget the start of a question by the time it had finished being asked. I struggled with one particular question because I didn't understand it. I was asked how I "could influence stakeholders." I asked for the question to be repeated, but despite prompting, still didn't understand what I was being asked. The term "stakeholder" wasn't in common parlance at the time. I didn't know what a stakeholder was, and I didn't know how I might be able to influence one. And to do what? Who did I need to influence in my work as a Knowledge Examiner? Still, I'd say I performed a little better than I did back in 2011.

Taxi for Mr Ackrill

One afternoon I received an email from personnel informing me that I wasn't being offered the position. I felt humiliated. I'd done the job for seven months as a temp, and eight months before that as a permanent employee. I did my job well, I was never late, and took little time off. I was a model employee. I have my own ideas as to what happened, but basically I believe that the Hard Knowledgeers didn't want any moderate examiners on board.

I decided to see the few weeks out on my placement, but in my mind I had already left. Those last few weeks were painful. I no longer took my coffee breaks with the others and withdrew into my damaged shell. On the Friday I left I only said goodbye to a few people, including the two ladies in the admin department who had always been good to me. I left my official Knowledge of London examiner tie and laminated ID card in my drawer, and slipped out the back door never to return.

Running London's transport system is a colossal undertaking and a thankless task. People only notice when things go wrong, and it's impossible to satisfy everybody. Transport for London do a lot of great work, but I'm highly critical of the way they've handled road modernisation schemes. On a more personal basis, I resent them for the way I'd been treated in my time as a temporary examiner. They broke the rules and paid me less than the other examiners, then insulted me with a one pence per hour rise. I was finally forced to leave after my job was effectively given to someone else. This wouldn't have happened if Nicola was around.

I was pleased with my performance and attitude as an examiner. As a Careers Adviser at Connexions I had stopped believing in what I did, and when the job was de-professionalised I reverted to the naughty boy I was as a teenager. I wasn't sure I'd be able to fit into employment again, and to adhere to rules and responsibilities, but I managed it at TfL. I enjoyed the work and I liked and respected my colleagues. The examiners had pride in their work and never sold out their principles. I was still a cab driver and I had been given the opportunity to do my bit to ensure that the London taxi trade remained the best in the world. I consider it a privilege to have been one of a unique group of people. How many people in the world can claim to have been a Knowledge Examiner?

A return to examining looks increasingly unlikely now. I could have applied for a different role within TfL, but it wouldn't be the same. Soon after I left they appointed an additional examiner; someone who was interviewed during the same recruitment process as mine. I later heard that another had been appointed. I never got the call. They clearly didn't want me around.

In a strange postscript to my time at TfL, I later applied to be a Topographical Tester. In a belated attempt to tighten up on private hire licensing, TfL decided to bring in geography tests for minicab drivers. I took an initial online assessment for the role. I had to put patterned boxes in order in some kind of logic test. What this has to do with finding your way around London I don't know. I failed it.

12

The Years of Change

Recession in the cab trade was biting hard now. Twenty years ago, if you dropped off at Waterloo in the late evening you'd see a line of people trying to flag you down on Waterloo Bridge on your way back to the West End. Now you could easily drive a mile further up to Euston and back again without a bite. The run-in to Christmas 2015 was poor. The traditionally slow Kipper Season of January to March 2016 was predictably difficult, and it barely improved as the year progressed. I was earning less than I was when I went back to the trade in 2010.

One thing London taxi drivers don't ask for when times are hard is higher fares. Trade had been depressed for several years, and fares had only been raised by a very small amount each year, or sometimes by nothing at all. We are realistic enough to know that higher fares put people off. Cab customers aren't captive like train commuters. They have options.

It's not that there are too many taxi drivers either. Driver numbers have risen little over the years. Many drivers are part-time, and they were staying out longer to make up their money. Weekend work used to pay better because there were fewer drivers around, but Saturday or Sunday became as poorly paid as a Monday, only with more road closures to contend with. Much of the competition was coming from the unrestricted licensing of private hire drivers, and powerful global players exploiting loopholes in taxi and private hire licensing law, such as Uber. More about them later…

The Cycle Superhighway and Other Crimes

Toxins from vehicle emissions were killing Londoners in their hundreds annually, and with increasing concern over road congestion and pollution, cycling was promoted as a green alternative. Now concerns were increasing over the number of cyclists killed on the roads. TfL's misguided response was to step up the rolling out of "road modernisation" schemes.

Many roads carrying two lanes in each direction were narrowed down to one – or one and a half. The rest of the carriageway was marked out for cyclists, sometimes with protective kerbing. In 2016, the controversial Cycle Superhighway opened East–West from the Tower of London to Westminster. This essential thoroughfare is used by commuter coaches from Essex and Kent, and has traditionally taken the weight off busy streets such as The Strand, Fleet Street and Cannon Street. The Cycle Superhighway is now congested for most of the day; and often well into the night, and at weekends.

At the western end of the East–West Cycle Superhighway, the innocuous left turn from Victoria Embankment on to Westminster Bridge was banned. There are no warnings, and the alternative isn't signed. Motorists with up to date sat navs realise that you have to turn right onto Horseguards Avenue, take another left into Whitehall, then a left onto Bridge Street and forward on to Westminster Bridge. If you get as far as Parliament Square on the Cycle Superhighway, you have to turn right onto Bridge Street, then drive around all four sides of Parliament Square to come back on yourself. It takes five to ten minutes to complete this manoeuvre. How much extra fuel is pumped into the air with these pointless diversions? How much time and money is wasted? You also have to be aware that Whitehall and Parliament Square are often closed off at the weekends for demos.

Many roads were being narrowed by having paving laid down the middle. This prevented an exit route on roads like Regent Street, where cabs could no longer make U-turns, and where emergency vehicles struggled to get through densely-packed traffic. If a taxi stops on Oxford Street to set down a passenger and process a credit card, the buses now have to sit behind you for a minute or so. The paved centre strip down the centre of Regent Street and The Strand encourages pedestrians to cross where they shouldn't, and provides a dangerous alternative route for cyclists and motorcyclists in a hurry.

I think ill-advised road modelling is as much of a threat to the cab trade than Uber and their ilk. A taxi meter runs on a combination of time and distance, and when a cab is caught in stationary traffic the meter still ticks over, albeit at a slower rate. A £10 fare can easily become £15 or even £20. No cab driver likes to get caught in stationary traffic, but it happens more and more. It's embarrassing asking for a large amount of money for what should be a short journey. Sometimes you want the road to open up and swallow you, you really do.

London is a complex city to drive around, and the authorities make it all the more difficult for those brave souls who attempt it. Some bridges are congested for most of the day since remodelling (narrowing). The Blackfriars area has become a complicated mess of car lanes, bus lanes and cycle lanes. At a junction, a driver would reasonably keep positioned on the left when turning left; but some left lanes have become contraflow cycle lanes. The hapless motorist making a hard left would now be confronted by a lane full of oncoming cycles. Different forms of transport have been given their own dedicated traffic lights. Pedestrians have their work cut out trying to judge when it's safe to cross the vehicle and cycle lanes controlled by separate lights. There are some sharp turns in the Blackfriars area, and accidents are averted only by motorists, cyclists, and pedestrians, all obeying their dedicated lights. People have already been killed here. Many cyclists campaigned for segregated lanes following some horrific accidents at junctions, but if I were a cyclist I'd find many of these new schemes complicated and dangerous.

At Blackfriars, a sign says it should take seven minutes to cycle to Tower Hill. Following extensive time trials set for this book, I conclude that this short journey averages around fifteen minutes in a cab. It isn't much better at the weekend. I have driven it in six minutes, but on a particularly quiet Sunday morning. This just isn't right.

I subscribe to few conspiracy theories, but I do believe that many of those controlling London want to eradicate motorists from London completely. They just want cyclists and buses on the roads, and they are making the driving environment as hostile as possible. They know we'll all be driving electric vehicles eventually, and it won't matter to them if we're all sat in stationary traffic all day.

Whatever you think about cycle lanes, while they exist, you should respect them, as they do help to keep cyclists safe: they should not be used by motorcyclists, or by drivers of the Number 3 bus taking a rest parked in Jermyn Street. Sometimes though, cycle lanes are absurd, and it's virtually impossible not to drive into them. One of many examples I can provide is on the Outer Circle, Regent's Park. Going anti-clockwise you have little choice but to ignore the cycle lane to get past a queue of vehicles aiming to make a right turn at York Gate. I try to respect cycle lanes, but in these cases common sense prevails.

Some important roads had been closed over the last few years, including a useful through route through Tavistock Place in Bloomsbury, which used to take some of the weight off the perennially congested Euston Underpass. A few years previously, Camden Council banned the left turn at Marchmont Street that affected traffic heading towards King's Cross and St Pancras Stations. Traffic now had to make a longer route to these busy stations. In November 2015, they closed the route west through Bloomsbury. In both cases, vehicles had to stay on the road longer, resulting in artificially manufactured traffic congestion and extra exhaust fumes. Bloomsbury is a pleasant and leafy area of Central London, but has become choked with traffic that doesn't need to be there.

Plans for the City of London to ban taxis from Bank Junction resulted in a series of demonstrations by cab drivers in the New Year of 2017. When Cannon Street is closed for any reason, what then? Your sat nav is not going to get you out of trouble. Indeed Cannon Street has been closed for two long periods since the closure of Bank Junction. During closures you are confronted by cones blocking the road, and signs warning that you can't drive through the junction. The common sense decision would have been to open up Bank Junction, at least temporarily.

Other damaging closures are planned, including restricting the major Central London thoroughfares of Tottenham Court Road and Oxford Street. Whenever you see a long line of red buses crawling along Oxford Street, think where they might go to should the mayor successfully close the Oxford Street as he said he would.

Finally, have you noticed that as the roads have become progressively smaller, vehicles have become progressively bigger? Look at how much bigger fire engines, ambulances, refuse collection vehicles and police vans have become over the years. An ambulance used to be the size of a Transit van. It's now a huge green and yellow monstrosity that looks like a Morrison's delivery truck, only noisier.

Credit Cards

On holiday to Majorca I didn't consider myself negligent for failing to research the island's transport payment requirements before boarding a bus to Palma, but a visitor to London would be ridiculed for not knowing that you can't board a bus with cash. TfL go on endlessly about customer choice, yet they won't let you pay for a bus ride with cash.

TfL then decided to dictate how we ran our businesses. In 2016, around 40% of London taxi drivers accepted credit cards. Before TfL made credit card acceptance mandatory in October of that year, we'd often be asked to stop at a cash machine. This wasn't an ideal situation for either party. The customer would need to pay whatever the meter ticked over while he queued at the machine, and the driver often had to worry about stopping on a busy road with parking restrictions.

I'd been able to process cards through the Computer Cab system for the previous five years. I wasn't asked to process cards very often because the public didn't expect cab drivers to have card machines installed. It served me well while I was part of a minority. On more than one occasion a hotel doorman would wave me in past a rank of empty cabs and load me up for a lucrative ride to Heathrow. I also got "roaders" to Oxford and Reading from the rank at St Pancras International Station on credit cards.

It's positive that the public now know they can pay by card, but there was quite a fuss at the time. Firstly, a credit card payment isn't legal tender and there is no compulsion to accept it under UK law. TfL are so arrogant they think their own laws trump UK law! (Incidentally, cab drivers can insist on the exact money: there is no compulsion to give change). Many drivers didn't want to be forced into agreements with finance companies, and they weren't happy about paying a commission for the privilege. None of us liked the idea that finance companies were profiting at our expense and effectively taking a cut of the metered fare. As the demand for card payment increased we also found ourselves maintaining a printer and buying over-priced rolls of receipt paper.

Business had always been a simple matter of taking cash and giving change as appropriate – and scribbling out a receipt on occasions. Credit card payments can be corrupted, systems can be hacked. We were open to a myriad of nefarious activities. Many of us mistrust technology. We know from driving our cabs that the more technology there is, there's more that can go wrong. And if a credit card machine fails, the driver can only get help between nine and five, Monday to Friday.

A lot of drivers hire their cabs, and even before the mandate, cabs sometimes came supplied with a card reader by the garage. Owner-drivers (Mushers) were threatened with having their card machines taken away by the finance company if they weren't being used enough, and pressure could also be visited upon the rental driver (Journeyman) through the garage who provided the card reader (this would put particular pressure on part-time drivers, of which there are many thousands). If the driver wasn't interested in processing cards the popular remedy was to put a plastic bag over the card reader and pretend it's out of order. Rather like Del Boy with the parking meters.

TfL were unnecessarily prescriptive by ordering us to install card readers in the passenger compartment. I had a hand-held reader sitting with me in the front. I'd pass it through the gap in the partition and the passenger would tap in his details. It worked fine, and if there were any problems I could deal with them at my end. Drivers complained that should they get into the back to look at a faulty reader they would open themselves up to all kinds of issues, particularly with lone women.

In order to publicise the taxi credit card revolution, TfL spent a king's ransom on posting out a large pack to every taxi driver in London. The pack contained four stickers and instructions on their use – you can't put notices up where you like in a cab; everything has to be approved and put in their prescribed position. We noticed that only four finance company logos were featured on the stickers. We wondered how the lucky four were chosen. Was a deal made with TfL to advertise? If so, would TfL be gaining advertising revenue at the drivers' expense?

There remains an issue over who pays for the service. Companies don't supply banking facilities and card reading machines for free. At one time I was forced to charge card customers an embarrassing 12.5%. We could no longer charge a fee to our customers, so it was the driver who was charged. The fee varied on which supplier we went with. Our argument was that we shouldn't be charged for making payment more convenient for others. However, it would make us more competitive when word got around that all London taxis accepted credit cards, so the issue of fees faded.

Looking at the pros and cons, I tentatively welcomed the move towards credit card acceptance as it was becoming expected by potential customers, and people now had the confidence to hail a cab without cash. I'm also glad that I now rarely have to wait at cash machines. I'm still not sure how someone pays by tapping their phone on my credit card reader, mind.

Political Correctness

Transport for London's Taxi and Private Hire department act as a licensing body, but they are also prone to censorship and applying political correctness. In 2017, some drivers started displaying the Licensed Taxi Drivers' Association (LTDA) publication *Taxi* on the back shelf of their cabs whenever it carried a prominent headline about our Uber friends. There have been plenty of headlines: the Cameron government pressurising Boris to leave Uber alone, Uber drivers implicated in terrorist attacks, and the shocking Uber-related sex crime figures that few people wanted the public to know about. Factual reports, but unpalatable to those charged with the responsibility of doing something about them.

It's good that TfL had expanded their army of enforcement officers, but they took things too far when they accused a driver of having "unauthorised signage" and removed a copy of *Taxi* from the back shelf of a cab on Harrods rank. They felt the headline "Rapist Uber Driver Jailed for 12 Years" was "misleading" and "not TfL's belief!" The headline was a fact, so not open to the charge of being misleading. The driver was effectively accused of not agreeing with the opinion of two TfL enforcement officers. TfL backed down in their threat to suspend the driver's licence.

TfL spooks are either known as enforcement officers or compliance officers in the media. I'm not sure which title is correct, but both sound rather militaristic and scary: what are they enforcing? What must we comply with: the opinions of TfL staff?

During this period, President Trump and Kim Jong-Un were swinging handbags over North Korea's nuclear rocket tests. When you think about it, North Korea and TfL are quite similar: both regimes have delusions of grandeur, and both supress free speech within a totalitarian state. Both regimes have far reaching tentacles. For a London transport licensing body, TfL have some strange outposts. All London cab drivers receive TfL documents originating from Sheffield. As a Knowledge Examiner I had to make phone calls to Sheffield to get clearance to use the photocopier. And it took a suspiciously long time to get security clearance and finally obtain my laminated identity card (007: licensed to print A4 sheets in black & white). If TfL operate out of Sheffield, why not further afield? Maybe they have an office in North Korea?

I wondered if anyone had heard from the harassed Harrods driver since this sorry incident. Perhaps he was whisked away to Pyongyang under the cover of darkness to undergo interrogation and brainwashing? I imagined grainy images of the arrested driver being shown on North Korean TV. In a stilted voice, and with a glazed expression, he could warn others thinking of displaying subversive publications on the back shelves of their cabs. Following ideological re-education he could be transported back to London to have his memory skilfully wiped by James Bond villain-type scientists. He would then be free to take his place as a servant of the regime. He might even be turned into becoming an enforcement officer himself.

There are cab drivers you see in the caffs who suddenly disappear. Perhaps they've retired? Perhaps they've gone to the great cab rank in the sky? Or their disappearance could point to something more sinister. Some of them were prone to express subversive opinions on the regime. I've said a few things about my licensing body so I'd better be careful what I say. I sometimes imagine I feel the presence of TfL spooks watching me from the shadows as I put the bins out.

Following the Harrods incident, drivers were even more aware of the advertising opportunities their back shelf provided, and it became standard practice to display newspapers and magazines with contentious headlines. The media continued to supply headlines on the shortcomings of Uber, and the LTDA ad-van was driven around to spread warnings of Uber even further. Transport for London's censorship had seriously backfired.

Cross-Border Hiring

It's understandable if nobodyoutside the cab trade has heard of cross border hiring. Any member of the public would reasonably expect all taxis and private hire cars to be only operating in the geographical areas they are licensed in. The idea that drivers licensed in one area are working in another area sounds both crazy and illegal, but it is happening all over the country, particularly in the private hire sector. Following deregulation, drivers who found it hard going in their own town, simply went to work in another town in which trade was perceived to be better. Drivers could even have had their licences revoked in one area, then gain a new licence in another area.

Usually, drivers licensed in smaller towns work in bigger towns or cities, though we also see large numbers of private hire cars licensed by Transport for London working in towns and cities such as Bristol, Birmingham, Brighton and Southend.

The satellite towns around Merseyside had drawn chancers in to Liverpool for many years. In December 2016, Knowsley Council suspended issuing new taxi licences after being swamped by applications. The council was receiving twice as many applications as they would normally expect. The suspension was only for fourteen days, but Knowsley Council were left scratching their head as to the reasons for such a surge in demand for licences. They didn't need to look far. Knowsley's sudden popularity was down to the council's lifting of the "Street Knowledge" section of the application process, and by the deregulation that allowed taxi and private hire drivers licensed in one area to work in another.

Word had got around the taxi and private hire world that drivers were free to work wherever they like. All you had to do was identify the licensing authority with the slackest regime and apply there. With the borders down, Transport for London unwittingly became a national licensing centre for private hire, supplying minicabs to the whole of the country. It's worth remembering that a London private hire licence also serves as a Congestion Charge season ticket.

Customers had been attacked after getting into "local" minicabs, unaware they were licensed in towns many miles away from the town in which they were booked. London-licensed Uber cars were operating everywhere, and were hard to spot as London minicabs are un-plated and carry few identifying marks. The tiny London private hire sticker is virtually unreadable, and often obscured by tinted glass.

It came to light that 177 private hire drivers residing in Sheffield were licensed by TfL in London. Over six months there had been a 330% rise in TfL private hire licences for drivers with a Sheffield address. In addition to the London licensed drivers, there were 400 private hire drivers with Sheffield addresses licensed by Rossendale, near Blackburn. Drivers were coming into Sheffield from many other places, including Wales.

Sheffield Council did nothing wrong. They tried to run a tight ship, only to have it overrun by pirates from foreign lands. Their reward was to be flooded by drivers who'd gained licences where the regulations were lax and where there were no restrictions in numbers, notably London. The situation was grim for genuine Sheffield drivers, and for the cab-riding public who might reasonably expect to be driven around by a local expert accountable to the local licensing authority.

Safety and standards were out of the window because Sheffield Council had no enforcement powers over drivers who are licensed elsewhere. An authority cannot carry out checks on vehicles or drivers that are licensed elsewhere, even when they are operating in their area.

In January 2017, Southend Council discovered that two minicab drivers it had banned for sharing penalty points with other drivers were back working in the town. They had simply applied for licences in London where TfL had earned the reputation as a soft touch.

In Southampton and Brighton, taxis and minicabs licensed by the council are required to have digital CCTV cameras fitted to their cars, at the driver's own expense. Southampton is now flooded with Uber cars licensed elsewhere. Drivers who were working, but not resident, in Southampton had no compulsion to adhere to local licensing rules and were saving £700 on a CCTV system.

I've lived in the small town of Leighton Buzzard since 2015, but I've little idea of what goes on past the train station. I won't be doing any cross-border work here. If I had to drive a cab here I would have no idea. You don't soak up the geography of a town just by living there; not for cab driving purposes anyway. The area needs to be studied and experienced. You need to learn every main road, every suburb, and every main route in and out of town to have any kind of acceptable working knowledge.

TfL either can't, or won't restrict, PH licences. It's absurd that they can totally transform London's road system as they see fit, yet complain that they need an Act of Parliament to restrict minicab numbers. London mayor Sadiq Khan claimed he'd asked for permission to cap private hire licensing, but was ignored by the government. Perhaps he did, perhaps he didn't?

Embarrassed by their reputation as the go-to authority for a quickie licence, TfL put up hurdles to try and stem the tide: things that the public should expect as standard; such as topographical testing, and a good standard of English. Whether or not licensing will slow down with the English language tests, who knows? When they're all speaking like Nigel Havers we could all be in trouble.

The War on Diesel

By 2017, the war on diesel was well underway and the eco-friendly tanks were rolling through the suburbs. The Mayor announced he was planning to charge cars over eleven years old £10 to enter Central London. The so-called "T-Charge" was introduced in October 2017. The previous Mayor, Boris Johnson, had already said that no new taxis would be licensed from 2018 which weren't close to zero emission. All cab drivers could do was look on in frustration. We only had two vehicles to choose from, and they were both diesel-powered. A Euro 6 compliant TX4 was available, as well as the Mercedes Vito van conversion – known in cab circles as the "Bread Van". From January 2018, neither the TX4 nor the Vito could be bought new. A new electric cab was launched and would represent the only new vehicle option at the start of the New Year.

Years ago we were encouraged to buy diesel vehicles, and this was incentivised by Gordon Brown of the Labour government. A car is a big investment, and a diesel car is what we were told to buy. A third of the population are living in in-work poverty, and many people can't afford to change up. I can't either.

At one time, the carbon dioxide emitted by petrol engines was held responsible for global warming. We then stopped hearing about global warming, and it was emissions from nitrogen oxide in diesel that was cited as the new evil. Had the taxi manufacturers known that before the diesel backlash they might have switched to petrol engine cabs – which were available in small quantities when I started out in the 1980s.

I always suspected diesel was dodgy though. I bought my TX4 (Euro 4) cab from new in 2011, but was alarmed at the amount of smoke that the greenest and cleanest London cab emitted. On its first two annual inspections it failed on the emissions test. My cab passed its next five tests after I added a bottle of Redex diesel treatment on the day before its inspection. If there's an additive available that cleans diesel, maybe the problem is with the fuel we are sold rather than the actual engine?

Diesel cars were still accounting for nearly half of all new sales in 2017, and drivers of most commercial vehicles had no choice in the matter. So, it's annoying hearing people on radio phone-ins clamouring for more fuel duty to be levied on diesel. We don't hear so much about those nose to tail convoys of red monsters dieseling along Oxford Street and Regent Street.

Early in 2017, the London mayor expressed concern over the air quality near schools. I find it ironic whenever I see a school bus. It's always the oldest, dirtiest, buses that sit idling by the school gates waiting to transport kids around.

Whenever the subject of air quality comes up, we hear experts telling us we should be walking and cycling to work, as if we all live in Mayfair. Are they so out of touch they don't realise most people working in Central London live in the outer suburbs, or outside London completely? Even if I had somewhere to park my cab in London, I couldn't cycle in from Bedfordshire, and if I cycled three miles to the train station, a train season ticket would cost a lot more than my diesel does. Even if you have an office job in the City and live next to Harrods, a bike's impractical if you're carrying anything bigger than a sandwich box.

The taxi situation was absurd. In 2017, there were no electric cabs available, and one solitary rapid charging point for electric cars in Central London. We knew nothing about electric cars, or how they might work. Would I be able to drive thirty-five miles into London, cover another sixty miles; then make the return journey home without recharging? What would I do if I ran out of juice? How would I charge a cab anyway? Run a lead through the letter box and hope next door's cat doesn't show any interest?

One reason why it took so long to introduce an electric taxi was because of the twenty-five feet turning circle requirement. Manufacturers were nervous about committing a new vehicle for such a niche market as taxi production. Our private hire competitors could chose whatever production car they wanted, and they could promote their green credentials with a hybrid or a fully electric car. With taxis outnumbered by many thousands of minicabs, I'd say it's private hire drivers that should pay over the odds for a car with expensive specialisms such as a twenty-five feet turning circle. And wheelchair ramps come to that. All this adds considerably to the price of a new taxi.

I don't fully trust electric or hybrid cars. They sound too quiet, as if nothing is happening under the bonnet. I'd worry they were going to cut out when stationary at traffic lights. I've driven enough cabs to know that when your cab develops a problem, conking out is a very real possibility (cyclists and pedestrians don't like electric cars either as they can't hear them coming. Incredibly, future electric vehicles are mandated to have noise built into them).

The government were also concerned about pollution from wood-burning stoves. Personally, I don't know anyone with a wood burning stove, either at home, or fuelling their cab. I don't think the Carriage Office would allow that, though I think I saw something like it on *Top Gear* once.

Launch of the Electric Revolution

From January 1st 2018, no new diesel-powered taxis could be sold for use in London. In preparation, the London Taxi Company changed its name to the London Electric Vehicle Company (LEVC) and opened its order books for its new range-extended electric taxi.

The taxi trade was underwhelmed on its unveiling. It was an impressive vehicle, but there were two big issues: the price tag, and battery charging. When the price tag of £55,599 was announced, the trade were not impressed. Sixty grand is only the half of it: with 90% of drivers relying on finance, the real cost, spread over four or five years, was staggering. 2017 was the worst year most of us had ever experienced in the cab trade, and we couldn't see how we'd ever get our money back.

On one hand TfL acknowledged the lack of charging facilities; but on the other they were forcing us to buy electric cabs. At the time of the new cab's launch, there were still no rapid charging points in Central London. There weren't even many slow ones.

There's a gap in my education, and I've no idea how electricity is produced. The National Grid said we were becoming increasingly reliant on imported electricity. I didn't know electricity was something that's transported around Europe on a lorry – and no doubt by foreign-owned companies. In Brexit Britain, I don't like the sound of that. Transport for London research is reported to have said that Britain would need up to twenty new power stations to service the electric vehicle revolution. It'd take more than a few fields full of plastic windmills then?

If a taxi is unable to complete a roader for fear of running out of electricity, our private hire competition will surely oblige. As yet, neither the private hire industries, nor buses, have any obligation to switch to electric. New motorways no longer have a continuous hard shoulder, but they could have been useful for proving sanctuary to vehicles caught short of electricity.

The move to electric vehicles is exciting, but it will take aeons to replace every diesel vehicle. During the long transition period we will surely see the number of charging points increase, though I don't know where they will find the space in London for the necessary number of bays. Local authorities don't want charging bays taking up valuable road space on city streets, as those spaces bring in money through parking fees. We'll also see a decrease in the number of conventional fuel stations. There could come a middle period where neither electric nor diesel drivers find adequate refuelling facilities.

The idea of a scrappage scheme for older taxis was put forward, but the benefits would be negligible. A new taxi is out of the pocket for most of us. Consequently, there is considerable demand for used taxis, and they are worth more than Mayor Khan would give us to scrap them. The trade needed bigger incentives. We'd all like to go green; we just can't afford it at present.

One factor that's not talked about much is the government's interest in going electric. Most of the price of a litre of diesel goes to the government in tax. If everyone goes electric, the government will be losing a lot of revenue. Tax revenue is the reason why the government keep people drinking, smoking and gambling. Keeping people alive too long is expensive. All they can do is keep making money out of people while hoping they die an early death. Electricity prices will rise, and so will the tax on that electricity. At about the same time as the launch of the electric cab, the UKs biggest energy supplier, British Gas raised their electricity prices by 12.5%. In the spring of 2018 it was announced that British Gas customers on dual-fuel tariffs were facing an additional 5.5% rise. Following hard upon that, npower announced a similar rise. As I was putting the finishing touches to this book in July, EDF announced a 6% rise for its dual-fuel users. This will affect 40% of its customers.

Are higher prices and taxes the way forward? I think so. We have little choice but to use electricity in our homes. If our vehicles become dependent on electricity they will have an even bigger mandate to charge us what they like. Then again, maybe we should think further ahead and forget about the electric car revolution completely. Aren't we meant to be calling up self-driving pods in a few years time?

Driverless Cabs

Non-cab driving friends often taunt me that self-driving taxis are on their way. I laugh off their claims. Even if taxis and minicabs were replaced by self-driving machines, would the public have enough confidence to travel in a cab with no driver? And has the personal touch been underestimated?

Human interaction is continuously being factored out of daily life through technology. Look at how few tills there are in your supermarket, and how we are encouraged to use the self-scanning facility. Apart from the frustration at being continuously told you've put your shopping in the wrong place, or have got the wrong bag, I find the whole experience depressing and impersonal.

I worry about the redundant staff who make room for the machines. Who benefits from replacing humans with robots? In classic Marxism, those who own the means of production own the power. It's highly unlikely that the remaining supermarket workers' wages have been raised through savings made on laying off those replaced by machines. You can be sure that the profits made go straight to the shareholders.

Uber's move towards driverless minicabs shows their intention to lay off all their drivers ASAP. The technology might be there to run cars around racetracks and on empty roads in California, under strict supervision (a driver), but I can't see driverless cars on regular city streets. There's no room, for one thing. In early 2018, a pedestrian was killed by a driverless car being tested by Uber in Arizona. There was a "driver" on board too. Uber suspended the project.

Many people rely on driving as their career, and there would be many thousands of people out of work. A driverless car would have to wait its turn at junctions, and wouldn't have the judgement of a human driver. Who gives way on a single-track road? Would a driverless car know that Savoy Court is the only road in London where you drive on the right? Would any resentful cab driver let a driverless Uber car out of a junction?

Let's look at other modes of transport. There are no conductors on London buses any more and no cash changes hands. We hardly notice the person with the gallant responsibility of driving the huge red monster. You're virtually encouraged to see the driver as a robot merely opening and shutting the doors. Please don't speak to the driver or distract his attention. Scan your Oyster Card and move quickly inside before you become another victim of London knife crime.

Air travel is an interesting one, as most of the flight is programmed by computer. The pilot's role is largely in taking off and landing. As a nervous flyer I don't like to think about that when I'm up in the air. I like to imagine two highly-skilled pilots deep in concentration. I hate everything about flying. I don't like the way they call the airport a "Terminal", and I'm struck by the absurdity of the safety demonstration. How many successful emergency water landings have you ever heard about? I can only think of the Hudson River one in 2009. Yet on every flight we're asked to pay attention while the attendant shows us how to blow into a tube before we spiral out of control and plunge into the briny.

Crashing into the sea is probably worse than crashing into a mountain. I like oceans, rivers and lakes, but I'm scared of them. Or rather I'm scared of drowning. When I was about six a kid pushed me into a swimming pool on a school trip and I haven't been the same since. I can still recall the panic and the horrible sensation of water up my nose. How some people enjoy diving for fun I'll never know. About fifteen years later I taught myself to swim in the sea in Spain, but I rarely go in above my knees. Before I could swim, people used to tell me that everyone can float. I never believed them then, and I still don't. If everyone can float, why do people drown? Can't answer that one, eh?

I also have a fear of sharks. Don't get me wrong, I love all of God's creatures, but sharks are always on my mind when paddling in eighteen inches of the Med. I watch *Jaws* every summer to get me in holiday mood. It's nice watching man-eating sharks in the comfort and safety in your own home, but it reminds you that all sorts of dangerous critters inhabit the underwater world. (I'm also a big fan of Jeremy Wade's *River Monsters*).

I feel sorry for the shark at the end of *Jaws*. In recent years I've seen the film as an allegory of the cab trade. It could be that the shark represents the over-fed complacent cab trade of old, and Chief Brody and his "partners" are Uber executives out to destroy it when it's forced to feed in shallow waters. No, it's more likely that Uber is the shark and the blokes on the Orca are cab drivers fighting for normality on behalf of right-minded citizens. The Mayor is clearly The Mayor. The Mayor of Shark City indeed.

It's probably best to try for a seat allocation close to the flight recorder. They say the black box always survives. I don't know why they don't make the plane out of the same stuff they use for the black box. Encountering turbulence I always look over to the flight attendants. Only if their faces aren't contorted in fear can I stay calm. No, we need the human touch.

Anyway, driverless aeroplanes? Would you trust an Uber-operated jumbo to perform an emergency landing on the Hudson River? You can almost imagine the surge pricing supplement should they manage to pull it off.

Developments in 2018

A strange thing happened at the start of 2018: electric vehicle charging points were mushrooming up like nobody's business. They were everywhere.

It was also reported that two new electric taxis would be available for use in London by the end of the year. One of the models was said to be coming out at about £40,000, about £16,000 cheaper than the new LEVC taxi.

Many of us are waiting for a sustained improvement in trade before committing to a new cab, particularly with three models to compare. I'm hoping at least one of the new cabs will be affordable. I sigh with relief every year my high-mileage seven-year old TX4 gets through its annual inspection. I feel I'm riding my luck. Every year the dents and the paint blisters get worse. Every year I worry that the gearbox or engine will pack up, and I'll be faced with the garage bill from hell, or the prospect of committing to several years of huge monthly payments on a new cab. Every year I promise myself a new cab if trade improves. At the moment though, the idea remains a range-extended pipe dream.

Living forty miles from Central London I'll certainly be researching charging points locally before committing. I haven't seen any in Leighton Buzzard yet, though we do have electricity. And colour television. I suppose a slow charger will give me an excuse to sit in a pub for an hour or two, but that novelty will soon wear off. Even waiting around for half an hour every day is a no-no for me. That's twenty-five minutes more than I currently spend refuelling. That's technology going backwards, surely?

I assume the current price to charge a taxi with electricity is an introductory offer? We're still in the dark as to how much this whole electric cab project is going to cost us day to day. One thing that is only just being talked about is the fact that to be allowed to charge up with electricity at certain sites you need to take out a subscription – up to £32 per month from what I hear. Maybe things will get more competitive? Possibly, but I wouldn't be surprised to find that by the time most of us have converted we'll be spending about as much as we're currently spending on diesel. We'll see…

The future is electric, that's for sure. A diesel cab will feel like the Flintstone's car one day in the future.

The closure of Bank Junction had been a contentious issue since the City of London made this crucial area of the financial district buses and cycles only for most of the day. From Monday 16th to Wednesday 18th April 2018, the City authorities opened up Bank Junction to all traffic. This was a temporary measure while dignitaries met for the Commonwealth Heads of Government Forum.

The City originally closed Bank Junction because they said it was dangerous. They cited public safety. In opening the junction up they were either saying it is not dangerous; or that it is still dangerous, but they are happy to put VIPs at risk with all those nasty taxis, minicabs and vans driving around.

The alternatives to Bank Junction include a slalom of chicanes and temporary lights on Gresham Street. Other difficult-to-negotiate roads like Lothbury and Bartholomew

Lane help form a treacherous bypass of Bank Junction. The scene is nothing like that depicted on a London postcard that Commonwealth visitors might have picked up on their last day: a few black cabs, one 1964 Routemaster bus, and near-empty streets. At least seeing these streets in person gives the opportunity to VIPs to experience modern London envisioned by TfL and its anti-motorist allies.

Access to Bank Junction is essential, and it should never have been closed. It adds insult to injury when roads closed for being dangerous are opened up temporarily to create a false impression to visitors. A couple of weeks previously we'd heard about Unilever's move to Rotterdam in order to escape the chaos of London's crazy traffic schemes. Those making the decisions aren't going to listen to cab drivers, but when major corporations move out because of roads are closed and systems made too complex, they should realise that something very bad is happening on our streets.

13

Uber

Mischievous customers sometimes solicit the driver's opinions on Uber. What they're after is a pithy soundbite to amuse their friends with later. Some drivers rise to the bait like the Sex Pistols did on Bill Grundy's *Today* show in 1976: "Go on, you've got another five seconds. Say something outrageous." Wiser heads learn to keep a discreet distance when urged to discuss sensitive subjects. Uber's quest for world domination needs discussion though, so here come 4000-odd words on the subject.

From the outset, I need to make clear that I've nothing against Uber drivers. I blame the game, not the player.

In 2012, the American Uber organisation was licensed as a private hire operator in London. From then on, Uber rode roughshod over legislation, and set about to destroy taxi trades in British towns and cities. They saw London as the Holy Grail as it had the most highly regulated and vibrant taxi service in the world. London's transport infrastructure is a honeypot, and if Uber could take over London's taxi and private hire trades it would have cracked the big one. Year by year, their presence was felt by lower earnings for both taxi drivers and those driving for traditional private hire companies.

Uber are a foreign company with money behind them, and friends in high places. They had the nous to get around existing private hire legislation. They had powerful investors, celebrity endorsements and enjoyed government protection. The London taxi trade's 24,000 individual driver-operators had their work cut out competing with the invader.

Forty thousand Uber cars parachuted in amongst 24,000 taxis is going to have an impact. Some people put the taxi trade's hatred of Uber down to a resistance to competition, but it was *unfair* competition that we objected to.

Taxi drivers were left wondering why we put ourselves through such an ordeal to get licensed. We signed up for a job for life in which taxi drivers have the sole right to ply for hire. That was the deal. Suddenly, 350 years of legislation was swept away when clever computer programmers from Silicon Valley got together to exploit a weak licensing body.

In the old days, a driver was aligned to a private hire operator (whether they were employed or self-employed remains a moot point and still subject to court cases.) A customer would phone a minicab office and a car would turn up. Alternatively, they could visit a minicab office and make a booking. The booking would be logged – as the law dictates – and when a car was free, the customer would be invited to proceed to the booked car. The customer would be invited to wait in the office if things were busy.

These days, there is no need for an office as all transactions can be done over the air. A private hire driver needn't align himself to one operator, but can subscribe to one or more phone apps and receive jobs electronically. TfL should've realised that the miracle of technology enabled immediate hailing to take place through an app, and they granted a licence even when Uber admitted that they didn't even accept advance bookings.

Uber rapidly built up a following of customers, and tempted drivers away from other private hire companies with unrealistic earnings claims. Once the drivers had committed themselves – perhaps by buying a smart black Mercedes in order to service top corporate accounts – it was too late. Uber lowered its fares and raised the commission it charged drivers. It didn't matter to Uber if its drivers couldn't make ends meet, as the British benefits system allows people on low wages to top up their money with tax credits. Supermarkets have exploited this system for years.

Uber told TfL they were a technology company, and their role was merely to introduce passengers to drivers like an agency, over a mobile phone application. If they were a technology company, they should never have been licensed as a private hire operator. Private hire drivers aren't allowed to respond to an immediate hiring, but this was exactly what was happening. A customer presses a button on his phone and a car is on its way. This is the modern equivalent of someone putting their hand in the air to hail a taxi. Once that button is pressed, it's an immediate hiring. TfL had been negligent in failing to keep up with technology, and had licensed an illegal operation.

Some towns and cities around the world banned – and continue to ban – Uber, but most authorities licensed them. Uber lobbied hard to get influential politicians on their side, and encouraged celebrity endorsements. Uber had the money and power to decimate the transport businesses in towns where existing taxi and private hire regulations were weak.

London Mayor Boris Johnson called taxi drivers Luddites for resisting the march of progress. Some drivers had expressed concerns over plans to make credit card acceptance mandatory, but the London taxi trade had been using computerised booking and despatch for decades. The trade also had smartphone apps. Taxis could be hailed electronically, but the practice wasn't widespread and there wasn't a coherent publicity campaign. Taxi drivers belong to a variety of different associations and subscribe to a variety of different booking methods. Uber were bigger than our myriad of booking systems and had the marketing power.

Traditional private hire companies were the first line of defence, but the flood of Uber cars affected the taxi trade too. In order to take over London, Uber needed a large and constant supply of drivers. They would be recruited from around the world, tempted in with claims of big earnings. TfL were licensing upwards of four hundred private hire drivers every week, and many of those drivers joined Uber. In keeping with the gig-economy model, Uber flooded the market with drivers working at, or below, national minimum wage levels. Over-supply pushed down pay and conditions, and ensured safety standards were kept low.

After talking with friends about their transport use, I could understand the appeal of Uber. One friend, Chris, lives in the Greater London suburb of Upminster and can find a taxi straight away. There's no problem with supply. The only issue is cost when he needs to take a longer than average journey. He spoke of wanting to get home one night from Liverpool Street Station in the City of London, about twenty-five miles away. He would take an Uber car as it only cost £30. He asked how much it would cost in my cab. I had to admit it would cost around £100.

How can Uber do it that cheaply? It must take the best part of an hour to get there. When you factor in the likelihood of returning empty to the City, you're talking £15 an hour. When Uber have taken their commission, it doesn't leave the driver with much. It's accepted that the only Uber drivers making a living are those working around eighty hours a week.

Fares are subsidised by huge, but shrinking, investments. The customers benefit for now, but the fare rate should be seen as an introductory offer, never to be repeated. The more power Uber gain, the more they will charge. The drivers sit at the bottom of the pile. Uber have lost court cases in the USA over unrealistic earnings claims, yet more drivers join their ranks. Driver dissatisfaction in the private hire sector had been well publicised, but Uber still managed to offer up an impressive brigade of drivers. Uber pride themselves on supplying car within three minutes, and my friend confirms they sometimes arrive within seconds.

It works by over-supply. It doesn't matter to Uber if they have thousands of drivers parked up doing nothing. It only affects the drivers. The customer wants a car within three minutes, and Uber can arrange it. Driver turnover is high, with new arrivals coming to take the place of those who have left disillusioned. There's always someone to drive you to Essex for a pittance.

Through over-supply, Uber can cover the whole of London, the airports, and any other town they fancy. Not every booked Uber car will turn up, and not every driver will know where they're going. The driver might be funny about guide dogs, or gays. He might try it on with lone females (all well-documented). He might throw you out if you criticise his choice of route (or his sat nav's). Thirty quid all the way to Upminster though – the customer will take the risk and pocket a sizeable saving!

People now know that the Uber organisation pay virtually no tax in the UK. They know their drivers are being exploited. They know Uber pay so little that many drivers claim tax credits. None of this matters to Uber's customers; they just want to get from A to B as cheaply as possible. On price, taxis can rarely compete. I'm no better. I use companies that dodge UK tax and treat their workers abominably. I know I shouldn't; but the price, convenience, and delivery times, sometimes overrides my conscience.

During 2016, Uber started to take a bigger cut of commission. This resulted in demonstrations by its drivers (called "partners"). Uber rides were usually cheaper than taxi rides, but at busy times they would use surge pricing and ratchet up their fares as demand rose. They drew criticism for hiking up their fares during tube and bus strikes, or in the wake of terrorist attacks. I feel uncomfortable if I gain work during tube strikes as it feels like cheating, but Uber were multiplying their fares by up to six times.

TfL claimed they couldn't suspend private hire licensing without an Act of Parliament. They had previously suspended issuing Suburban taxi licences for a while in certain sectors, and that seemed easy enough to enact. In recent years Suburban drivers have had it particularly hard. If All-London green badge drivers were having it tough, yellow badge Suburban drivers were having it tougher. A Suburban taxi driver in Merton can't survive on Wimbledon fortnight alone. Greenwich drivers can't survive on the flow of tourists in the compact oasis of Greenwich town centre or events at the O2 Arena. Newham drivers can't survive by relying on occasional events at the Excel Centre. TfL didn't seek to get the necessary Act passed to restrict private hire licences in a similar way.

Tightening Up

TfL realised they never should have licensed Uber, but it was too late. They had investors in Cameron's government who would ensure Uber's status. All TfL could do was embark on a belated tightening up process.

Under pressure from taxi trade organisations, some established private hire elements, and other bodies concerned about traffic congestion and pollution, TfL announced a tightening of regulations. Private hire driver applicants from abroad would need to sit English tests. Drivers certainly need an adequate grasp of English, but I have to agree with Uber that the proposal to force drivers into taking a test costing around £200 to prove GCSE level English was a bit overzealous. A simple test would be adequate. There were also proposals to bring in stringent topographical testing.

Since the private hire trade was licensed in 2000, things had got slack. TfL merely tried to raise standards to the level that the public could reasonably expect as a matter of course. Uber wanted regulations as slack as possible for their drivers, and made an appeal. Some of the private hire fraternity saw the new regulations for what they were: a raising of standards that could only enhance the public's perception of minicabs. After members of the taxi trade discovered that private hire drivers were working with inadequate insurance, TfL tried to tighten things up here too. Private hire drivers were reported to be buying insurance policies that could be switched on and off. It appeared that no insurance company could legally issue such insurance.

Uber had taken on the body that had controversially awarded them an operating licence. They were biting the hand that feeds, and they were fighting wars on all fronts. Now it was the turn of two Uber drivers to take Uber to court to claim they were employees and not self-employed. The drivers won, which meant Uber drivers would be entitled to a working wage, holiday pay, sick pay, maternity and paternity pay; and all the other benefits that employed staff enjoy.

Uber later lost an appeal against this, but the matter is still being appealed in the courts.

In early 2017 Uber won their appeal over insurance. Drivers could now legally arrange monthly insurance policies.

The Downfall of Uber?

"[Uber] rides are so cheap essentially because it has used twenty-first century technology to erode twentieth century workers' rights." (Richard Godwin, *Guardian*, 5th June 2018.)

Make no mistake, Uber are the poisoned froth on the lager of capitalism. They were never going to be presented with an *Investors in People* plaque for their office, if they actually have a London office. Uber's business model started to be questioned more intensely when issues around self-employment, zero hours contracts, and the "gig economy" became discussed. "Uberisation" was a new word used to describe the way big corporations exploited tax loopholes, and gave their workers self-employed status to avoid responsibilities around employment law. Uber claimed its drivers were self-employed partners, yet they were dependent on Uber for work, and had to adhere to strict controls.

By the end of 2016, the tide seemed to be turning. Uber had been feted as trendy and progressive when they started, but bad publicity was coming thick and fast. Uber were criticised whenever they hiked their fares up during difficult times; and a string of well-publicised assaults by its drivers did a lot of harm. That, and the legendary long routes that Uber drivers sometimes took.

In March 2017, Uber lost their appeal regarding English language requirements. Their drivers were compelled to pay for English language exams. In the same week, Uber's Chief Executive, Travis Kalanick, was filmed getting into a heated argument and abusing one of his own drivers/partners.

Should Uber ever succeed in their aim of becoming *the* de facto cab service, do their users think they will keep their fares as low as they currently are? They put up their fares during public transport strikes, and immediately after the Manchester and the London Bridge terrorist attacks in 2017. Will they not find any excuse to implement surge pricing? Will all their cars become wheelchair accessible like taxis? If not, where will that leave the disabled? Those with limited mobility find it difficult to find an accessible private hire vehicle, and assistance dogs are still being refused.

In 2017, the bad publicity kept coming. Only 15% of Uber's tech staff were female. Around twenty employees were fired after and numerous female workers complained of sexual harassment and discrimination.

In India, a woman passenger was raped by an Uber driver. The driver was eventually jailed for life, for this and other crimes, but not before an Uber executive managed to access the victim's medical records in an attempt to discredit her. The executive, Eric Alexander, was sacked after journalists heard of the incident. Other powerful people in the Uber hierarchy left, including Head of Public Policy and Communications, Rachel Whetstone. Whetstone was a personal friend of the previous Conservative Prime Minister, David Cameron, and was godparent to Cameron's late son, Ivan.

Uber's Operator's Licence was up for renewal at the end of May 2017. TfL enigmatically chose to grant Uber a temporary four-month licence rather than a new five-year licence, saying that this "will allow us to conclude our consideration of a five-year licence". Taxi trade groups naturally pressured TfL into providing details of what exactly was going on.

Backers realising their investment was becoming more toxic by the day, asked Uber's CEO, Travis Kalanick, to resign. He did so, in June 2017.

Not one London taxi driver was charged with a sexual assault in 2016. Complaints about taxi drivers are handled directly by TfL. Complaints about private hire drivers are handled in-house by the operators themselves. Uber considered it optional whether they escalate complaints up to TfL or the police.

In August 2017, the Metropolitan Police claimed Uber were failing to pass on allegations of driver misconduct. This included at least one sexual assault, and another involving a weapon. In one instance, Uber took no action against a driver accused of sexual assault by a woman when the driver denied it. The driver went on to commit a more serious attack on another woman.

The Met's Taxi and Private Hire Unit were made aware of six sexual assaults, two public order offences and one assault in 2016, which Uber initially kept from the police. The delay meant that certain cases – such as the two public order offences – could not be pursued because the six-month time limit for such offences had passed. An Uber driver was allegedly involved in a road rage incident in which pepper spray was used. Despite pepper spray being classed as a firearm, Uber would only give information to the police when formally requested to do so under the Data Protection Act.

The Metropolitan Police were thoroughly fed up of them and were snowed under with investigating complaints against Uber drivers – those complaints that they were made aware of. Inspector Neil Billany, head of the Met's Taxi and Private Hire Unit claimed in a letter to TfL that Uber "seemed to be deciding what to report" and only informed the police about the "less serious matters" that would be "less damaging to their reputation."

Taxi drivers have to renew their licences by first applying for an enhanced criminal record check through the Disclosure and Barring Service (DBS). It became apparent that Uber drivers could go through an agency, said to have links with Uber itself. TfL considered the situation dubious and forced 13,000 drivers to apply for new enhanced DBS reports.

Instead of using their four-month temporary licence period to get their house in order, Uber's arrogance was such that they behaved even worse.

Shock Decision

The Licensed Taxi Drivers' Association (LTDA) and other London-based taxi groups had put sustained pressure on

TfL over Uber's licensing, and TfL had finally been shamed into doing the right thing. On September 22nd 2017, TfL announced that they would not be renewing Uber's operating licence.

Most people were shocked, including many in the cab trade. The reasons given were related to safety, and to Uber not accepting corporate responsibility. Issues include Uber's approach to reporting criminal offences, concerns over how drivers' medical certificates are obtained, and issues over drivers' enhanced Disclosure and Barring Service checks (DBS).

TfL also cited Uber's use of Greyball in London as one of its reasons not to renew their licence. Greyball is a tool used to stop Uber being spied on by government officials and law enforcement agencies. Using a digital map, Uber would flag up individuals as hostile agents should Greyball identify requests for service originating from the area around a government building. They would also search social media in an attempt to identify potential law enforcement agents, and try to identify the cheap mobile phones used in sting operations. Greyball had been used in the USA as early as 2014, but it didn't become public knowledge until March 2017.

In the days that followed, the Uber licensing issue became the dominant subject in London, eclipsing even Britain's negotiations to leave the European Union. I allowed myself a celebratory light ale that evening, but few of us in the taxi trade thought the game was completely over for Uber.

Over the next twenty-four hours, around half a million people had signed a petition against the decision: people who clearly don't know that TfL listen to no one. Uber complained that if the decision was upheld it could put 40,000 of its drivers out of work. In reality, many drivers only worked part-time, and they could easily return to the traditional private hire companies from whence they came.

And never mind that Uber wanted to put 40,000 drivers out of work by investing big in driverless cars. Go on, waste more money on the driverless minicab fantasy. I don't know what Uber's drivers think about their plans to make them redundant!

It was no good blaming TfL, the LTDA, or taxi drivers agitating for a ban on Uber; it was Uber themselves who let down its workforce by it belligerent attitude. The question was, was it a hard refusal or a soft refusal? The London taxi driver knows that if he is judged to be an unfit operator, his licence will be immediately revoked. Why were Uber allowed to carry on operating? All their drivers with suspect criminal checks were allowed to carry on working too.

Most of us thought Uber would make concessions in order to be relicensed, and that this was just a shot across the bows. What some people didn't realise was that Uber had the warning shots back in May: they were given four months in which to improve things, but they chose not to. When it transpired they were covering up sexual assault allegations, there was an increasing public clamour for something to be done.

Before TfL's decision turned the spotlight on Uber's affairs, many people thought it was just taxi drivers whingeing (plus the 80,000-odd non-Uber private hire drivers whose businesses were being undermined). The general public aren't particularly interested in what constitutes plying for hire, whether a mobile phone can be used as a taxi meter, or whether a London-licensed minicab can legally work in Brighton. But people now had a bit more awareness of the taxi and private hire trades, and the roles and responsibilities within them. People now know there are issues over Uber drivers' insurance, questions over criminal record checking, and the fact that Uber were picking and choosing what criminal allegations to report to the police. These were the issues that made people sit up and think. Everyone could now see how government interference and having friends in high places has protected them.

People could see that the headlines on taxi magazines were true: Uber hadn't been checking criminal records properly. They really were ignoring criminal allegations. An Uber driver really did try to cut someone's head off at Leytonstone Station while shouting "Allaha Akbar." Another was nicked after waving a samurai sword around outside Buckingham Palace just weeks before TfL licensing decision. Those with a conscience could see how they were exploiting not just tax and VAT loopholes and a spineless licensing regime, but also its drivers – who they wanted to replace with driverless cars ASAP. LBCs radio presenter James O'Brien likened Uber to a Victorian mill owner. I like the analogy, although mill owners were locally-based and paid their taxes in the UK.

By the time Uber had meetings to discuss their non-licensing, they did something they'd not done before: they apologised for their behaviour. So what? Taxi drivers know that if we had a string of serious complaints against us we wouldn't get four months in which to put things right. We know if every box wasn't ticked, once that four months had elapsed we wouldn't be getting our licence back, however much we said sorry.

In November, while Uber were crawling to TfL in an attempt to save their licence, it transpired that 57 million customer and driver accounts had been hacked. Uber had paid $100,000 to the hackers to destroy the details, and had tried to hide the whole affair. It took them a year to come clean. At the time of the breach, Uber were being questioned by regulators in the USA over data mishandling, privacy violations and security complaints. 2.7 million people in the UK had their names, addresses and email addresses compromised. If I had an Uber app on my phone I'd worry about how I'm being spied on, and how my data is being used.

As the year 2017 closed, those who chose to look were to seeing right through the Emperor's clothes, and what they saw disgusted them.

In February 2018, Uber were still crawling to TfL. They told TfL that they would from now on report criminal allegations directly to the police. Meanwhile, the stories of rape, assault and terrorism, continued. TfL couldn't possibly hand their licence back, could they?

Appeal Hearing

In June 2018, Uber started an appeal process in Westminster Magistrates' Court. In a desperate endeavour to get their licence back they admitted a string of safety failures, and said it agreed with TfL decision not to renew its licence back in September (!). The organisation claimed it now had a 24/7 phone helpline for passengers and drivers, and it would now be reporting serious incidents to the police. It was revealed that 2,500 Uber drivers had been investigated for suspected offences, including sexual assaults and dangerous driving.

Uber claimed to have changed its ways though, and was now fit to be licensed.

On the second day of the appeal, Uber were granted a fifteen-month operator's licence. The decision didn't come as a surprise to a jaded and deeply cynical cab trade. Uber should never have been licensed back in 2012. TfL know it, everyone knows it (and even Uber admit it); but the organisation is too powerful and has too much protection to be stopped now. A lot of powerful people have their grubby fingers in the pie. Nobody is going to stand up to them now. As Johnny Rotten might have sneered: "Ever get the feeling you've been cheated?"

Maybe things will change if Uber are weakened? *If* they follow the rules from now on, they will be weakened, as their business model won't be so easy to sustain. Private hire driver licensing has slowed. It's saturated. Drivers are unhappy, and there are fewer signing up. Uber have peaked, and I believe their best days are behind them. In London anyway. Should TfL ever find a way to put a cap on PH licensing, this will harm their model of over-supply. There are still appeals in the pipeline over their drivers' employment status. This one will cost them dearly should they lose the appeal.

Anyway, that's all I have to say on the matter. Let's move on…

14

The Future

The drivers of the 60s and 70s had it easier: less traffic; fewer madcap road systems; and less competition from private hire. The work was always there. Even when I joined in 1988, cab drivers were still earning enough to secure a mortgage on a London home. Some would enjoy long holidays abroad, golf club membership, and the ability to earn an income superior to many people in occupations regarded as working class.

Other self-employed artisans had it good too. For a while, public sector workers belonging to strong trade unions also enjoyed a decent wage and a degree of job security. That's largely gone now, as wages have been driven down and the unions have been stripped of their power. Job security has been replaced by zero-hours contracts where the boundaries between employment and self-employment are blurred. Many workers are part of the gig economy, where you complete one task, then have to scour around for your next. London cab drivers have always worked this way, as the next job is never guaranteed. Early cab drivers lived hard lives, but the modern self-employed driver has never felt downtrodden. Being truly self-employed gives us autonomy and helps self-esteem; but with jobs being fewer and more widely-spaced apart than in earlier times, the stress is sometimes felt. We don't feel as secure as we used to.

The likes of Uber made a mockery of the training we've all been through, and have undermined the service we have provided for over 300 years. When we looked to our licensing authority for protection they did nothing. Cab drivers have committed significant time and effort in order to ply our trade in London. Fewer than 24,000 taxi drivers are in competition with over 113,000 private hire drivers. Around 40,000 of that number are driving for Uber, and it's competition that is neither fair nor legal. We went through the Knowledge palaver because we understood that only taxis had the right to ply for immediate hire on the streets. That was the deal. But Uber cars are available for immediate hire at the press of a button. They should never have been licensed as a private hire operator, but TfL listened to the big guy with the power and the money.

Over time, people will notice that the arriviste app-based minicab services are not as cheap as they used to be, and that the service supplied by an overworked, demoralised, driving force has plummeted. People sometimes get the service they deserve but that is scant consolation for us. I shouldn't be sanctimonious, as I have unwittingly helped the supermarkets drive local greengrocers, butchers and fishmongers out of business by my shopping habits. I am painfully aware of my own hypocrisy when I complain that the tomatoes at the supermarket aren't as cheap as they were before the family greengrocer was driven off the high street. Perhaps taxis will also be driven off the high street and be reduced to becoming a heritage attraction like the horse-drawn buggies around Central Park in New York?

TfL's anti-car agenda has compounded our problems. Traffic is now moving at seven miles per hour in Central London. It's nothing to be proud of. Congestion costs us all. People are put off using us, and it's embarrassing charging someone over the odds because the traffic has run up the meter so much. There are fewer vehicles on the roads now, but the congestion is worse. TfL have artificially engineered congestion through ill-thought out road modelling. How much longer can we continue to offer a service to people at seven miles per hour?

These traffic schemes cost the motorist time and money. As our cabs burn more fuel, the cost is passed on to the passenger. The resulting pollution costs us all. I have no time for Uber, or the shoddier elements in private hire, but traffic congestion costs us dearly.

TfL are an unwieldly organisation, and they hold too much power. The taxi and private hire elements should be separated and returned to the control of the Metropolitan Police. If the taxi trade ever folds I put the blame on Transport for London.

I don't have the definitive answer. Like Brexit, nobody really knows how things will work out. Shouting abuse at Uber drivers and customers isn't the answer though. We need to provide the best service we possibly can, and constantly work on improving ourselves and the way we work. Taxi trade organisations are keeping the pressure on TfL to curtail the illegal activities of Uber. They need our support. Drivers and customers must respond more to traffic consultations, and feedback complaints to TfL, and other authorities, when we feel they are doing something wrong.

Cab drivers are fiercely independent, and our independence is both a strength and a weakness. Businesses don't like us because investors can't move in to exploit us. Rapacious corporations can't make a profit off our backs – this is why there was so much suspicion over having to enter into commercial deals with credit card companies. But we've never harnessed our collective power as much as we should have because we can't agree on a political viewpoint. Some of us believe in negotiation, others in militant action. Hopefully we can reach more of a consensus in the near future.

No Country for Old Men

Although most cab drivers are independently-minded and resistant to authority, many hold education in high esteem. Those with kids often put them through university. A new graduate is fresh and ambitious. When they emerge with a degree and a funny hat they are unlikely to sign up for another three or four years of hard graft to follow in their parents' footsteps.

I was twenty-six when I completed the Knowledge. There are few cab drivers starting at this age now. Many finishing the Knowledge are already approaching the regular state retirement age. Retirement is now a luxury for many people. It was something that those fortunate to enjoy secure work were able to save for. That work is less secure now. The pension pot has shrunk. The pension that people were promised when they signed up has been denied them. The goalposts have been shifted. People now work until they drop. Driving a cab is a hard job, but it's become seen as a retirement job to top up a paltry, or non-existent, pension.

People signing up for the Knowledge lack the assurance that I had when I started about the worth of the green badge. Unless cab driving becomes an attractive career choice again, this great old trade could simply die of old age.

It's not a perfect job. It never was. When I joined, older drivers had already pronounced the game as dead and did nothing but moan about it. The number of applicants for the Knowledge is falling. Becoming a cab driver should become quicker, but what kind of trade are people coming into?

I don't know whether the trade will ever be as strong as it was when I entered it in 1988. I suspect it won't be; but it still might be better than many occupations.

For those thinking of starting the Knowledge, what other options are there? Stay in your current job and hope the company stays afloat? Constantly worry that you might be made redundant when the firm is downsized? Or replaced with someone younger, sharper, and more dynamic?

You could put yourself in £50K of debt by going to university. If you do it while you're still young you could join the corporate ladder. Often, it's a ladder to nowhere though. I've seen better men and women than I put out to grass in the professional world following many years of loyal service.

The job has changed, and it will change further. Everybody's job has changed, and I'd venture that change happens quicker outside the cab trade. For cab drivers the changes are acute because until 2016 things had changed so little. My Careers Adviser job no longer exists. I needed to commit to a one-year postgraduate diploma course to enter, but the careers service was de-professionalised. There are now people doing a similar job without the diploma. Mini-Careers Advisers if you like.

Publicity

Is the Knowledge still relevant? In practical tests by Lancaster University, researchers ran twenty-nine journeys around London, using a car with a GPS app competing against a cab driver equipped with the Knowledge. The specialist knowledge of the cab driver was shown to better navigate complex routes faster. A sat nav is no substitute to the analytical skills of a London cab driver's brain.

In 2017, the trade had a boost with C4's television documentary, *The Knowledge: The World's Toughest Taxi Test*. C4's jolly little programme reminded the public what taxi drivers go through to gain their licences, and showed a heart-warming human story of struggling to better yourself. It was a privilege to see Knowledge candidates being interviewed as to the reasons why they took on the Knowledge. We squirmed on our sofas as we watched a variety of people being interrogated by the examiners on the Floor of Fear.

In September of that year, Jack Rosenthal's 1979 *The Knowledge* was adapted for the stage and ran for a couple of months at the Charing Cross Theatre. Directed by Jack's widow, Maureen Lipman, the play gave the trade another little boost. The publicity was timely as war was raging between the taxi trade and Uber. The play had opened just a few weeks before TfL refusal to re-licence Uber after the expiry of their four-month temporary licence. It was an affectionate, heartfelt, play, with a lot of humanity. It did an admirable job of reminding us all that the Knowledge affects everyone around it, and not least the girlfriends, boyfriends, wives and husbands, of those who complete it.

Will the London Taxi Survive?

Yes, but in a more competitive and demanding market. Uber, as they stand now, can put competing PH firms out of business in the race to the bottom. We're in a stronger position as we can ply for hire in the traditional way. Our numbers might be gradually reducing, but there's still a trickle of new blood through the Knowledge system. Those of us left standing will still be able to respond to street hails and service the many hotel and station ranks. That work won't necessarily go to Uber.

The drivers who are left could find they have more work than they can handle, but the downside is that the trade could be weakened. Fewer taxi drivers means less collective power. The numbers really need to be maintained. While minicab licensing is unrestricted, private hire have an unfair advantage.

New companies will muscle in on taxi work in the wake of Uber. They will have learnt from Uber's mistakes and gain operators' licences. If Uber continue, or another organisation takes their place, they will carry on the aim of trying to obliterate taxi businesses around the world. The customer might get a good deal at first; but should any one organisation become dominant, fares will inevitably rise. There will be shocking fare spikes whenever demand is high. The disabled will be side-lined.

Private hire licensing reached saturation point in 2017 and has now slowed down. Fewer people are seeking licences as too many drivers are chasing too few jobs and no one is making any money. There's such a vast conveyor belt of drivers required to maintain Uber's model of over-supply, that if licences are capped, the company will be weakened.

Uber will no longer be able to guarantee a car within three minutes – a pretty impressive selling point to be fair. Its drivers might be less inclined to put up with current working practices should they become more sought after.

Generally, I think things will become less favourable for the private hire trade; particularly for Uber, as they'll no longer be able to continue with the same business model. With Uber weakened, many drivers will return to the more respectable private hire companies. Things might settle down in the taxi and private hire world and go back to where they were a few years ago. At the time we didn't realise how good things were when all we had to worry about were Addison Lee.

London Mayor Sadiq Khan isn't happy about the traffic mayhem and pollution that unrestricted private hire licensing has caused. Nobody thinks having 114,000 minicab drivers on the streets of London is a good thing, and if licensing picks up substantially again, something will have to be done. Most people don't stay in the private hire trade for long. If PH licensing is capped, the number of working drivers will reduce further. Many of those already licensed, but no longer actively working, will still renew their licence every year should they ever want to return in the future. A private hire licence also serves as a Congestion Charge season ticket – who is going to give that up?

Ever since private hire started, the two services have appealed to a different clientele. Some people only use a minicab, some only use a taxi. There's a floating middle, which use both. We'll probably never win the custom of those who just look at the bottom line, but we could win over the middle ground if we put the effort in. In the years when things were better we lost some of the middle ground while chasing the top end.

We don't need to work harder, just smarter. We need to use technology to our advantage, and we need to be involved in trade matters. By 2017, we were all accepting credit cards, and our apps were getting known. We need to consider fixed price fares on occasions. We must respect and value our customers and provide a quality service at all times. A century or so ago, we appealed to the gentry because a gentleman could get into our cabs without taking his top hat off. In order to wear the trousers, we have to remember that gentlemen no longer wear top hats.

Become a Writer and Make Millions

Of course you could opt out of work completely and become a writer. Imagine swanning around in your dressing gown, tapping a few words out between lunch and dinner time, then spending the evening in your local ale house editing your work over a few pints of Riddles Very Peculiar. No, it's not really like that. You still need to work your writing around a full-time job, and you're unlikely to make a steady income – particularly once your over-priced printer ink has been factored in.

Before I embraced the punk ethic and decided to self-publish, I sent sample chapters out to twelve literary agents and one small publisher. I received polite – and sometimes helpful – rejections from those who took the trouble to email back. Agents invariably said they liked my writing, but couldn't see where it fitted in commercially. Readers aren't interested in the common man doing mundane work anymore. It's all about riding the zeitgeist, the big issues of the day. Or lame ghost-written celebrity novels.

If you've persevered with this book, I'm proud of you. It'll probably run at a loss, and I accept that. I'm really writing it as an intellectual exercise and as a testament to my career. A legacy if you will.

I'm likely to end my days driving a cab. I've got a lot out of it really. I moan about the job. We all do. But sometimes it's great. Nobody tells me when to get up, and I don't have to ask the boss for permission to go home, or take time off. I don't have to suck up to management or screw anybody over in order to succeed. I live on my wits. I do good honest work; something I believe in. When you've had a good day, your customers have been nice, and you get a job going your way home at the end of the day, it's the best job in the world. There's always the feeling of freedom. Newcomers might not find it as easy, or as lucrative, as it once was, but the game is far from dead.

It was passing the Knowledge that gave me the confidence to consider university as a serious option. Back then I felt the need to prove myself intellectually. I did indeed learn a valuable lesson at university. When the mystique of education was shattered I realised that I'd already proved myself by passing the Knowledge. Had I put the same effort in at university as I did on the Knowledge I'd be Headmaster of Oxford University by now.

It's ironic that I escaped the cab trade to enter a conventional profession, only to make the return journey eleven years later. The so-called professional world wasn't what I expected it to be. The grass wasn't greener, it was just manicured better.

Ultimately, the cab trade was my salvation. I appreciate more than ever how noble and honest our work is. I appreciate how we are a collection of free-thinking individuals who plough our own furrow. For better or worse, I now know that that cab trade and I belong together.

If you've been affected by any of the issues raised in this book – or on a kindle, you modernist types – you'll find more to read and discuss on my website: pubcat.co.

I'll add a "Making of…" series of articles, some outtakes; and at the risk of attracting cougars I'll put some photos up too.

Afore ye go, look out for my other writings. They're all under my own name, though if you spot any Letters or Top Tips from Mr L. Buzzard in *Viz*, that's me too.

Q & A

If I've done my job properly, you will now have a good grasp of what it's like to drive a taxi in modern London. You'll know how the cab trade works and you'll have a good understanding of the Knowledge of London examinations. You'll also know a lot about the things that can annoy us and turn a good day into a bad one. This section will recap what we've learnt so far. I'm sure you still have questions, so as promised, this Q & A section should cover any outstanding issues. Come on, don't be shy – what do you *really* want to know?

What do cab drivers earn?

Barefaced cheek, I like that. It's an obvious question, but one that's rarely addressed. Some members of the public like to think we are all raking it in; that we all live in big houses in the suburbs, and we take three holidays to Florida every year. Maybe that's what it was like forty years ago, but it's certainly not like that now.

It's difficult to compare regular employed earnings with variable self-employed takings. The Income Tax and National Insurance schedules are different. The self-employed can claim tax back for costs incurred in running the business. With each driver working different hours and at different times of the day, you can only, at best, consider things by way of hourly takings. This still won't give you much of an idea. For example, I could drive you from Central London to Heathrow for sixty quid. If we encounter any turbulence it's likely to take an hour. You might imagine we pick someone straight off the Heathrow rank and trouser another £60 going back. You therefore get the impression we are on £60 an hour. It doesn't work like that. As we've already seen, I might have to wait two or three hours to get onto the rank. The figures don't look so good now, do they? Anyway, I'm a town driver; I only go to Heathrow once a month. A £60 job is an exception. There are plenty of times I've sat on the Pancras rank for half an hour, only to get a £7 job to Euston. As the hourly rate varies so wildly, it's impossible to put figures on it, but take it from me, there are more drivers on £7 an hour than on £60.

Am I dodging the question? C4's 2017 TV documentary, *The Knowledge: The World's Toughest Taxi Test* put it in the public domain that cab drivers have an average salary of £37,000. I don't know where they managed to find the average salary (I'm certainly on less than that). In any case we're not on a salary. It's a possibility for drivers that work longer hours than I do, but that's gross takings. There are a *lot* of deductions to come out of that 37K.

Do taxi drivers hate minicab drivers?

Almost all taxi drivers alive today have spent their working life alongside minicabs, and most recognise their right to exist. We all believe there are too many private hire drivers licensed in London – as do many private hire drivers. Most of us dislike Uber and believe they should never have been licensed, but it's important to blame the game and not the player. We are not anti-competition, just anti-unfair competition.

Do all cab drivers live in Essex?

Pretty much so. Some still live in the East End, but it's become an expensive place in which to live. The cab driver's spiritual home is now further out in the proud county of Essex, where many of today's Knowledge Boys come from. When I became an examiner and a candidate had an address in the Greater London part of Essex, around Hornchurch, Romford or Upminster, I'd ask what school he went to. Every one of them was a migrant from the East End, and none had been to a local school (my school was Dury Falls Comprehensive in Hornchurch. It doesn't exist now).

Older drivers who bought property in better times might live in the suburbs of North London, or in Hertfordshire. Many drivers live much further out. I recently met one of my old Knowledge customers who had moved to Northumberland, five miles from the Scottish border. Quite a few drivers live in Spain, and my man in Northumberland assured me there are people who sleep in their cabs at Heathrow who live in Cyprus and Thailand. I reckon there are a few in Florida too. Florida seems to be the Essex of the United States.

Do you get free cab rides from your colleagues?

Don't be silly. If you provide a free, or discounted, ride, you are going to make a loss, as you are using your time; time that should be used conveying fare-paying passengers. There is no physical product that can be sold to you at trade price.

Occasionally I pick people up who I suspect are cab drivers. This makes me nervous as I don't want them criticising my route. Similarly, should a customer be outed as a cab driver on a day off, he would feel under pressure to provide an above-average tip. Cab driving passengers don't usually reveal themselves.

Actually, I did accept a free cab ride once when I was a Knowledge Examiner. A cab driver who knew me offered me a lift back to the office from Capital Kebabs in the rain. He no doubt tried to impress me with his local knowledge of the backstreets of Southwark. If you're reading, I was duly impressed. Thank you, and well done.

Don't cab drivers spend most of their time in greasy spoons?

With toilet facilities at a premium, cafes situated in streets away from the roving eyes of parking wardens are popular for short visits. Only a small minority excessively spend their quality time in cafes these days. Most drivers are focussed on paying off cab loans and mortgages. The cab trade has an ageing population though, and many drivers are semi-retired. These drivers have the time to chat with their mates. Some drivers use cab driving as an excuse to keep out of the wife's way. You'll know a cab café if you accidently walk into one. Cafes frequented by cab drivers are noisy places as cab drivers tend to be on the loud side. Why sit with your friends and talk normally when you can shout across from the other side of the room?

Can the driver make the meter run faster?

Absolutely not. Inside the meter is a computer chip. It's smaller than the SIM card in your phone, but smarter than your cab driver's brain. My meter company sends me a little plastic chip every year and I plug it into the meter. The chip works out all the calculations. It knows all the bank holidays for that year, so knows precisely when to change tariffs, or set extras at Christmas. The meter is sealed and certified every year, and can't be tampered with. You'd need a PhD in maths just to understand the formula used to set the tariff. Even if you unsealed it, you wouldn't be able to make it run faster. All the driver can do is switch it off and on. The meter works on a very complicated combination of time and distance. The faster the wheels move, the faster the meter runs. It also runs when the cab is stationary. At certain times, such as after 8 pm, at weekends, or on public holidays, the tariff increases. This is done automatically by the meter. The only thing that can make a meter run faster is if the driver drives faster. And asking the driver to go faster isn't something I'd advise. The driver will proceed in accordance to the prevailing traffic conditions, and the law. There are always cameras watching you in London.

The meter tariff is reviewed every year. In my time, we've had modest increases, and occasionally no increase at all. In recent years, drivers haven't generally clamoured for an increase. Some drivers think the fares should be lowered.

I took a cab to Ealing/Finchley/Barking/Croydon. The driver got lost: don't they learn the Knowledge these days?

Although we're obliged to take you twelve miles out, we're only examined on our detailed knowledge of a six-mile radius of Charing Cross. All those places are well beyond six miles. Our day to day expertise is in negotiating the complexities of Soho and Mayfair. I've never been asked to go to Barking, and most cab drivers would get lost in Croydon.

Do taxi drivers sometimes take you the long way round?

Only if he expects the journey to be quicker. We're trained to use the shortest route, but often a longer route on roads that are less congested pays dividends. If the driver's analysis works out and the longer route proves quicker, it shouldn't cost you extra. Even if it costs extra, it might save you time. And time is money. If the driver's cunning plan doesn't work, he'll get it in the neck, so it's good practice to agree to any contentious route in advance.

Do taxis go south?

Sometimes. Most of our work is in Central London, north of the Thames. Many of us don't relish a trip to South London because it means queuing on bridges to get there. We're likely to have an equally tortuous journey back, and as South London isn't prime cab riding territory, we're likely to drive back empty. Also, as we don't spend a lot of time south of the water, we are less familiar with the area. Most of us like to stay within our comfort zone.

Often, the journey isn't as bad as we imagine though. You should find that most drivers will take you south with good grace.

I like the look of that nice green cab – can I pick any cab I want?

It's the customer's right to choose whichever cab he likes from a rank. You won't make a driver happy by rejecting his cab, but if the interior is full of rubbish or he has a plastic bag over his credit card reader, feel free to pick another one.

Can I bring my pets with me?

Yes, you can bring your dog, cat, rabbit, or any other pet, with you. It's the humans we're suspicious of.

Can I bring up a crate of Guinness?

So long as the bottles are in the crate, and the crate's on the floor of the cab. If you are pregnant with a crate of Guinness and you are about to give birth, please be aware that I can charge a £40 soiling charge.

I've heard that it costs double to travel at Christmas?

Not in London. At certain times around Christmas and New Year we can charge an extra £4 per hiring.

I bet you love the rain!

I hate it. Visibility is reduced, the windows steam up, and the traffic slows. It's difficult to drive in the rain, and it's depressing. Contrary to popular belief we don't get more customers when it rains; just wet, depressed ones.

I put my hand out but the cab didn't stop!

It's likely that the driver didn't see you: maybe he was concentrating on avoiding that family wheeling pushchairs between those buses. Maybe he was daydreaming. Maybe it was a limp-wristed hail.

"But I'd just come out of Selfridge's and waved my arms like a mad woman – he definitely saw me! And the next cab didn't stop either!"

"Selfridge's, did you say?"

"That's right! Both cabs saw me! Is it because I'm black/transgender/act like a mad woman/have facial tattoos? &c…"

"Ah, that's because there is a taxi rank at Selfridge's. Should a passing cab stop for you when there are cabs waiting on a nearby rank, the driver would be contravening etiquette. He'd get a mouthful of abuse as minimum."

Cabs should not stop to pick up on the opposite side of the road too. That side of the road is served by cabs coming that way. Unless there are no cabs in sight.

As soon as the driver saw me, he switched his light off and drove past!

Generally, a cab for hire displays an illuminated yellow roof light, and a "For Hire" light in his nearside window. He might have decided to call it a day and head for home the second you hailed him, or he might have just accepted a radio job. OK, he might not have liked the look of you, but the other two explanations are the most likely.

I'm a nice person, why shouldn't he like the look of me?

I'm sure you are, sir, but consider it from the driver's point of view. You are a member of the public; a stranger, in a big city full of freaks and weirdos. The driver needs to satisfy himself you are not likely to give any problems in the confined space of his £40,000 taxi. A quick risk assessment is made as the driver approaches you. It's not scientific; it's just a brief visual scan. If you are out of context the alarm bells will be ringing: for example if you are wearing a hoodie in the City or Mayfair.

I stopped a cab in Oxford Street, but he directed me to the one behind. Why was that?

Because Cab A had passed Cab B further back. It was Cab Bs job. The driver of Cab A was being courteous.

The yellow light wasn't on, but he still stopped for me – why?

On my radio circuit, I get job preference if I am in "Radio Only" mode and my "For Hire" light is off. I'm probably in "Going Home" mode too, which means I am looking to go north. If you are in a one-way street heading north I might stop for you. I say "might" because once I've stopped and engaged with you, I am compelled to take you anywhere you want to go to within twelve miles. It would be bad form to refuse you after stopping for you, so I don't often take the risk. And it is a risk, because many wily coves trick drivers into thinking they are going in a particular direction when they're not.

I got a London Taxi from Luton Airport and it was a lot cheaper than the one I got going back. How come?

Because it wasn't a London taxi, lady. Luton Airport is in Bedfordshire. Luton, actually. They call it London-Luton Airport as a tourist scam. You got a Luton taxi, which has a lower tariff than London. Anyway, are you sure it was actually a taxi? Addison Lee minicabs are allowed to operate at Luton, and they're cunningly painted black like a taxi. This is another cynical marketing scam.

Only London City Airport has a London postcode. Heathrow has a Twickenham postcode, but is in Greater London and offers London taxis. All other airports sold as being in London are in other counties. There are no rank for London taxis at Stansted, Luton or Gatwick.

Why wouldn't the driver let me put my bag in the boot?

Taxi boots are tiny, and what space there is, is largely full of the equipment we're compelled by law to carry in order to be fully accessible; such as wheelchair ramps and a harnesses. There's a designated space for luggage next to the driver.

It's only a short one – is that OK?

No job is too small, and your job probably isn't the shortest one I've done: that was when a fat Arab boy persuaded his mum to get him driven half way around Portman Square.

Can I smoke?

Absolutely not. Even if you open the window. It's against the law. Vaping is also against the law, according to a sticker TfL made me put in my cab.

Can I eat and drink?

I'll let you eat a sandwich, something like that, and a drink, yes. I don't want kebabs and burgers in my cab though. Not just because of the possibility of mess, but because of the smell you're inflicting on my next valued customer (curries will be confiscated and taken home for the cat and I).

Any anti-social behaviour will get my back up. Remember, my cab is my office. You wouldn't like it if I turned up at your place and moved your stapler and photographed my arse on your photocopier.

Sorry, I only have coins, is that all right?

Coins are great! Some days you get nothing but £20 notes. £5 notes are often in short supply, and so are £1 coins. I'm always happy when the pound has had a good day.

Can I pay in Euros or US Dollars?

I'll take Euros, but please ask first. My exchange rate is 1:1. I'll only take dollars if I have a holiday to the USA booked. I'll take Scottish banknotes, so long as they haven't got Nicola Sturgeon's face on them. Northern Irish, Jersey and Guernsey notes? I personally don't take them.

APPENDIX B
(FOR HARD USERS ONLY)

Tips for Knowledge Students

Throughout my Knowledge-handling career I have been asked many questions surrounding the frightening world of the Knowledge. Many questions asked were based on ancient myths that I am surprised are still circulating. So, I think it'll be useful to look at some of the issues raised, and expel some myths about Knowledge Appearances:

- You are not obliged to wear a suit and tie, but I would strongly recommend it. The rules say you should dress in a smart, professional, manner. I know, professionals don't all wear suits and ties these days, but it's still the 1950s up at the Towers. Most of your examiners feel the need to maintain archaic traditions, and they expect it of you too

- Examiners are not told what they can ask. Your first Appearance will be based on the Blue Book. After that you can pretty much be asked anything, so long as it's within the six-mile limit

- If you think your examiner has made a mistake, politely point it out. If unsatisfied, ask to speak to the manager ASAP. Your query will be taken seriously and it won't go against you

- There are no quotas: examiners don't have to pass or fail a certain number of people in any given period. There are no quotas for men or women either

- If you can't decide what route to call it's probably because I've given you a "Dilemma Run". If I've sent you up to Hampstead from Regent Street it doesn't really matter what way around Regent's Park you go. You'll face the same choices driving a cab. Have confidence and just go!

- Examiners sometimes ask obscure Points that are unlikely to be asked by a cab customer. Examiners know you spend longer on computers or in a school than you do on your bike. Every day, they see candidates who roughly know where a Point is because they've looked it up on a computer, but they don't know exactly where it is because they've not seen it with their own eyes. Never guess a Point. If you own up immediately, you'll only lose one mark. If you get a guess wrong you will lose a lot more

- Never call a right turn from Piccadilly into Stratton Street. Yes, cabs do it, but its highly illegal

- You are judged only on your current Appearance. Your previous Appearance sheets are scanned and attached to your file. Files now only exist on computer. Your examiners sometimes look to see what Runs you were asked previously, and they might exploit your weak spots. Generally, all an examiner knows about you are the questions you've previously been asked, and your scores. Don't worry about your last Appearance, just concentrate on the here and now

- Examiners don't say bad things about you on your file. The days are gone where your weaknesses and attitude were commented upon. Occasional comments on your performance are made on your Appearance sheet, but these are brief and strictly factual. In the spirit of transparency, any comments will be repeated on your feedback sheet

- There is no date in your file suggesting your Req date. The idea makes me laugh, but candidates still believe this ludicrous rumour. Once you've gained enough marks you get your Req.

I often read web postings where students worry about very trivial problems. There is always more than one way of driving a Run, either virtually or for real. The important thing is to connect the two Points. Keep it simple if you don't know the name of every little cut-through road. Use the oranges and lemons if you're not sure.

Finally, a bit more about confidence. In many cases, a bad Appearance is caused by being excessively nervous and lacking confidence; things that are virtually impossible for me to cure. You're nervous, because it means a lot to you. A touch of nervousness is good, it sharpens you.

Some people always study harder than you, or at least they say they do (sometimes it's quantity over quality). Don't compare yourself with others. If you've studied as hard as time and resources have allowed, you've done your best. Be proud. You have made it this far and have earned the right to be confident. Ignore the myths and rumours. Think of your examiners as fellow cab drivers who want you to succeed. An Appearance is your opportunity to shine. Good luck.